TALES and TOWNS

of

NORTH

The late John A. Logan Johnson, of Lambertville, graciously supplied the old pamphlet entitled *The Old Pig Drover of Log Gaol,* linking such colorful names as "The Devil's Kitchen," "The Dark Moon Drive," and Log Gaol itself. Log Gaol is the old name of Johnsonburg, in Warren County, at the end of the rolling road over from Allamuchy.

TALES and TOWNS

of

NORTHERN NEW JERSEY

by

HENRY CHARLTON BECK

with Photographs by

WILLIAM F. AUGUSTINE

RUTGERS UNIVERSITY PRESS

New Brunswick   *London*

Seventh printing, 1994

Manufactured in the United States of America

Library of Congress Cataloging-in-Publication Data

Beck, Henry Charlton, 1902–1965.

Tales and towns of northern New Jersey.

Includes index.
1. New Jersey—Social life and customs. 2. New
Jersey—History, Local. 3. City and town life—New
Jersey. 4. Legends—New Jersey. I. Title.
F134.B46   1984   974.9   83-10984
ISBN 0-8135-1019-8

British Cataloging-in-Publication information available

*Dedicated with Affection to
my Grandson*
DAVID ERIK PHILLIPS

Other books by Henry Charlton Beck

Jersey Genesis
Forgotten Towns of Southern New Jersey
More Forgotten Towns of Southern New Jersey
The Jersey Midlands
The Roads of Home

Contents

Tales and Towns of

NORTHERN

NEW JERSEY

N

Coleville

Smith's
Clove

Sussex
(Deckertown)
Beemerville
Vernon

Ringwood Manor
State Park

Pellettown
(Ackerson)

Suffern

SUSSEX
(Wantage)
Stockholm
(Snufftown)

PASSAIC

Newton

Wanaque

Park Ridge
(Pascack)

Blairstown

BERGEN

Hainesburg
(Sodom)
Johnsonburg (Log Gaol)
Lake
Hopatcong

Mount Herman

Hawthorne
(Hopperstown)

Englewood
Dock

Hope
Vienna
Waterloo

Hackensack

Delaware
Petersburg
(Caddington)

MORRIS

Great Meadows
(Danville)

Rutherford

Morristown

ESSEX

WARREN

Mendham

Weehawken

Ralston
(Roxitious)

Orange

Hoboken

Stewartsville
Glen Gardner
(Sodom)

Jersey
City

LONG
ISLAND

Phillipsburg

HUNTERDON

STATEN
ISLAND

Frenchtown
(Alexandria)

Ringoes
(Ringo's)

Trenton

Christie McFall

FOREWORD

The reader will perhaps understand my delight in the publishing of *Tales and Towns of Northern New Jersey* when he learns that it approaches the attainment of an objective set twenty-five years ago. At least two books on North Jersey were planned as part of my lifetime project of unearthing and recording the folklore of New Jersey. At the same time, the reader may sense two aspects of what has become a race with time: first, that *Tales and Towns* does no more than mine a portion of the richness of North Jersey folklore, and so must be followed by *More Tales and Towns;* and second, that some additions must be made to what has been discovered, or rediscovered, and reported in these chapters. I am happy not only that *More Tales and Towns of Northern New Jersey* is well under way, but that in this introduction I am able to tie off the loose ends left in three of the chapters of the present book.

In early researches made for this book, as complete as they seemed to be when the record was compiled, at least two important narratives end in an atmosphere of mystery, and another may seem inaccurate in the light of recent developments. Books are not made in a day, and after many days and months of traveling the old roads, seeking and finding many clues and some answers, I had to come to a stopping place. But changes came even as the book was being put together.

In the first chapter, "Gentleman in Disguise," you will read that the old milestone bearing the inscription "2 mi. to L.G." is missing from its site on the road from Allamuche to Johnsonburg. I can now tell you that the milestone is back where it came from, mended and burnished and free of the lichen which came with the years, and which made it, in the estimate of one historian, "the oldest thing in Warren County."

In Chapter II, "The White Pilgrim of Dark Moon," the Christian, or *Christ*-ian, Church, is described with almost contradictory phrases and without reference to its history outside the local area where it was once active. About this Church (as it appears in the towns through which we travel in these pages), I have learned that there is a *now* angle, as

John Ehrhardt calls it, inasmuch as their descendants are the Disciples of Christ, the church to which President Johnson belongs. "Their present organic formation," John wrote me from Madison, "dates only from the mid-1800's, when they were known as 'Campbellites,' after Alexander Campbell, who founded (according to their official history) a church in 1809 at Brush Run, Pennsylvania. However, the history is more complicated than that, and various names were used before the union was effected . . ."

The oldest section was made up of "Republican Methodists," who seceded from the Methodist fold in North Carolina in 1793; they were more or less joined by some dissident Baptists in Vermont in 1800, and received another accretion from seceding Presbyterians in Kentucky and Tennessee in 1801. The union of the groups as the Christian, or *Christ*-ian, Church, or Disciples of Christ, began in 1827. Whatever has been inherited in areas of New Jersey touched upon here would seem to have varied from place to place, sometimes making the *Christ*-ian Church seem to be a catch-all for those leaving other churches for one reason or another.

"However," John Ehrhardt further informs me, "they follow a strictly congregational form of government and their centralization is little more than a loose federation. Their only agreed-upon creed seems to be 'The Bible without comment.' Some of their congregations are very close to the Unitarians in their ideas." The Exodus of Methodists from their church to form a *Christ*-ian Church because of the appearance of a woman evangelist would seem to have been a local matter, then, in New Jersey's Vienna region.

Finally, in Chapter V, "Frenche's Castle and Waterloo," I reported that this charming Canal village faced eventual obliteration. I have recently learned that Waterloo's restoration as a typical early American village, associated with what was the only canal in the world to climb and descend mountains, seems assured through the means and planning of one content to put things back as they were. So far, there seems to be no prospect of the intrusion of the kind of commercial enterprises which Bill Augustine refers to as "tourist traps."

HENRY CHARLTON BECK

Hillcrest Farm,
R.D. Robbinsville, N.J.

TALES and TOWNS
of
NORTHERN NEW JERSEY

Mystery still surrounds this impressive house in Johnsonburg, long proclaimed to be an early Episcopal church, a pre-Revolutionary outpost of the Society for the Propagation of the Gospel in Foreign Parts. Authorities of the Society in London may yet find a record of such a church in this village.

Chapter I

GENTLEMAN IN DISGUISE

North and east of a great expanse of ink-black prehistoric lake bottom called Great Meadows, the road comes meandering down from Allamuchy, or Alamuche, to Johnsonburg—Log Gaol in the days of the Pig Drover. Great Meadows, once a regional name, by now has displaced the Danville of Daniel Vliet in Warren County, its railroad station maintained mostly by a freight agent—there is no passenger service. On the crest of a hill behind it is a firmly planted house that looks for all the world like a Swiss chalet, taken for granted in this land of magical names—Waterloo, Stillwater, Hope, Yellow Frame, and even Gratitude.

Mr. Finley's often brittle and delicately hand-colored map of New Jersey in 1834, prepared for Tom Gordon's *Gazetteer* and printed by Daniel Fenton in Trenton that same year, was already proclaiming Fredon as if it were Freedom, which it is frequently mispronounced, and, to the southwest of the Sussex-Warren border, Tranquility, which seemed to be the charmer of them all. Surely, I have thought recurrently, this was an appropriate objective, and perhaps the expression, of those early travelers who had passed successfully beyond Great Meadows, called by even the most venturesome "The Shades of Death."

As recently as 1872 the Beers, Comstock, and Kline *Atlas* maps, which I almost always take along to confuse those who continue to tell me that I really ought to equip myself with something more up-to-date, were calling Caddington *Carrington*, which it never was; Greendell *Greenville*, which I suspect it may have been; and an elusive crossroads called Southtown

3

was given the same typographical status as Johnsonburg itself. But only from the lips of the reticent, who remembered what grandmothers and grandfathers had said, and in the text of a little-known pamphlet, was I to hear of caves under limestone ledges celebrated as "The Devil's Kitchen" and "The Devil's Wheelwright Shop" on a road called "The Dark Moon Drive" which wound out of Johnsonburg. More surprisingly, for most of two centuries there was a narrow passage close by referred to by those who know it well as "The Pass of Thermopoly." My most impressive dictionary would indicate that "thermopoly" is a place of radiant heat, but whatever it is or was, I feel sure that with all the others it was well-known by one who was known far and wide as "The Old Pig Drover of Log Gaol."

All this is important to setting the scene, but, beyond that, the thrill of folklore, or perhaps it is the fun and adventure of it, lies in the certainty that once a clue turns up, there's no telling where the trail may lead, or how much time or geography may be eaten up before the tale, neglected or glossed over by history, is complete. Even then, there is no way of being absolutely sure. The keys to the solution of so many lingering enigmas of New Jersey history are often in hands that do not know them for what they are or, in knowing, try to make them a private matter. If their owners only knew, they would experience the true satisfaction which comes when this insatiable curiosity about what used to be, develops new friendships, even reunions of family or old friends for which no formal plans were made.

This is how it was with the story of *The Old Pig Drover of Log Gaol*, a copy of which came to me first in the autumn of 1950—not from Johnsonburg, or from Allamuchy, but from Phillipsburg, far over on the Delaware River, when the late and revered John A. Logan Johnson sent me the pamphlet I never had seen. Although John had died before Phillipsburg could celebrate its own anniversary among reminiscences of days when Indians had called it Chintewink, his gift was a thoughtful expression of appreciation of a meeting long before and of a continuing quest—or so he wrote me. I have treasured his letter for many years, folded away as it has been in the booklet itself.

The pamphlet, originally a paper read in 1913 before the Woman's Branch of the New Jersey Historical Society by W. H. Vail, was printed in the proceedings of the Society the following year. Mr. Vail, it is reasonable to assume, was kinsman of one of the principals concerned with returning the Pig Drover to his rightful character and faraway home. I read it through quickly and discovered that here was much more than the story of a man who drove pigs to market and, in intervals between journeys, fascinated the neighborhood of Johnsonburg with stories told from the two-storied piazza of the old hotel. First, there was the "mystery" of the old "2 to L. G." milestone, then reference to another older tavern outside the village, an establishment first described to me as "Dark of the Moon Inn," and then another concerning "the original Hardwick Church," which long ago had been removed "to the ridge" to become "the far-famed Yellow Frame Church."

I remember that I had begun with a search for the milestone with its curious inscription, then an unsolved riddle, long before I knew of the paragraphs buried in a weighty history of the area in which the Pig Drover emerged as little more than a "Peculiar Person"—all the detail of contrasting color removed. No one to whom I spoke referred to the Drover in any way, and it was long, long after that when I was led to the barren site where the church had first stood, a place called (with appropriate whispers, it seemed to me) the "Dark of the Moon Graveyard." Yellow Frame Church is far away from Johnsonburg, but it has at least been moved across the drive from the tombs its proximity so long protected.

It is good to remember that the "2 to L. G." milestone was where it always had been when I saw it first on the Allamuchy

Road, even though at that time there was evidence of a mending after the first senseless attack by vandals. The day was one on which I had admired the slim spire of the Methodist Church in Tranquility, as well known to the countryside as are the "Lord's Auctions" in August each year. I had lingered again beside the second grave of The White Pilgrim in the walled graveyard down the hill from the "Christ-ian" Church of Johnsonburg. What is more, I looked upon the house of those memorable Johnsonburg physicians, Roderick Byington and William Penn Vail, as well as the impressive stone house which, it was said, had been an early Episcopal church. Recurrently referred to as a "mission," it was, I was told, an early outpost of the Society for the Propagation of the Gospel in Foreign Parts, which sent missionaries to this country in pre-Revolutionary days; however, the archivist of the Society in London has been unable to find any record of its presence there.

The "2 to L. G." milestone, which had "disappeared" when last I went questing in the vicinity, is as important a part of the backdrop as are the almost forgotten church and "the house of the doctors next-door," as it was sometimes called. The Pig Drover, followed by cunningly corn-fed porkers, certainly passed and repassed the milestone, whose "L. G." was to identify him, on his way to and from the tavern in the heart of Log Gaol where he told his stories. Few, if any, of his narratives had anything to do with New Jersey, a fact that was quickly noted by a few listeners long before he was aware of it, and this, oddly enough, proved his "downfall"—which, actually, was anything but that. It was the village physicians, one undoubtedly the student of the other, who compared notes with an early schoolmaster and realized that the tales told by the Pig Drover had, almost without variation, the Old South as their locale.

I doubt if anyone can give a precise date for the Drover's earliest arrival in the neighborhood, safely ensconced in the valley lying between Mount Rascal on the south, and a line of

low, limestone hills on the north—these are Mr. Vail's own
words, and I wonder what he would have thought of a more
recent debate that there were no rascals, really, but that the
name originally belonged to a family named Rascall. This
variant was maintained as gospel by my late friend, Arthur
Daly Minton, almost to the day of his death. However, from
all I have heard and read, I would judge that the Pig Drover
was at least known thereabouts, and by such a name between
1825 and 1830, and probably earlier. It is a matter of record
that when the "2 to L. G." stone was erected, Log Gaol was
the most prominent place in that area of the state and "contained the only gaol of any kind in northern New Jersey."
Whenever it was that the Pig Drover put in an appearance, he
found in Log Gaol the place where, incredibly enough to us
now, "two stage lines converged and crossed" near the tavern
that was to serve him as his own kind of theater.

In those days it was at the tavern that "all important transactions took place." Wrote the author of the paper that became
a brochure, "All the public meetings, other than religious, were
held at the tavern. It was there the caucuses and elections
were held. And the training days drew great crowds, from near
and far, to the taverns, and there are a few individuals still
living"—this was written more than forty years ago—"who can
remember those days when the farmers and laborers gathered
with their flint-lock muskets across their shoulders, and the
marshals drilled them in the early hours of the day, because by
the afternoon the Jersey whiskey had rendered them incapable
of marching, for by that time they resembled the poor, tired
Hessians at Trenton. . . . The tavern usually contained the
largest assembly room in town, and therefore it was the place
where dancing parties were held, and all political meetings,
where questions of public welfare were discussed and decided. . . ."

One of the stage routes ran from Albany to Philadelphia by
way of Log Gaol, and the other came over from New York

Peter Billow lives within sight of the inn in Log Gaol, now Johnsonburg, where the Old Pig Drover paused on his journeys. The stone walls of the Billow garage were part of the jail itself in a period when there was no other in northwestern New Jersey and when Log Gaol was the county seat.

City to Stroudsburg "and thence through the beech woods to Slocum Hollow (now Scranton), Pennsylvania, and thence to western New York State. It is readily seen," our Mr. Vail has pointed out here, "how these facts conspired to render Log Gaol a very important and prominent place." To which I hasten to add that it was a place of even greater importance on the days, and more especially the evenings, when the Pig Drover was there. He always was assured of an audience, probably made up of a miscellany of travelers, but I must also conclude that he warmed to a large and receptive crowd as the night wore on and the store of liquor was worn down—although I hasten to say that there never was an occasion when the Drover couldn't "hold his liquor." Minehosts of the old inn, which, although changed in many ways, is the only one that ever was on the property at the end of the road over from Alla-muchy, surely looked upon the Drover as "good business."

I must admit forthwith that I hold a special affection for Log Gaol, no matter what the arguments are about the tavern's having been the original, because it is easy to imagine the Pig Drover in action there and because, for the most part, a mantle of reflective quiet has settled on the village like the dust of a dried-out road. This in itself matches the innate mod-esty of those who have been kind, but reluctant to speak of what had been taken for granted for so long a time. Yet, all the while, there was Peter Billow and his good wife, living almost opposite the inn until they moved to the tastefully reclaimed and restored house that I did not know was the old Billow homestead until Iver Billow in Rockaway told me. And, up the road out of Johnsonburg and opposite his farm, Russell Hen-dershot was waiting for the right questions at the right time to show me where "Dark Moon Tavern" had been, not far from the broken stones of the Dark of the Moon Graveyard. He told me he wished he had saved some very old bottles he had found on the corner and that he had caught whoever it was that smashed the tombstones, with nothing less than a crowbar, where the Yellow Frame Church first had stood guard.

It is more than likely that Peter Billow and Russell Hendershot, who told me he was the Mayor, were as sure from the beginning, as was W. H. Vail, of the tavern and the old houses. There seems to be no doubt that what used to be the Peter VanNess or Vanness house was the old church, although it has been referred to frequently as "the mission" and although in the late 1930's a local official was quoted as saying "that denomination sorta got pinched out in this vicinity." It had served, apparently, from about 1781 to 1850—and that is why I believe that the Society for the Propagation of the Gospel had a work there. The Episcopal Diocese of New Jersey was not organized until 1785. Mr. Vail, who himself remembered the evidences of the church in "the pulpit, high up, against the end wall" about ready to fall into the basement with the flooring, declared boldly that the date on the outer wall, 1781, had been altered from either 1731 or 1751.

The old church, no matter what records in England do not say, had become a house when I was there with its gracious owner purveying antiques and wondering, even as I would, about a strange bulge in one of the thick inside walls. There was no counterpart on the outside where, before she came there, the very ancient date stone of which Mr. Vail wrote had disappeared.

The Billows, the Hendershots, and others had heard snatches of the Pig Drover story through most of their lives, but beyond the bits of information I had strung together, many seemed to have no complete narrative of the man who was not, I must point out, an aged wanderer. Thus I have decided that the whole of it, with as much continuity as can be supplied only with the help of our unquestionably trustworthy Mr. Vail, shall be given to the Billows, the Hendershots, and all the rest —including those who know the true solution of the vanishing

This milestone, with its inscription "2 to L. G.," was long protected as one of the oldest objects in Warren County, repaired more than once by farmers nearby. It disappeared mysteriously for a time but is now back in place, considerably cleaned up, and protected by a little fence.

"2 to L. G." milestone. After all, you have been waiting (patiently, I hope) for too long a time.

I can safely pass over the years in which The Old Pig Drover of Log Gaol went unchallenged, or at least unquestioned, as a pig drover who could tell good stories from the porch of an inn and, I have no doubt, from the warmth of its bar-room and adjacent parlors, when the weather was cold or inclement. It well may be that either Dr. Byington or Dr. Vail, or both, had begun to have misgivings about the Pig Drover, whose stories they had heard. However, it was not until William Rankin arrived, working his way up from Greenville, East Tennessee, by teaching along the way, that the seeds of what was to be the great silence, or denouement, were planted in one blunt statement of devil-may-care analysis. Born the son of a Revolutionary soldier in 1799 William had left his home in the spring of 1828, with almost no money and little except a "settled purpose to graduate from Yale College. Arriving in Log Gaol on a warm August day, he applied for an appointment as a teacher in the school.

"It was on this day that Dr. Vail, just returned from visiting some patients," says the 1913 account by the doctor, written almost a century later but hidden away in the Historical Society's brochure, "noticed this young man coming up the road, poorly clad, penniless, foot-sore, unkempt, weary and hungry. It was thus that these two young men met for the first time, and it was thus that a life-long friendship began, between two individuals who were not only to be bound together in friendship but who were, under God, to become the most important factors in framing and directing the course of the educational development of northern New Jersey for a long time to come. . . ." This, indeed, is a sweeping statement, but it is one that is illustrated, you might say, by two or three departures in the same little book—the "residence of Drs. Byington and Vail" and "The Old School House at Log Gaol."

"It was several years before Mr. Rankin reached Yale College, and then to spend only one year there, but he became in after years the Principal at Sussex, Chester, and Mendham, New Jersey, and many of his pupils, living today" revere his name and influence as an educator. But let us return to the story of the Pig Drover.

"Dr. Byington was the examiner for teachers and Dr. Vail suggested to the Doctor that if the young applicant for the school had not good parts, to let him pass along, for they, the two doctors, were the only persons in the hamlet who had received a liberal education, and no doubt the new teacher would board at the tavern, the center of the village life, and Dr. Vail was anxious that the coming teacher, whoever he might be, should be possessed of good conversational ability. The examination naturally took place at the tavern and attracted a large crowd, who expected good sport, at seeing the awkward and uncouth backwoodsman 'put through,' as they termed it, by the well-educated examiner, Dr. Byington.

"But the anticipated merriment was short-lived, being very quickly changed to surprise, and then to admiration, when in addition to a thorough knowledge of the elementary branches, he proved himself equally at home among the classics and sciences. . . ."

I must confess a debt to Mr. Vail for including this among the word pictures of this occasionally poetic record, for it gives some estimate of the character of the ultra-modest man who was to be the prime-mover in the kindly action which revealed who the Pig Drover truly was and which also restored him to the home and family to which he belonged. Few phrases can equal those of the tattery brochure, and that is why I make bold to use them so liberally. However, let me jump ahead a little to tell you what we know of the Pig Drover, the recruiter of pigs. He seemed to be about fifty years old, "was of burly appearance, laughter loving, and in a high degree had the gift of inciting others to laugh. . . ." Whatever other details there may have been have faded away in the passage of time.

I think that The Old Pig Drover of Log Gaol is the name he gave himself, for it seems to have that quality that the Drover could have given so easily to the title of one of his own stories.

William Rankin had been hardly launched in his work as teacher at the one-room school, now a little house off a road corner that once had a "snake fence" of rails on one side and a barrier of stones on the other, "when toward evening one day, as he was seated upon the tavern porch, with Dr. Vail, enjoying the beauties of the glorious sunset, along came the Old Pig Drover, and Dr. Vail said to Mr. Rankin, 'Now for a good time, for I never met anyone who possessed the power to interest people in telling stories equal to this pig drover.'

"The arrival of this personage was always the occasion for a great gathering of the story loving public, for let us remember that this was before the age of the daily papers, when even books were few, and thus they who possessed the faculty of narrating events in an interesting manner always commanded large audiences at the town tavern, specially if the narrator had lived, or traveled, in a distant part of the country, or in foreign lands, and so possessed the advantage of being able to add embellishments accruing from such experiences. Novelties are always in demand, be they in the shape of large hats, or hobble skirts, only so they are the latest fad in the world of fashion. . . ." I can only guess what Mr. Vail would have said in one of his amusing asides in an age of radio and television, when almost every area of the world is in almost instant touch with every other area. "As we proceed," he went on, "we shall see where the charm of the pig drover's stories lay.

"As soon as the supper was over the pig drover appeared on the scene, with its tavern porch filled with anxious persons ready for the performance. No 'reserved seats' there. No boxes to be rented for the season, and no music necessary to usher in the performance or the performer. The rule was, first come, first served. Only one thing was certain, that whenever the pig drover appeared at the tavern to tell stories the seats were

always full. . . ." Two things at least, my restive mind suggests, were as uncertain as ever: First, from what family source
did our Mr. Vail gain his intimate details, and second, were
the Drover's shoats out back while the presentation proceeded
out front? Although there seemed to be little difficulty in gathering together the pigs after the sessions of story-telling, I
wonder if the performances were not reserved for the evenings
of return trips from the cities.

"The location of most of his stories," continues the memoir,
"was in distant southern portions of the country, and the names
of many of his heroes were familiar to Mr. Rankin"—the schoolmaster from the South. Here it was that a castle began to
crumble. "It was evident to Mr. Rankin that the pig drover
had not always been in his present ragged and dirty condition.
When animated in conversation, relating incidents that had
been familiar to him in his past life, he would kindle into true
eloquence, his eyes would dilate and flash with excitement,
and his face would beam with the expression of a soul asserting
its native dignity and power. He had heard with appreciative
sympathy (as was learned afterward) such orators as Patrick
Henry, and others from the Southland, and he loved to im-
personate them, and could do it effectively. To listen to him
at these times was no small enjoyment. One could but regret
that this man, possessed of such powers, should have fallen
into vagrant and reckless habits. . . ."

William Rankin's reaction was entirely different. "That man,"
he observed quietly to Dr. Vail, on the very night of the first
performance he had witnessed, "is not what he pretends to
be. He has a history."

What had given distinction to the Pig Drover's stories until
then—plots and people from the South, mostly connected with
the times of slavery—became something more for the teacher.
"Mr. Rankin," we are told, "having come from that land, and
from the very section in which some of the names were famil-

The inn and post office in Johnsonburg, where the Old Pig Drover told his colorful stories many years ago. This is where the Pied Piper of the Pigs was revealed as a businessman of the South, who, having lost his all, took to the road in embarrassment.

iar," became intensely interested in what to him was a mystery, a puzzle to be solved. Somehow it transpired that "when the merry glee had subsided, and all retired to rest," William Rankin found that he and the Pig Drover had the tavern porch to themselves. The schoolmaster lost no time in asking the Drover if he knew anything of the characters of his stories and if some were not still alive.

"At this the pig drover immediately changed his whole aspect, exhibiting surprise and emotion. He gave no reply to the inquiry, but, in his turn, asked his questioner if he had lived in

Southern Virginia or East Tennessee. Mr. Rankin replied that
he had traveled through those countries. The pig drover's un-
easiness evidently increased. He at length rose to his feet, and,
in a style altogether different from that in which he had just
addressed the merry company, bade Mr. Rankin good night.

"They parted, but the Pig Drover (as Mr. Rankin learned
afterwards), before retiring, repaired to the kitchen, and
learned all he possibly could respecting Mr. Rankin. The next
morning Mr. Rankin rose early, and took a seat upon the same
porch. In a few minutes the pig drover made his appearance,
and with countenance lighted up, he rushed to Mr. Rankin,
and taking him by the hand, addressed him by the epithet of
'countryman.' He playfully upbraided Mr. Rankin for having
lost the frankness of a southern character, and assuming that of
a Yankee. They took their seats and Mr. Rankin was now
happy in the thought that all difficulty had passed with the
night, and that they should have a frank conversation of other
times and places. But no, the pig drover's countenance immediately overshadowed, as if with a veil of thoughtful melancholy.
Soon they parted. The pig drover collected his drove of shoats,
and started for the city, while Mr. Rankin returned to the day's
duties. . . ."

That was when William Rankin began writing letters. At
the same time he began collecting all that was known in the
neighborhood about the Drover along all the roads where he
had become a friendly and familiar figure. Stagecoaches began carrying notes to friends in Abingdon, Virginia, in Tennessee towns, and even further away, describing an eloquent
Pied Piper of the Pigs who said his name was Samuel Fulton
but whose highly entertaining tales, the envy of any rustic
raconteur, bubbled over with familiar names and events. Beside the shaft that is a memorial to Judge Mushbach in the
Christ-ian, now Christian, Church in Johnsonburg, I remembered that it was the Judge who told the schoolmaster that
"the pig drover had been known for a number of years previ-

ously in that section of the country, and all this time he had followed the same humble occupation of purchasing shoats and driving them to market. . . ."

He was thought by the farmers he served "to possess a kind of witchery in his mode of driving his pigs. His little flock, consisting sometimes of as many as thirty pigs, would run before him, or follow him, with a docility perfectly astonishing. His method was to carry, slung over his shoulder in a careless manner, a bag containing some shelled corn, and dropping this corn, little by little, as he walked along, the pigs formed the habit of running with him. . . ."

William Rankin was quick to learn that Samuel Fulton, alias The Old Pig Drover of Log Gaol, always paid "with exactness the price of everything he purchased, and was supposed to possess money. He would collect a drove, drive them to market, dickering all along the road, from Pennsylvania to Newark and Elizabethport, and return to Log Gaol, about every two months. He was known to use ardent spirits, for refreshments, as he termed it, but he never became a sot; though sometimes he would become pretty hilarious, if not boisterous, and then he would upbraid his hearers as being 'mudsills of the north,' while he was 'a Southern gentleman to the manner born' and on such occasions, it would seem to me, the Drover almost gave himself away."

Judge Mushbach once admitted to Mr. Rankin that he as well as others had "surmised that the pig drover was a character in disguise"—however, he was accepted by the community "as a person of lower grade" with a bearing that was such that "he commanded the respect of everybody, unless, upon such occasions . . . when he imbibed too liberally of that too common article, 'Jersey Lightning,'" I include this passage for a special reason. So many have insisted to me that "Jersey Lightning" as a term, if not a product, was associated only with Down Jersey. This, however, is important:

"The pig drover continued to make his periodic trips, always tarrying, as he passed, at the Log Gaol tavern. He maintained great uniformity in his deportment and business transactions, *but never held another storytelling soiree* after the time Mr. Rankin questioned him. The two met occasionally and exchanged a few polite phrases but that was all. William Rankin kept his investigation to himself, of that I am quite sure."

Among other revealing aspects of the tale of one who may have been the first wandering story-teller in all New Jersey, even if the narratives were from afar, it notes what was to be the last meeting of the Pig Drover and the schoolmaster. This will seem a little strange, at first, when it is realized that Mr. Rankin was more responsible than anyone else for Samuel Fulton's eventual return to himself and his people. The teacher, returning to the tavern between morning and afternoon sessions of the school one day, was told that the Pig Drover had arrived, that he appeared very ill, indeed, and that he had been taken to the tavern's poorly kept garret.

"A few squalid rags had been spread on the dirty floor, and his own wallet (for he always carried a kind of knapsack) was placed under his head for a pillow. It was at this moment that young Dr. Vail arrived, with William Rankin, almost in tears, about to run off with a second summons. The teacher asked if the Pig Drover was dying. The doctor replied that he thought not, that the attack was a rush of blood to the head. As to the cause, the doctor replied that it had an element of mental emotion. . . ." The schoolmaster concurred, for he, more than all the others, knew the probable cause of the Drover's anguish.

I have suggested that the innkeeper looked upon the Pig Drover as "good business," but I would have hoped that it was more than that by this time. Perhaps, inasmuch as the Drover no longer told his stories, this attitude had changed. Now the Drover, flushed and feverish, was unable to speak. "Do you think he has any money?" asked the hovering minehost. Mr. Rankin countered with a question as to whether the Drover owed him anything, and the answer was "No." "How then,"

asked the teacher, "does it concern you or me as to whether he
has any money or not?" The owner of the hotel said uneasily
that he was afraid the old man might "fall sick on my hands.
Will you go his security?" he demanded to know. William Rankin stared his reply and "all hastily went downstairs. . . ."

There it was that the tavern owner exclaimed, "If no one
will be his security, I'll have him immediately taken to the
poorhouse." As a result, young Dr. Vail may never have attained a moment of greater, more memorable dignity. He said:
"That threat of the poorhouse will not rashly be carried into
execution. He is my patient, and shall not be removed without
my permission." Whereupon William Rankin hurried back to
his school, and, returning just as anxiously in four hours, he
was startled all over again. On "inquiring for the sick man, he
was told that he had recovered, gathered his herd of shoats,
and was gone. . . ."

As those chronologies so often unfold, the next day's mail
brought a letter for William Rankin, not from Abingdon, Virginia, but from Fayettesville, Tennessee, signed by James Fulton. "Mr. Fulton stated that he had received the letter that
had been written by Mr. Rankin, and sent to Messrs. Holt and
McIntyre, as it had been forwarded to him. He further stated
that the person described in the letter was undoubtedly his
father, whose name was Samuel Fulton. He also stated that in
the great financial depression that fell upon the country at the
close of the war of 1812, his father failed in business, and after
almost superhuman struggling, was unable to meet his obliga-
tions to his creditors. This broke his heart, and he withdrew
from the world, and the knowledge of his friends and family.
He was last heard from"—the letter went on—"in Pennsylvania, still adventuring, but in vain, to repair his ruined fortune. About twelve years previously, his friends received a
newspaper which stated that a man by the name of Samuel
Fulton had died. After this, no further hope of ever seeing

him again was entertained" and he was numbered among the dead.

James Fulton added that "his mother was still living, and received the intelligence that her husband was yet alive as a voice from the grave. He said that the connubial relations of his parents had been without a flaw until the day of his father's departure; that his mother was enraptured with joy at the hope of again rejoining her long lost husband. Mr. Fulton also wrote that he would never rest until he procured the return of his

The house of Drs. Byington and Vail in Johnsonburg remains today much as the Old Pig Drover saw it and as it was when Dr. Vail, sensing that Samuel Fulton's stories marked him as a man of gentle background, worked with William Rankin, a young school teacher, to restore him to his family and home.

father and restored him to his family and friends. There were
at that early day no railroads and very few stages. Long journeys were mostly performed on horseback. The distance from
New Jersey to Western Tennessee was about one thousand
miles, but this did not deter this dutiful son from accomplish-
ing his purpose. . . ."

I have been tempted to draw the curtain on the final scene
without ceremony or the pathos that throbs in all the details—
but that is impossible. William Rankin left the school at Log
Gaol soon after the first letter came, taking a post of assistant
in the school of the Reverend Clarkson Dunn in Deckertown,
now Sussex in Sussex County. He was greeted at the door one
day a month or more after by a gentleman who identified himself as Mr. Buchanan, from Western Tennessee. With him was
William's oldest friend from Log Gaol, Dr. Vail. The physician
informed the schoolmaster that Mr. Buchanan was a messenger
sent by James Fulton "to convey" the Old Pig Drover back to
his home and family in Fayettesville. Mr. Buchanan revealed
that he and the man who had delighted in the name of The
Old Pig Drover once had been partners in an extensive mer-
cantile business, but they had failed. Whereupon Samuel Fulton vanished.

Returning to Johnsonburg in May, 1829, Dr. Vail and Mr.
Buchanan set out to find the Pig Drover. He was found, at
last, working on a farm in Knowlton Township on what I have
called "the forehead" of New Jersey, a farm owned and occupied at the time by one Harrison Blair. "It was at the beginning of the corn-planting season (and as it was too hot to
prosecute his usual vocation ·of driving the shoats) and as
he also could obtain better wages," the narrative in Mr. Vail's
paper goes on, "it was his custom, each year, to hire himself
out to the farmers, for the demand for workers was great.

"Upon the day in question the pig drover was planting
corn, and as Mr. Buchanan approached him, it was evident
that he was being watched sharply. 'Is this Mr. Fulton?' asked

Mr. Buchanan. 'So they call me,' answered the drover cautiously and the visitor declared with enthusiasm how happy he was to meet the object of his search. 'You seem to know me,' said the old man, 'but I have no knowledge of you. Who are you?' 'Don't you know me?' asked Mr. Buchanan. 'Take a good look at me. Why, my dear sir, you used to know me well enough. You have done me many favors that I shall never forget.' The pig drover's curiosity was now at fever heat. 'Tell me,' he said, 'who you are.' At the announcement of his name, the old man dropped his hoe, and grasped Mr. Buchanan's hands. The old pig drover had a thousand questions to ask as they walked to a retired spot. . . .'

There were mingled tears and, at the beginning, an adamant refusal to go along home with Mr. Buchanan. Samuel Fulton said that he could not return "in this plight" and that there were "small sums along the route" owed by him to others and by others to him "not only in this county, but also in Morris and Essex Counties." "Very well," replied Mr. Buchanan, "you get measured for a new suit of clothes, then go over your route settling up all your accounts, and by the time you return I will have purchased the horse and trappings, and we will start for the old home in the Southland." This is how Mr. Vail quoted Mr. Buchanan, but I must admit to you that I somehow miss the appropriate fanfare of trumpets and the lingering roll of drums.

Mr. Vail's brochure ends with a series of letters over which I must pass quickly, for we have far to go and many other places and people to see. Naturally enough, Dr. Vail invited William Rankin to come to Log Gaol to witness the Pig Drover's departure from the heart of the land he had learned to love. The schoolmaster, content to remain detached from what he had accomplished, replied: "I believe, in view of propriety, it will be impossible to attend at Johnsonburg on the present occasion. But my whole soul goes out in favor of the good cause

of restoring the unfortunate old man to more desirable circumstances. . . ."

Beyond that, William Rankin somewhat bluntly stressed the
fact that a visitor, also from Tennessee, had taken up much of
his time so that he could not leave his teaching. Mr. Vail had
Mr. Rankin's letter when he wrote his paper, as well as a longer
communication from Mr. Buchanan in which he dwelt on the
hardships of the return journey and concluded with the meeting of Samuel Fulton and the wife who had believed him
dead—a reunion that he and the others tastefully chose not to
witness.

We can go across the road and ask Peter Billow about the
walls of Log Gaol, once part of an old barn, now a garage at
the edge of the lawn of his house; we can frown and scold
with Russell Hendershot about broken tombstones at the Dark
of the Moon Graveyard and a missing milestone not far away,
and we can linger again beside the Johnsonburg grave of The
White Pilgrim. But now, as we pause, there are three scenes
here, one at Log Gaol, another at Fayettesville, and a third in
Hackettstown, which stay with me. In Log Gaol an old man,
merry again, rode his new horse up and down in front of the
tavern, calling out among the cheers of his friends, "What has
become of the Old Pig Drover of Log Gaol?" In Fayettesville
the quiet graves of the Fultons, Samuel and his wife, are appropriately side by side, but, I am told, the epitaph supplies
no answer for the Pig Drover's last question at Log Gaol. In
Hackettstown, J. Harold Nunn, author of several books of history and an officer of the Warren County Historical Society,
ignored all the political dust stirred up by the vanishing "2 to
L. G." stone.

"I know where it is," he told me simply. "It has been mended
once again and all cleaned up." Inasmuch as the cleaning
process included a mention of the use of steel wool, I must

presume that the lichen and other marks of weather of more than two centuries have been removed. It was clear that the stone, wherever it was, would not be returned to its familiar setting on the Allamuchy-Johnsonburg Road. "Somebody would be sure to smash it up all over again," Harold Nunn insisted.

Chapter II

THE WHITE PILGRIM OF DARK MOON

Now that I have shared with you the full story of The Old Pig Drover of Log Gaol, remembered in a way I hope will please him, if ever there is occasion to tell it from the two-decker porch of the inn at Johnsonburg, I must admit in all conscience that I had not planned to begin in Log Gaol.

That just "happened"—but, as I warned you at the start, one clue inevitably leads to another, one new friend to several more, and then, suddenly, the honest researcher has covered much more ground, in related legends and territory, than ever he intended.

Samuel Fulton called himself "The Old Pig Drover," and I must conclude that he would be content to be so recalled, at least in New Jersey. But I cannot say the same for Joseph Thomas, the wandering preacher from Ohio, in his regard for the name I have given him, "The White Pilgrim of Dark Moon." He was celebrated in his day merely as "The White Pilgrim," and I am the one who has extended the sobriquet because, after his one and only service in the Episcopal Church at Johnsonburg, perhaps borrowed to accommodate the size of the crowd, or congregation, "the Dark of the Moon Grave-yard" is where they took his body, struck down by virulent smallpox after one sermon.

I must suppose that there was a superstition abroad that even the dead in the better-cared-for cemetery in Johnsonburg, downhill from the "Christ-ian" Church, might have been con-taminated—although it is further recorded that Mrs. Thomas and the children were not permitted to visit the out-of-the-way grave that was to conceal the Pilgrim's bones for more than ten years.

By now you know that the Dark of the Moon Graveyard had been left behind by a church that had been moved to the Sussex-Warren County line, where its name, "Yellow Frame," assumed all the importance of a town, even on modern maps. You may not have known that the county line cut directly through the church in front of the pulpit, so that the pastor, until the church was moved a second time, had the dubious distinction of standing in one county and preaching to a congregation in the other. Assuredly, you were not aware that the name of the Dark Moon Tavern attached itself to the graveyard up the rise when the then untroubled graves remained obscurely behind, after the church had been moved. Although the temporary burial of The White Pilgrim among the shadows of the "Dark Moon Drive" is an indictment in itself, I doubt if Joseph Thomas would have relished any association with Johnsonburg's second inn, even as I doubt if the Pig Drover would have been concerned by it in death or in life.

Actually I was on my way down by favorite back roads from Blairstown when I made my decision to give the Pig Drover priority. I had come upon so many who, in that special way of country people, first said that they knew the old story and then began asking for details with which to knit the reports and rumors together so that I was sure the whole of it should be assembled again in one place. The White Pilgrim had remained, even for me, a hazy legend until later. The strange reflection now is that in the beginning I had set out for neither the story of the Pig Drover nor that of the White Pilgrim but, instead, for a place revealed on older maps, especially those I saw from the 1860's on, as Carrington; I was determined at the same time to discover, or rediscover, a village called Feebletown, or Febletown, somewhere up from Hope, the Moravian town. It is probable that the Pig Drover and the

Russell Hendershot, whose farm was across the way from the first site of the Old Yellow Frame Church, broods on Dark of the Moon Graveyard, its stones much damaged after repeated invasions by vandals. The church was moved long ago to the Sussex-Warren line.

White Pilgrim never met, but it is likely that they both knew the same old roads.

I had gone to the scaled-out location of Carrington, out of Hackettstown, where a newer name, Petersburg, had appeared, but no one I could find there admitted to any knowledge of Carrington, spelled in that or in any other way. Just after that H. Ben Hill, Sr., of Blairstown—he told me he signed his name that way because there were "just too many H. B. Hills"—had indulged some reflections in a somewhat spidery hand. But neither Ben Hill, nor Floyd A. Linaberry in New Jersey's Vienna, nor Mrs. Elizabeth Cool, in Stewartsville, far down at the other end of Warren County, had the slightest idea that they would be joining forces, as the weeks and months went by, in recalling The White Pilgrim as I wanted to recall him. Ben wrote to Floyd, and Floyd wrote to Mrs. Cool—and I went on from there.

I had heard of The White Pilgrim before, and I had seen his memorial obelisk, erected at last in the Johnsonburg cemetery, but I think the first stories were part of a false trail. Legends seemed to link him too quickly, I am sure, with the ways in which Hainesburg had become Sodom. There were at least three Sodoms in New Jersey—devastating names applied, they told me, by traveling evangelists treated in unmannerly ways in some of the villages they visited. A variant has been that pioneer surveyors, and not the wandering preachers at all, were to blame. Some of these, unwilling to work harder than absolutely necessary, were said to be content to accept answers to questions about this or that town, if they were in a hurry to be on their way. "What's that next village?" they would ask. "Sodom" frequently would be the reply, and Sodom it would remain at least long enough to go on maps and into crude records. Even so, Tom Gordon lists two Sodoms, one in Hunterdon, where now it is Glen Gardner, and the other in Warren County, and I have heard rumors of at least a third.

Now I know that there was a kind of "Black Pilgrim" working as assiduously in the same general region, and the blame could be attached to him with as much convenience. Finally, to dispose of the matter and go on, it is always possible that what went on in these places in their earliest days induced the Bible-pounders here and there to consign neighbors they disliked to Sodom and its lake of burning pitch.

I had let it be known that I had come to the conclusion that "Carrington" had become Petersburg, although there was little at the corners there to indicate anything resembling a village. At the same time, I pressed my inquiries concerning Feebletown, just north of Hope, spelled *Febletown* on the Beers *Atlas Map* and by almost every writer of the same era. Concerning Feebletown I had heard everything from the explanation that it was the area of a town on the "wrong" side of the tracks to the alternate, offered in Hope, that Feeble or Feble was a family name, although I never have seen it by any spelling on a tombstone anywhere. The late Arthur Daly Minton had said he remembered a Feebletown in Washington, "just the other side of the Morris Canal," and Ben Hill, in Blairstown, had talked with people there who spoke of another Feebletown, not far away. Here and there I must share a few letters with you, if for no other reason than that their writers did not know how much they were giving to the story of The White Pilgrim—although momentarily the circumstances must seem roundabout. Ben Hill wrote:

"Going from Vienna on the second farm on your left, there is a quicksandy 'boiling' spring of some size. From this were taken mastodon bones, possibly a whole skeleton—these bones are preserved in the State Museum in Trenton. Similar bones were taken from a swamp along the Hope-Johnsonburg Road, just east of Kolsenby's Tavern.

"Danville, for which you have been looking, became Great Meadows, a post office name change, fifty-five years ago, give or take a year or two. I never heard who Dan was. . . ."

I soon was to hear with considerable certainty and with some personal delight, for already I had hazarded a guess after seeing an old tombstone, that of Daniel Vliet, at Great Meadows. Ben added that Vienna had been Cumminsville in earlier days, and here the family name, Cummins, was to prove important because of an episode, brought to me later by Floyd Linaberry, concerning The White Prophet. Ben Hill went on: "The first farm I have mentioned was considered an Indian encampment by the late Charles A. Philhower. I spent my summers between 1900 and 1918 on a farm outside Vienna and I never heard the name Carrington mentioned. For that matter, I never heard of Feebletown, or Febletown, near either Hope or Mount Hermon. There was, still is, a section of Blairstown known as Feebletown, or Slabtown, or Skunktown, whichever come to the tongue first. Possibly any section on the 'wrong' side of the hill picked up the name from its more prosperous neighbors."

It will not be spoiling matters, although I must retain something of an air of suspense, if I tell you that by this time Ben Hill and I and some others think we know why the name Feebletown came into being, and, further, that there may have been many Feebletowns, a name tossed about neither in jest nor ridicule. However, we have found no explanation at all as to why map-makers and historians resorted, over and over again, to the spelling *Febletown*.

At this point and in this area Townsbury seemed to be an odd redundancy, and Ben, who had been a teacher, informed me quickly that once it had been Meng's Mill, for John Meng, who had built an old stone mill there. Later John and Benjamin Town owned it for a few years, and they lost no time in changing the name to Townsbury. After that there was a series of short notes in which Ben supplied names of those in their eighties or more to whom I might turn. Herein lies the tragedy of it all—and you may find me saying this, one way or another, many times as we go our way—in that as quickly as I acted, more than one had died before I could see and talk with them. Of the others, some would be productive, I felt quite sure, because the report that so many *never* had heard of Carrington or Feebletown or any of the incidentals between has recurrently proven the kind of challenge that starts even the rustiest wheels of memory turning. At last Ben Hill wrote, with a fragment of a modern map pinned to his note: "According to the following mentioned persons Feebletown is where the road from Silver Lake meets the Hope-Blairstown Road. I have placed a red mark on the map. It might have extended a bit towards Blairstown to where an abandoned road used to connect the Hope-Blairstown Road with the Hope-Mount Hermon Road."

Ben Hill's list included the names of Miss Eloise Lenhardt, compiler of a weekly column, "Seems Like Yesterday," for the Blairstown *Press;* Elmer Jones, retired rural delivery mail carrier who "served Feebletown all the while he was R.D. carrier"; and Jacob Maring, a farmer and substitute carrier on the same route. "All state," Ben reported, "that they have known the name all their lives, family knowledge, but cannot explain the origin."

Then there came a rewarding letter from Floyd A. Linaberry in Vienna and now I can tell you that for all the erudition of those who made those ever-challenging maps for the Beers *Atlas* in 1872, there never was a "Carrington." "Caddington" was the true name of the village northwest of Hackettstown, and the name by this time has been supplanted by Petersburg, which, Floyd insisted, was known as Cat Swamp, too. What continues to offer confusion is that there is no particular place known as Carrington, Caddington, Cat Swamp, or even Petersburg, which, I have been assured, is thought of as more of a region. I have come on that explanation time and again, and there would be more like it. The Great Meadows of the present—and a wholly pleasant village it is—was Danville, and I say this to reassure those who may have thought that I was referring to *Den*ville all the while. Perhaps at one time Danville and Denville caused confusion.

As I have suggested before, this time a blind guess, a hunch, was right on the very day I walked, for the first time, down the green "aisles" of those buried behind and beside the Presbyterian Church at Great Meadows. An impressive building of stone, it was no longer in use when I went there in mid-1962, as attested by a State Police warning, tacked across the crevice of the front door. Presbyterians in Great Meadows, I was told at that time, had reverted to churchgoing in Hacketts-town, where their ancestors who established this mission had lived in much earlier days. Later in 1962 I noted that the building had been taken over by an Eastern Orthodox congregation.

Here is where I saw the impressive marker to the memory of Daniel Vliet, for whom Danville, predecessor of Great Meadows, the postal town, was named—it is to the left of the church itself. And, not too carefully concealed behind the church itself, as well as in a back corner of the cemetery, were stacked-up tombstones, some broken, some with aged inscriptions remembering Danville pioneers. I always have been haunted by the thought of a departed spirit, wandering about in dismay and fruitless search for his (or her) name, or perhaps that of an old friend.

Thus I hurried off to see Floyd Linaberry, not knowing that before the hunt was over I would know more about The White Pilgrim than ever I had known before, in still another town, Stewartsville, which many find difficult to believe was once more important than Phillipsburg. When I met Floyd and Mrs. Linaberry in the morning quiet of their Vienna house, I found that I was next-door to what once was the "Christ-ian," or Christian, Church, now a well-ordered apartment building, with what could be to many a bewildering cemetery of its own out back. Floyd wrote this preamble: "I have known

Harold Ben Hill all his life—also his sister, Gertrude, his parents, and his paternal grandparents. My information might vary some from Harold's, but it is well to remember that no two witnesses will give the same report."

The friendly Linaberrys were a little surprised that anyone would act so quickly on an invitation to share what could be remembered of the fading lore of the land. My answer, I soon discovered, was one that had been borrowed by Floyd himself from the Parable of the Feeding of the Five Thousand—someone must gather up the fragments so that nothing be lost. Somehow the words very quickly brought us close together.

"First let me say that I never have heard of Carrington," Floyd Linaberry said, in his precise way. I replied that Caddington, an alternate name that Ben Hill had remembered in the interim, by this time is Petersburg and that even those who live in and near where it must have been do not know its story —or, if they do, would not admit it to me beyond pointing out some ruined walls which, they said, had been part of the old school. All Ben Hill had told me in passing was that he had suddenly remembered that his mother had gone to church in *Caddington,* not Carrington, and that it had been an offshoot of the Methodist Church in what had been Cumminstown, or Cumminsville, and now is Vienna. After a time, he had added, she had resumed "being a Methodist."

"I have wanted to know," I explained to the Linaberrys, "what the background of the Christ-ian, or Christian, Church is, not only because it has an association in my mind with The White Pilgrim in Johnsonburg but also because I would like to know why, in the 1840's at least, the hyphenated spelling of the name was adopted." Here I relied heavily on my old friends, John Barber and Henry Howe, of *The Historical Collections,* for proof on this point. The answer, if there is one, or more than one, never has been entrusted to me with complete definition, and so I am left to wonder at the number of churches calling themselves "Christian," seemingly without relationship, as well as at the "Christian Methodist Episcopal Church," as listed by the National Council of the Churches of Christ in the U.S.A., especially in the light of what was to be revealed in Vienna. And I have wondered, in the meanwhile, if the early pronunciation was different, even to the extent of calling it *Christ*-ian.

Floyd smiled knowingly and, for the most part, came to the point. "About 1838," he told me, "Mrs. Abigail Roberts, an evangelist, was refused the pulpit of the Vienna Methodist Church. Several of her followers met at the home of Matthias Cummins at Caddington, and services were held in the barn that then was owned by Christian Cummins." I asked immediately about the great stone barn that I had seen where the road bends in Petersburg, but later, when I returned there to ask even more pointed questions, answers were less than helpful. "A Christian Church was erected at once, and parts of the foundation are still in evidence," Floyd Linaberry told me. "The first floor was used for worship services and the basement as a school." I have seen the ruins near Petersburg.

All of which would indicate that a few boards, a kind of crude roof laid across the remaining walls, have made what used to be a church and school into a garage on the corner of what must be the heart of Petersburg, old Caddington. No one that I could find had heard of anything formally referred to as a church, although one or two "seemed to recall" the ruins of "the old school." The latter unquestionably outlasted the former. "Mrs. Lewis Ayers, who was Mabel Frace," my friend continued his story, "tells me that her father, born in 1853, attended this school. My own father, John A. Linaberry, attended classes there, too.

"In 1858 the members of the Caddington Church erected a church in Vienna and dedicated it, on February 1, 1859, with the Reverend Moses Cummins in charge." I asked about the Cumminses and the prevalence of the name, and Floyd said that he thought the family came from Alsace-Lorraine. The church was remodeled in 1883 and again in 1909. Worship services were discontinued about thirty years ago, and the building was sold for an art studio about fifteen years ago. About ten years ago," Floyd added, "I bought and remodeled it so it would be two comfortable apartments. People didn't seem to mind the cemetery in the rear. . . ." Although The White Pilgrim was in his temporary grave in the "Dark of the Moon Graveyard three years when Mrs. Roberts, the woman preacher, came to town, at least the legend persists in saying that he had something to do with the establishment of the church in Caddington.

In spite of the remodeling, the lines of the former church in Vienna reveal what it used to be, and I had no difficulty in identifying it, before I met the Linaberrys or saw the little graveyard and what would be to many just another house. One of the monuments, impressive in its height and polished granite, bears the name Cummins, and under it, Jakob and Maria. "These people," Floyd explained, even as we lingered there, "aren't here any more, although the stone would seem to say so. The bodies were removed to Pequest after the church was closed—by the way, there was a time when this whole vicinity was known as Pequest." Pequest, the name of a river, naturally adapted itself to the country through which it flowed, and hence the vicinity retained its name. I was to come upon that situation recurrently, especially in Wantage.

"But you'd think," I suggested, "that more people would recall just what happened—after all, much of all this isn't so long ago. I realize that the attitude of Methodists toward women in the pulpit has changed, even as it has with the Presbyterians, and the Abigail Robertses may have had a different reception in this day and age, but there are other questions here. Was there a different way of doing things that made these followers in the splinter group call themselves Christian— or *Christ*-ian? For that matter, what was the background of The White Pilgrim, and what did he teach? After all, the church in Johnsonburg knew his name well, and so did another in Hope. What made the Pilgrim so welcome in a dissident group calling itself Christian when members of other churches must have maintained with equal vehemence even then that they were Christian, too?"

That was when the Linaberrys, especially Mrs. Linaberry, promised to find me more on The White Pilgrim. Floyd went on unperturbed. "Prior to the Revolution," he was saying, "Bishop Asbury and others held worship services in the home of Philip Cummins, which resulted in the erection of the Methodist Church in Cumminstown, now Vienna, in 1810. At first this was called 'The New Jerusalem.' The Methodist Society of Trustees then included Philip Cummins, John Cummins, Christian Cummins, and James Hoagland. . . ." That was when I risked an interruption to point out that the Cumminses of Cumminstown had Methodist matters pretty much their own way, and Floyd merely replied again that the family had come from Alsace-Lorraine. If there was some connection, it remained obscure. Meanwhile I have been told that a variety of congregations have adopted the name of "Christian" for almost as many reasons.

This first Methodist church, which at a later date was to be the center of a squabble over a woman preacher, was, as they say, "enclosed at once," but, Floyd told me, "for a time a carpenter's bench was used as a pulpit." This means that religious fervor, at least as expressed here, could not wait for the building to be finished. This church "faced the village of Vienna." In 1854 it was torn down, and the present church was erected in its stead—the dedication came on January 8, 1855, with the Reverend John L. Lanhardt, Chaplain of the United States Senate, as the principal speaker, and with the Reverend James L. Tuttle in charge of the devotions. "Whereupon," Floyd said, "the Vienna Methodist Church became the head of the Circuit."

The infiltration of an earnest foreign-born population, attracted to the area by the living to be gained from the black muck of the ancient lake bottom—such soil produces lush crops of lettuce, onions, celery and other vegetables and spawns allied industries as well—is sweepingly "blamed" for the changes that intruded and even closed a church temporarily. This is only one aspect of the story, which includes, on the one hand, easier means of transportation, and, on the other, such differences in religious practice that minimize or preclude the loss of ceremony. Even a guidebook of 1939, which pays tribute to Dr. J. Marshall Paul, of Belvidere, who, single-handed, began a reclamation of this New Jersey lettuce land in 1850, significantly concludes a paragraph this way: "A Greek Catholic Church [in Great Meadows] offers a surprising architectural note: a silvered Byzantine cupola atop a severe wooden frame."

No architectural changes had been made in what once was the thriving Presbyterian Church at Danville and what was, for a long time, the idle, though not abandoned, Presbyterian Church at Great Meadows. Floyd Linaberry, who seemed to have all such matters readily on tap, gave me its history in this capsule' fashion: "The Danville Presbyterian Church was erected in 1824 and at first was a mission church of the Presbyterian Church in Hackettstown. The church was remodeled in 1868. Worship services were discontinued a few years ago, and now the church is again under the supervision of the Hackettstown Presbyterian Church." This was almost on the eve of the new arrangements by an Eastern Orthodox group to use the building.

It was also Floyd who told me, without equivocation, that my so-called hunch had been right and that Danville had been named in honor of Daniel Vliet, who surely must have been one of the pillars of the church in which services were recently revived. After all, there had been another Daniel, Daniel Van Buskirk, who was Danville's first postmaster—and some postmasters have been sufficiently lacking in humility to

name places in their own honor. The classic example, I always
have thought, was old Middle-of-the-Shore down in Burlington County, where Ebenezer Tucker, objecting to the second
name of Clamtown, soon devised ways to make it Tuckerton.
"I have not been able, so far, to learn how the name Mount
Rascal originated," Floyd confided sadly. Mount Rascal isn't
far from Hackettstown, and for those who inquire, two schools
of thought emerge on the subject: one says that there was once
a sure-enough rascal who lived somewhere atop an elevation
that today is beautiful to behold, and the other argues that
there was a family name involved—spelled Rascall. The late
Jack Minton always argued for the latter, but I must admit
that I never have seen the name on any of the monuments,
modest or impressive, in known or hard-to-find graveyards of
the neighborhood. The Recklesstown of Anthony Reckless, now
Chesterfield, and threatened by a traffic circle as I write, is
one thing, Mount Rascal something else again.

Floyd Linaberry and his wife continued with a miscellany
of loving remembrances after that, before the "concert" was
subdued and the "lights turned low" for what I should have
sensed to be the key revelation: as complete a story of The
White Pilgrim as I have had. The unintentional setting of the
stage came with more revelations on "the Skunktown locality";
a batch of information inherited by Floyd from his mother
with a bearing on the Feebletown mystery; still another mastodon skeleton gathered up from the fields on the Theodore
Barker farm halfway between Hackettstown and Vienna and
crated for a museum in Boston before Trenton was aware of it;
and ways in which Warren natives tell newcomers from old-
timers by ways in which they speak. A newcomer, I was informed by Ben Hill as well as Floyd Linaberry, speaks of
Paulina as *Paul-eena*, but the native sticks to *Paul-eye-na*. For
years I had been calling Alphano *Al-fah-no*, and if I had been
born or had lived nearby, I would have pronounced it *Al-fay-*

no. When you go up or over that way, you will have to decide for yourself whether you wish to go native or not.

There was a pause, and then there came a brief note from "F. A."—Floyd Linaberry—with the Vienna postmark, now familiar, urging me to see Mrs. Elizabeth Cool, in Stewartsville, without delay. He and Mrs. Linaberry were keeping a promise —remember?—and they had discovered that Mrs. Cool had a fragile clipping which had everything to do with The White Pilgrim. What was more, although I might copy what had been written at my leisure, there was attached a "Lament" for no less than the Pilgrim himself, set to a tune which Mrs. Cool remembered her grandmother singing. I am forced to conclude that the clipping had yellowed and become brittle because it had been tucked away in the intervening years in Grandmother's Family Bible. I think I was right on all counts.

I found Mrs. Cool with mixed emotions one summer's morning shortly thereafter. She was still distraught by the tragic drowning of a young man of whom the whole village had been fond, yet already busy with part of the preparations for a wedding to be held at the Stewartsville Presbyterian Church that afternoon. For the most part, however, she was graciously concerned because I had come "so far" for what, she said, might "turn out to be so ordinary a tale, even with the forgotten 'Lament.'" But you shall presently judge of that.

I reassured Mrs. Cool when I said that I had been seeking more details on the life of The White Pilgrim for many years, and I was hoping, at the same time, to learn what he and the Christ-ian Church taught. I had not expected to find such answers in Stewartsville, which, until then, had been a very old town principally identified with the Morris Canal, now traceable only in a tree-grown depression across some pastures north of the village. I should have known better. This was Greenwich Township, Warren County, pronounced *Greenwitch*, and not *Gren-nitch*, as in Connecticut or sometimes even in New Jersey's own Cumberland County. This is where the old Greenwich Presbyterian Church happens to be and, across from it, deserving of special treatment later on, an old mill and the miller's house, dated 1677. On the property are abutments of the bridge of an old but forgotten road that had been an Indian trail and that came up as a road from Flemington.

"There is more to history than what the historians would like us to know," Mrs. Cool told me, "and I am still looking for details of the history of the old tavern down at the corners." She gave me a copy of the centenary booklet published by the Stewartsville Presbyterians in 1950, but not before she had read from one of the pages these words, given new warmth in the quiet of a country parlor: "In 1844 Stewartsville was a flourishing village with forty-five dwellings, and, at the same time, Phillipsburg had only thirty-five homes, thus, believe it or not, Stewartsville was at one time larger than Phillipsburg."

"What I'd really like to get," Mrs. Cool added, "is, as I've told you, the history of the very old tavern up at the corners— it's several apartments there, now, and the date, 1814, seems to have been scratched in the plaster near the roof-peak. And there's always that story of the two young men hanged on the village green in Newton for a crime that they didn't commit. . . ." Mrs. Cool smiled as she passed me a second yellowing clipping from another old book, knowing full well that some day I would go on from there.

The invaluable cutting presumably recounts as much as was known of The White Pilgrim, and may have appeared older than it was because of the quality of the newsprint, but that must remain as much a mystery as the name of the newspaper from which it came and the wanderings, equally uncertain, of its subject. The Pilgrim dressed all in white because, in the gossip of the neighborhood, the color white was impervious to the world's evils; in his estimate—at least until his last conscious hours on earth—white was also a barrier to all contagion. The manner of the Pilgrim's death was surely a contradiction of any such theories and, quite as certainly, could have been of little reassurance to his followers.

In reflection, it is a wonder to me that among the rampant superstitions which surrounded the death and burial of The White Pilgrim, not one, insofar as I know, attributed anything sinister to the borrowed use of the Johnsonburg Episcopal Church, at that time an outpost of the Society for the Propagation of the Gospel in Foreign Parts in England. Here are the words of the clipping:

"Considerable local interest attaches to a movement to inaugurate a pilgrimage to the tomb of Joseph Thomas, in the cemetery at Johnsonburg, Warren County, next April, the eighty-third anniversary of his death. Thomas was known as 'The White Pilgrim' eighty years ago because of his custom of wearing white clothing, including white hat and boots, and riding a white horse. This was very unusual for these times and Thomas is referred to by a historian of the early part of the nineteenth century as 'a living oddity.'

"Joseph Thomas was a native of Ohio, born about 1790. While a young man he became impressed with a call to the extension of the Kingdom of God and became an itinerant preacher. He traveled up and down the country, preaching his doctrine wherever he could find an audience, and, garbed as he was, this was not very difficult. His fame always preceded him.

"When he made his first visit to New Jersey in 1835 he was everywhere given a respectful hearing and made many converts. The reason of his visit to Johnsonburg at this time was no doubt due to the existence of a Christian Society there, such an organization being instituted in 1826 by the Rev. Simon Clough and his colleague, Rev. J. S. Thomson. . . ."

The story gives no indication of an alternate spelling which appears in *The Historical Collections* and other historical records—*Christ-ian*—and I am still left wondering where this was first used and why. There is sufficient proof, however, I think, that The White Pilgrim, whatever his "doctrines" may have been, did not establish the church, either in Johnsonburg or in Caddington, now Petersburg. It is more likely that he was welcomed even as was Abigail Roberts. The account continues:

"The articles of faith of this society were at one simple and comprehensive. They read 'We covenant together to take the Scriptures as our rule of faith and practice, and agree as far as in us lies to walk by them, allowing to each other the right of private judgment in matters pertaining to conscience.'

"The White Pilgrim's work was about finished when he reached Johnsonburg. He preached but one sermon there, and that was delivered in the old Episcopal church. A few hours afterward he was stricken with a virulent attack of small-pox, which, in the absence of competent medical treatment, soon ended his active and useful life. His body was buried in the Dark Moon burying ground. . . ."

Unless my arithmetic is off, The White Pilgrim was either forty-four or forty-five when he died—so just what does the statement, his "work was about finished," mean? Was this the end of his itinerary in New Jersey and did he have plans for resuming elsewhere, or did he, in reality, linger only where his reception was enthusiastic? Further, here is evidence that "the Dark Moon burying ground" long survived when the church behind which it had been established had gone. By now, as I may have told you, even the corner that once was occupied by the tavern is empty, except for a hardly discernible cellar hole, and you may have two choices concerning "the Dark Moon" as a name. Either a "dark moon" was painted on the sign-board of Johnsonburg's "out-of-town" inn, surely not the one where the Pig Drover told his stories, or part of what became known as the Dark Moon Drive rarely saw the light of sun or moon. When I went there last, its most darksome curve had been cut from the main road so that in any light it remained

Mrs. Elizabeth Cool, of Stewartsville, near the banks of the old Morris Canal, was a saver of clippings and referred to little-known details of the life of The White Pilgrim and the ballad that was written about him after his death in Log Gaol.

darker than ever. Russell Hendershot, who lives across the way from where the curve was cut away from the road that still goes climbing up toward Yellow Frame, prefers the latter. The story continues:

"The most pathetic phase of this incident is the fact that this earnest preacher of the gospel died among strangers, far away from his wife and children, whom he left in Ohio, and who were not permitted to be with him in his last hours or even to visit the grave of their loved one.

"During the convention of the Christian Church held in 1846, the remains of The White Pilgrim were removed from the Dark Moon burying ground to the cemetery of the church at Johnsonburg, where his last sermon was preached. The sum of $125 was contributed by the people of the neighborhood for a suitable monument which was erected shortly afterward. This monument bears the following inscription, '*Joseph Thomas. Minister of the Gospel in the Christian Church. Known as The White Pilgrim by reason of his wearing white raiment.'*. . ."

I am sure that I saw the monument that first time I saw the Log Gaol milestone, and the inquiry followed, step by step. I have been told from time to time that I have confessed utter ignorance in admitting that I have obtained so little of the lore of the primitive Christ-ian Church, but, at the same time, I have been assured by others that the sect, under its rule of conscience, holds to a variety of beliefs and practices, depending on circumstances and the neighborhood in which it happens to be operating. Each time I suggest that a group, holding to the original tenets that barred a woman "with a message" from the pulpit, has all but died out in New Jersey, I am informed that I err gravely, that there are those who keep it alive, here and there, perhaps under the old name that by now means many things, and with little association between one church and another. The article Mrs. Cool loaned me in Stewartsville attached the "celebrated" lament, by which she set great store:

I came to the spot where The White Pilgrim lay
   And pensively stood by his tomb,
And in a low whisper a voice seemed to say:
   "How sweetly I sleep here alone."

The tempest may howl and loud thunders may roll
   And gathering storms may arise,
But calm are my feelings, at rest is my soul
   The tears are all wiped from my eyes.

The call of my Master compelled me from home,
  I bade my companion farewell;
I left my sweet children, who for me now mourn,
  In a far-distant region to dwell.

I wandered a stranger, an exile from home,
  To publish salvation abroad:
I met the contagion and sunk in the tomb,
  My spirit ascending to God.

Go tell my companion and children most dear
  To weep not the loved one that's gone;
The same hand that led me through scenes dark and drear
  Hath kindly conducted me home.

The name of the melancholy minstrel had been revealed in
these lines:

"Shortly after his death (April 9, 1835) The White Pilgrim's
grave was visited by J. Ellis, of Irvington, who composed and
published the following 'Lament' which became so popular that
it was sung to a tune that is still remembered by some of our
older residents. . . ."

And so I have shared with you the words of the ballad in
full, not only because composers of those days seized upon
all such occasions, national and rural, to burst into mournful
phrases, with music to match, but also because this particular
composition—and I shall certainly continue to seek out the
tune—must surely be classed as an early New Jersey folksong,
of which only too few have been kept intact. Or are some of
them, at least in text, hidden away in clippings such as this one
guarded well by Mrs. Cool, of whom I would not have heard
if it had not been for Floyd Linaberry, who, in turn, had been
alerted by Ben Hill's admission, perhaps contrived, of what he
was not sure.

I did not ask Mrs. Cool if she recalled the melody her

grandmother had sung. Perhaps I will some day. But the time of bereavement in her community that week had taken its toll, without the further intrusion on the memory of words gloomily associated with the death and first burial of that strange and ascetic wanderer, The White Pilgrim.

Chapter III

THE SHADES OF DEATH

It is easy to become a name-dropper in this kind of gentle probing, especially along the old roads traveled by such memorable wanderers as The Old Pig Drover and The White Pilgrim—to say nothing of the postal riders and the drivers of careening coaches who had to know their way. I can say truthfully that it never has been my purpose to drop the name of a place for mere impression's sake, and yet we will link together the legends and their variants, even though we may not learn all we wish to know overnight.

Rock-studded fields will yield the blue and white of summer's ragged robin and Queen Anne's lace to the winter's snow, folding its own spotless blanket around the stones of otherwise forgotten graves, but place names as certainly linger, either in dimming memories or on yellowing maps. Meaningful names like Shiloh, or Mount Hermon, or Buttermilk Pond stay much longer than those who named them and knew why. Thus I hope always to see, in what there is, at least a wavering shadow of what there used to be.

Glancing back along the ways by which we have come so far, I find references to Waterloo, Stillwater, Yellow Frame, and Gratitude as well, and soon we must go and see what they are and were. We know now that Carrington must have been a slip on a mapmaker's drawing board, that Freedom has been inexplicably cut to Fredon, and that "The Devil's Kitchen" and "The Devil's Wheelwright Shop" were caves better known to incautious but more respectful boys of another time. And the Wershings, having reclaimed the church, where The White Pilgrim preached his last and fatal sermon in Johnsonburg, the old Log Gaol, into Johnsonburg House where antiques are purveyed informally, are now convinced that the most important antique of all is missing: a date plate bearing the numerals 1781, which competent authorities and even history argue should have been 1751 or even 1731. Helen and Robert Wershing have been too cautious in subheading Johnsonburg House with a mere "Circa 1770," and I am seeking evidence at the offices of the Society for the Propagation of the Gospel in Foreign Parts, in London, to prove it.

Now, on a homespun diagram fashioned for me by kindly Floyd Linaberry are shown the ways to Belvidere, the Warren County seat with its quiet square or green recalling New England villages; to the Danville that became Great Meadows; and to the Cumminstown that is Vienna, not because of those who live there but because Jakob Cummins thought more of the old Vienna he had loved than of a memorial to himself. In this Warren region, called Pequest before the Revolution, I find strange fascination in the "Shades of Death Road," which skirts the blacklands of the Great Meadows as the rim of a cup, a feeling that is oddly akin to the spell cast by the name of the River Styx, which flows into Lake Hopatcong. If memory serves, both names were first mentioned to me by John B. Ehrhardt, of Madison, who through the years has acted as a special kind of prompter in matters like this. Even as the name, or nickname, of Feebletown (or the many Feebletowns I'm sure there used to be) now suddenly seems to take on a meaning we had all but lost, I like to think of Hope as most appropriately at the upper end of the Shades of Death Road, even though the Moravians who founded and built the town probably intended no connection at all.

John Ehrhardt's interest in the whole of the Great Meadows area was caught, he told me later, by "a little line on one of the maps of the Jenny Jump State Forest, designating an unimproved road at the base of the mountain as the Shades of Death Road. I inquired about it," John said, "and heard one fantastic story about some people killed by wildcats many, many years ago. Only recently I heard a somewhat more credible story of a series of murders in the vicinity—this last fragment of 'folksay' from a lay preacher of a Methodist church that then served the area as it probably still does. However, the nearest I came to a reasonable explanation for the Shades of Death was in a little booklet given me by a neighbor, Luther C. Scull," who, John explained further, was a rose-grower by profession and a geologist by avocation, "the man who would like to demonstrate his ability to grow roses under-

There are already several variants of the legend of "The Shades of Death," the name given the black mucklands up from Vienna and Great Meadows—everything from malaria to murder. Drainage turned the "Shades" into rich truck gardening lands.

ground." Knowing John as I do, I was interested in trying to knit his report on the Shades of Death into the pattern because it is likely to mingle such oddments as geology, politics, reports of pioneer physicians, and even some religion, with the lore of the land.

Luther Scull showed John Ehrhardt the report of the state geologist for the year 1884, as a starter, and this included a summary on the drainage of The Great Meadows, a project which cost New Jersey the then "stupendous" sum of $108,241. "Some obscure notes in Luther's books seemed to shed light on the Shades of Death," John explained. "They quoted Dr. William I. Roe, of Vienna, as saying, in 1877, that almost thirty years before he had been in practice for two years at Danville, on the lower border of The Great Meadows. 'At that time,' Dr. Roe said, 'the prevailing diseases were, for the most part, malarial in character. The intermittents were very severe and many of the residents expected the usual attacks of chills in the spring while a family moving into the neighborhood from a non-malarial district seldom escaped the ravages of miasma in one form or another.' "

John Ehrhardt found that another physician, Dr. E. T. Blackwell, of Hackettstown, had turned in this report: "In 1849, I passed the year at Townsbury and saw the influence of The Great Meadows. The health of the community was good until the middle of August, when malarial diseases in great variety and of all grades of intensity became extremely prevalent. Until winter, this outbreak continued, prostrating in some instances three or four members of the same family. The year, 1850, I passed at Danville, immediately on the edge of The Great Meadows. My experience with malaria here was repeated in an intensified form.

"During the preceding epidemic, by shunning exposure in the nighttime and, when this was impossible, wearing a handkerchief as a respirator, I was able to avoid the worst effects upon myself. Here,"—at Danville—"all devices failed; and I experienced in my own person its poisonous results in an attack of fever.

"It appeared to me, while sojourning in this neighborhood and marking the blighting effect of these influences upon the health of the people, that I could perceive in the lessened vigor and robustness of many of the residents, the results of this insidious and baleful poison. According to my observation, this is by far the most malarious district in this part of the State. The outbreak of malaria always occurs when the overflow of the Pequest, drying up, leaves its sedimentary matter as well as the earth saturated with deadly gases to the full influence of the fierce autumn sun."

John Ehrhardt was troubled at the time, his notes indicate, by Tom Gordon's slight reference to Danville in his *Gazetteer* of 1834: "Danville, postoffice, Warren co." John happily adds, however, that by 1844 John W. Barber and Henry Howe in their *Historical Collections* were not only more generous in their report on Warren's Independence Township, but they made mention of a church that revealed to John immediately where Danville was, and remains, under its new name, Great Meadows. "They wrote: 'Danville, on the road to Hope, on the western line of the township, 5 m. from Hackettstown, contains about 16 dwellings, several mechanics, and a Presbyterian church built of stone. Vienna, 1 m. E. of Danville, on the same road, is a village of about the same size. . . .'"

In summer the graveyard of the church is well cared for and kindly vines conceal the jumble of discarded and displaced tombstones that bother one in winter's exposure of so many things. There are many Revolutionary veterans buried here beside the road which, apparently in the beginning, turned up to Hope by way of The Shades of Death, and it is good to know that they are still shepherded, inasmuch as there is no such thing as *absentia* in such a state, by the Reverend John Rosbrugh, Presbyterian chaplain in the Continental Army who was bayoneted by Hessians at Trenton January 2, 1777, according to a memorial stone near the gate at the left of the church. However, the burial was in Trenton.

A passage from Barber and Howe is of special interest here: first, because Danville is definitely recorded as having been on an early road that swung up to "the North Country," which Floyd Linaberry had said was Shades of Death Road. Second, because John Ehrhardt had remembered the stone church and therefore the malarial Danville of old. He had used the direct road through Great Meadows to the Delaware Water Gap, that mecca of holiday seekers amidst the lost glories of the railroad era at its peak. You may remember one reaction to the events that led to that era, curiously similar to the sentiment that preceded the automotive age, the age of air travel, and now, the age of space. One writer said: ". . . But much of the natural beauty of this region has been destroyed recently by the building of the Delaware, Lackawanna & Western cut-off, running from Lake Hopatcong to the Delaware Water Gap. Modern enterprise lays her hands ruthlessly upon the beauties of nature, and the sentiments of localities, caring for none of these things, as long as the ends of commercial interests can be accomplished. . . ."

I cannot help but wonder what the same writer would think of the great mound of stones, the old roadbed, virtually a wall cutting across the countryside like a giant mole's burrow, with a tunnel here and there one carriage wide on roads that must have a way through. For now it is a mountain surmounted by one surviving track, where once there were two and even three, if long, impressive sidings are to be counted, with once countless, once elegant stations now dusty, dreary, boarded up, or pried open by vandals. We will visit some of these later, but I doubt if there will be any point in waiting for a passenger train.

John Ehrhardt was fortunate to be in Great Meadows in time to talk with John A. Cummins, a member of the family whose convictions compelled a resentment of the expulsion of

Abigail Roberts, the woman evangelist, and of the subsequent, if fleeting, establishment of a little church in Caddington, now Petersburg. "Like most good men," John Ehrhardt reported afterward, "John Cummins was rather reticent, insisting that he could lead me to a man more venerable who would be a better source of stories. When he said, however, that he was the great-grandson of the first permanent settler in the area, I decided to look no further."

"My great-grandfather," he told John, "was Jakob Cummins, an Austrian. He settled a few miles east of here, and a group of houses sprung up around him. Folks called it 'Cumminstown,' but when they wanted to put it on the map, my great-grandfather said, 'Don't call it Cumminstown; call it Vienna.' That was after the city he lived in in the old country. . . ."

When did Danville become Great Meadows, and why? John Ehrhardt talked with John Cummins in July, 1953. I did not meet Floyd Linaberry until 1962. Both men were precise in their statements, and if there were any slight discrepancies, I was concerned only by one of them. Any interruption in a narrative at such times often proves fatal, but, even so, I could not help but wonder about Floyd's linking the first Cumminses with Alsace-Lorraine and John Cummins' placing Jakob in Vienna. Not until much later was I to hear the explanation and know that both Floyd Linaberry and John Cummins were right. In 1953, John said that Danville had become Great Meadows seventy-six years before. "The railroad came through here, and they wanted one station for both Vienna and Danville," he said. "People up to Vienna wanted the station named for their town; so did the people at Danville. That was when the president of the Hudson & Lehigh stepped in and said: 'I'll name the station myself.' He called it Great Meadows, and it's been Great Meadows ever since.

"Of course, inasmuch as the station is really here in Danville, it wasn't long before the whole town took the name, even the post office. . . ." Apparently the malarial reputation that had oozed from The Great Meadows wasn't referred to, nor was the road called Shades of Death. There is evidence, however, that some older residents rarely connected the badlands with what their doctors said, or, if they did, they expressed agreement. John Cummins told John Ehrhardt that the name Shades of Death was derived from a series of murders there.

"There were three or four in my time and two of them are still unsolved," said this amiable descendant of the Cumminstown Cumminses with no quibbling at all. "One of them that was killed was a relative of mine, and we always suspected a neighbor who knew he had sold his crops and had seven hundred dollars in cash on him. But we couldn't prove anything."

But, John persisted, wasn't the name Shades of Death much older than that? "Oh, sure," John Cummins was quick to agree, "but that was before my great-grandfather's time around here. Used to be, I've heard tell, there was a whole colony of squatters who lived up that way. They kept pretty much to themselves, they did. Used to be said they had a lot of women, and they used to fight a lot over the women. Every so often somebody would be killed, but the law never could get anything out of the witnesses. But that was long before *my* time."

What about wildcats? What about the story that a lot of people had been killed by wildcats and that that was where the name Shades of Death came from? "Never heard of any in The Shades of Death [Great Meadows], but we had a-plenty in Petersburg," John Cummins replied easily, folding up his forehead in a special way he had. "Used to call it Cat Hollow," he added, and I remembered Floyd Linaberry's reference to Cat Swamp as an earlier name for Caddington and Petersburg. "Last one we killed, I'd say, was maybe forty years ago. They used to have his head in the big greenhouse in Hackettstown. . . ."

John Ehrhardt, persistent in his conclusion that the name Shades of Death had drifted down from pioneers who knew malaria well and came to "expect" it as a kind of seasonal plague connected in some way with the undrained bottom of an ancient lake, put this question: "What do you know about the time they drained The Great Meadows?" John Cummins was full of answers to that one and hesitated only an instant to begin with some of them. "That was in my grandfather's time," he replied. "One night a bunch of men came to the house and asked my grandfather to sign a petition asking for the drainage work. Grandfather told them to leave their paper and he would sign it, probably, in the morning—that is, if he thought it was all right. He wanted to sleep on it, he said.

"But he wanted to do more than that. Next morning, early,

The station and some of the houses in Vienna have the air of the Old Country.

John Cummins, of what used to be Cumminstown and now is Vienna, said that his great-grandfather, Jakob, urged that the new name recall his native Austria rather than the family.

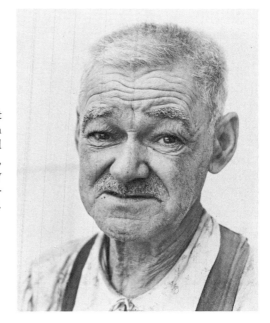

Grandfather took my father in the rig and went to see Dr. Ephraim Sampson. Now Dr. Sampson was the minister of the Presbyterian Church and a regular D.D.—but he farmed just like the rest of us. Dr. Sampson said, 'I won't sign that paper, and I wouldn't want you to sign it. If you sign, they can assess you for the work!' So Grandfather didn't sign, and he and my father and the Dominie rode around to talk to those who hadn't signed yet, to warn them about the assessment.

"Sure enough, when the work was done, the state tried to assess the cost against everybody they said was benefited. Took it to court, too, they did, and Dr. Sampson himself helped with the defense. The court ruled that everybody above the bridge had to pay whether they had signed the paper or not, but only those below the bridge who had signed the paper had to pay. You see, we were below the bridge—and we did not pay anything.

"Some of those who were assessed refused to pay, so the

state took their land and sold it at auction. There was one fella in particular I remember. He was a big Irishman named Paddy Welsh. He refused to pay, and they took his land. Some Ukrainians bought it, and they were the first Ukrainians around here. That's when—" John Cummins broke off thoughtfully, and, equally as thoughtfully, John Ehrhardt, who knows his churches, allowed his gaze to rest on the appropriate and prophetic onion-like spire of the Eastern Orthodox Church down the road.

How about malaria before the meadows were drained? That was the next question, pertinent enough from a newspaperman who, when I first knew him, was calling on doctors for a pharmaceutical house. John Ehrhardt would not be one to surrender easily to tales of murder and wildcats if malaria, after all, was the true explanation for the name Shades of Death. John Cummins, with the steadiest of steady looks, gave him no solace at all. "Never was much around here that I heard of," he replied. "Never needed much draining, either. Big red house across the way used to belong to a rich man named Sweasy. He drained most of this land at his own expense. Used oxen for some hand-ditching, he did."

John Ehrhardt, never a man to let a story stand one-sided, told me that after he had listened to what John Cummins had said about the assessment appeal of so many years ago, he decided not to pursue the matter further. "However," he told me, "I think the record is entitled to show what some other residents of The Great Meadows area thought about the drainage. Certainly," he said, "when I visited there I saw no sign of the 'lessened vigor and robustness' that had disturbed Dr. Blackwell more than a century before. Instead, in the black muck land, a compound of sand and decayed swamp vegetation, are raised first-quality onions, celery, spinach, carrots, and lettuce for the city markets, often running to two crops each year—a rare occurrence in this climate. Laughing women and children offer their wares from the side of the road and assure you that the vegetables came 'out of the muck' as a sign of true vegetable nobility."

Then John remembered that John Cummins had told him of the "muck works" down from the Shades of Death Road and that this is now the plant producing a special kind of fertilizer. I have found this true even on prowls on county roadways that provide startling views of the carefully ditched inky-black oblongs from almost every direction. John Cummins dismissed the idea by saying that mixed dried muck with over-ripe fish and chemicals was prepared and sold to city gardeners in little tin cans. "Used to get twenty dollars a ton for the stuff," John Cummins said, "before they started putting it in cans." There was nothing in the way of legend here, of that I was assured.

The way John Ehrhardt put it at the conclusion of his report was this: "Whence all this prosperity in an area where it was once fearsomely fatal to live? The books suggest the answer. 'The Great Meadows,' reported the state geologist in 1884, 'are lands bordering on the Pequest River, and its branches, Trout Brook and Bear Creek, in the townships of Independence, Allamuchy, and Frelinghuysen in Warren County, and Greene, in Sussex County. The southern end of the meadows is at Danville, and they extend upward on the main stream to Tranquility; up Trout Brook past Allamuchy, and up Bear Creek well towards Johnsonburg.

" 'The extreme length is 8.25 miles and the breadth varies from 1.75 to 0.25 miles. The area covered by them is assessed at 6,038.14 acres. . . .' " And the report goes on to relate how, in 1808–1810, Richard Addis had attempted to drain the area without success, followed by the workings of Amos Hoagland, Joseph Coryell, Thomas Fleming, David Menell, Nathan Hoagland, Samson H. Albertson, and John Stinson, many of whose names I have seen in the graveyards of the neighborhood, wishing each time that I could have known them and their trials. At least those who have been remembered here had to watch their money wash out at the ends of crumbling and useless ditches. None of their work produced permanent benefit, but between 1830 and 1840, Dr. J. Marshall Paul, of Belvidere, the only one who seems to have been singled out in even recent guidebooks, "achieved a yield high enough from the drained land to suggest that great economic benefit could be obtained from the work. However, Dr. Paul's money ran out, too, and his works were allowed to revert to nature. . . ." Oddly enough, although John Cummins made not the slightest reference to it, the Cummins family is credited as being the only one to keep the ditches open and the land drained with private capital from the 1840's on. Momentarily, you will know where.

With Dr. Paul, the prophet without honor, the state stepped into the picture in 1870, launching a dredging project that included the formidable removal of as much as five and a half feet of earth and boulders from the channel of the Pequest River. The work was completed in 1884, and, by 1886, Dr. John S. Cook, of Hackettstown, was able to write: "I think I can say that there has been a great decrease in the malarial diseases along the course of the Pequest since drainage was accomplished. These diseases are no more prevalent than in any other well-drained county. My own experience, and the reports of other physicians, confirm me in making this report."

If I have said that the flats, the meadows of Newark, have their own kinds of beauty, depending on the season of the year and mindful that it was expediency and man's greed that here destroyed a great cedar forest, then such an appraisal goes double for The Great Meadows of today where man commendably has reversed the process. Here, where even the height of The Shades of Death Road provides a panoramic view comparable in appearance to the contrasts of farmlands seen from the air, even the mists veiling the highest ridges of Jenny Jump Mountain offer no deterrent but, rather, something that is breathtaking, not by any means the leftovers of malarial days. If there are more legends of the mucklands concerned with wildcats or murders or even the fears that came with railroad intrusions, I am convinced that few who now live in The Great Meadows know them, or, if they knew, will have much more to say about them. Certainly these do not know the folksay around and down from the checkerboard mucklands any better than John Cummins, or Floyd Linaberry, or even Ben Hill in Blairstown, who sent me to Floyd.

One day, when I made another circuit of The Great Meadows, I came in from still another direction, across the old lake bottom from the Shades of Death Road. I had Floyd Linaberry's hand-drawn map with me, to make sure of Alphano (Al-fay-no) and where it was, when it had been Arnoldtown and, before that, Meadeville. Here, in what easily could have been another Cumminstown, I came upon the secret in the name, even though John Cummins had not remembered it. As usual, Bill Augustine was with me and it was he, as we came in from the north, who remarked again on the impressive stone house that commanded a long view of the mucklands. "Looks like a proprietor's house," Bill said, and I knew he was thinking of the forgemasters' houses of the old big ore towns. It was a house that still held the authority of an owner who had considered the possibilities of the mucklands long ago and had lived where he could watch the development of at least as much as he owned.

Men in the dooryard sent us to the house itself, and there we were met by a young man whose flashing eyes and soft voice I always will remember. He said that he was Arthur Anderson and that his mother had been a Cummins. The house? Yes, it was a Cummins house, built in 1854. The builder had been Nelson Cummins, who had owned about three hundred acres of The Great Meadows. "I am making sure," I explained, "that I know where Alphano is. . . ."

"This," Arthur Anderson replied, "is Alphano—although most

of the houses are down there—you can see them from here. Why the interest in Alphano?"

It was more than that, I said, and I told him of our many journeys around the Shades of Death, of what Floyd Lina-berry had said, and all that no less than John Cummins had added. "But I am still puzzled," I confessed, "by a number of things. First, there was Floyd's reference to the family coming from Alsace-Lorraine, and then, in the next breath, the old Vienna was mentioned. And I would like to know more about this Christ-ian Church with the hyphenated name—almost as if the name of Our Lord were said in its usual way."

"As I have read of it," Arthur answered easily, "they were the result of an early split with the Methodists." I knew that was true as far as the area was concerned, when a group, mostly Cumminses, went off to Caddington, the Petersburg

The Presbyterian Church in Great Meadows was once a mission of the church in Hackettstown, but it became inactive and now is used by members of the Eastern Orthodox Church.

of today, and held their own meeting rather than allow a woman evangelist to speak. "As for the Cumminses," Arthur went on, "they were Huguenots, and the good people of Alsace-Lorraine took them in when they fled religious persecution. Those were days, you see, when the oversight of Alsace-Lorraine was vested in the government of Austria. . . ."

Thinking back, I must have stared a little, for Arthur Anderson smiled and added, "At least that is how we've pieced it together in the family and from what I've studied. As far as we know, the Cumminses took their name from the place from which they had come, Comines, or Commines, actually in Belgium."

"You mentioned studying at a college on Long Island," I put in when I had recovered from surprise, surprise in the simplicity of it. "What are you studying?"

"I'm going to be a priest," this kinsman of the old Huguenots said, quietly but proudly, as well he might. "I hope to be ordained in October." I showed my pleasure, and we shook hands.

Chapter IV

SNUFF AND SNUFFLE

I don't know just when it was that I first became aware of the name of Snufftown on some of the older maps of New Jersey. Certainly without the variant, Snuffletown, or "Snuffle T.," as it appeared on Mr. Finley's map made for Tom Gordon's *Gazetteer* in 1834, it was one of those irritants in a name which, like Ong's Hat, Hockamick, or even Mendham, presented its own riddle, demanding solution. Peculiarly enough, the quest began in Snufftown, Sussex County, many years ago; it did not come to a conclusion, at least for me, until 1962—and that was in Changewater, on both sides of the Musconetcong River in Warren and Hunterdon Counties. Snufftown, I now have been assured, never had a snuff mill; Changewater had a mill, and it still stands, like an idle red barn.

Although there were a few who said, at the beginning, that Snufftown might have been merely a nickname, this was not to prove the exact answer, although it was closer than the idea that a simulated snuff might have been made at odd moments at the tannery. I remember pointing out that I knew of no other place in New Jersey with even the nickname of Snufftown, not even Helmetta, of the George W. Helme Company, which still makes snuff for a sizeable market. The Helmetta post office has known of letters directed to Hell Meadow, even when my friends of the Order of St. Helena had a convent there.

Tom Gordon took no notice of Hockamick as a name, or, indeed, of any of the legends surrounding Ong's Hat, which run a fabulous gamut from a hat in a tree (that still is there) to a Little Egg Harbor wanderer, Jacob Ong, but he offered

64

an immediate challenge by spelling Snufftown *Snuffletown*, with map to match. By 1844 John W. Barber and Henry Howe, glowing in the glories of the Hamburg and Wallkill Mountain, as well as the "high eminence" called Pimple Hill, lingered a little at Ogdensburg, Sparta, and Franklin before writing their estimates of Hardiston Township in Sussex, ignoring Snufftown and Tom Gordon's *Snuffletown* altogether. James P. Snell in his *History of Sussex and Warren Counties* of 1881 offers contradictory descriptions of Snufftown while the Beers *Atlas* map shows that it was, a few years earlier, the post town of Stockholm.

More than ten years ago, John Dixon Neel wrote from his retirement hideaway near Woodglen, once Whitehall, in Hunterdon County to enlist my help in weaving some regional folklore into a little brochure he had been asked to produce. The main theme of the little book was to have been the history of the Changewater Methodist Church, celebrating its fiftieth anniversary in 1951. When I hastened to see "Mr. Neel," as the whole neighborhood knew him, he told me that lack of funds on the part of the Changewater Church had curtailed the original plan, and I shared his disappointment. What emerged was little more than the story of the church as part of the program. Even so, one fact stood out in that story when it came to me: There *had* been a snuff mill in Changewater, and, what was more, its operator had given the land on which the church was built, in addition to a sizeable donation of money for the building fund.

So, for the longest while I had it on my mind that snuff had had something to do with the whole business. I had been to Snufftown, miles away, only to be told that no one knew where, or if, snuff was made there, and in the midst of the chronicle of those days, a quiet-voiced old lady told me briskly enough that "everybody took snuff." I had been in Changewater much more frequently, but no one, at least then, singled out the place where snuff had been made. I had grown up in a town, much further to the south, where it always had been said that the fashionable church of the community derived much of its well-being from the liberality of the snuff-and-tobacco tycoon. It was natural, then, for me to wonder if the snuff chapter of the Changewater Church had had something to do with reducing a little book of folklore into a paragraph in mere program notes. But Dick Neel had assured me since that it did not. Even so, it was friendship of the late John Dixon Neel, "J. D.," that pulled Changewater and Snufftown together, no matter how much "geography" there may be in between.

Truly, under the Stockholm label, Snufftown is still there. Not long ago, I looked in on the pastor of the Stockholm Methodist Church, which, I was quite sure, had lacked that identification when I was there in the beginning. "This *is* Snufftown, really," he said. I was to learn, only moments later, that he had just concluded what he called a "Snufftown Fair" for his church. Still striving in my stubborn way for some strange connection between church and snuff, I was told merely that perhaps some support for the church had come from those who "made or used it." I came home as baffled as ever and decided, on the way, to pay another call on Dick Neel.

Meanwhile I had been trying to learn something of the transition of Snuffletown to Snufftown. My fat dictionary said that *snuffle* had been "an (or the) act of snuffling" at least as early as 1764. There were other definitions, all accompanied by an illustrative quotation, "She has at present a little London cold, but her Grace says that it is only the snuffles." The snuff that was "a preparation of tobacco for inhaling through the nostrils" went back at least to 1683 and could be "any powder used like snuff for medicinal purposes." "Snuff," said still another reference, "is a fine powder made from the stems and leaves of the tobacco plant. The tobacco is first fermented by heat and moisture, and then dried and ground. Snuff is sniffed in through the nostrils, or chewed, or rubbed on the gums.

Various mixtures of flavors or scents are added to make the powder pleasant. At one time each person carried a snuffbox and it was considered a matter of etiquette to offer 'a pinch of snuff' upon meeting a friend. This practice is still carried on in southern Europe." I was now sure I knew much more about snuff than ever I did before, but where was it getting me?

My suspicions of a Snufftown that had seemed to be so evasive about its snuff mill, if indeed there was one, were magnified. Was the name that Tom Gordon had recorded as Snuffletown correct, and did it denote a village where nearly everybody had the sniffles? Could the same equipment used in the grinding up of bark for the tanning of leather serve to turn out a simulated snuff or even the real product if tobacco were grown nearby or brought in? I consulted one of my doctor friends who said he had treated many wartime soldiers who had acquired the habit of rubbing snuff on gums behind lower lips, and he shook his head. No bark, however treated, he was quite sure, could be passed off as snuff.

My call on Dick Neel was delayed, and I can blame nothing but a combination of faulty memory and stupidity on my part. I had forgotten the odd operations of the United States mail in rural areas as compared with the simplicities of yesteryear. John lived on the Hunterdon side of the Musconetcong, and although Changewater's post office may seem nearer, I was told that those living "across the water" could get their mail at Changewater only "by special arrangement." The postmaster there sent me to Hampton, and a postal clerk there sent me to Glen Gardner. By that time it was too late to retrace my steps, but at least there was a rural delivery man who recalled the way to Mr. Neel's house. I wrote to John Neel immediately upon my return. Almost by return post there was a reply.

"Yes, I am still in circulation, but not very much," Dick's letter said. I had asked a number of specific questions, one of which had been uppermost in my mind in the interval, as I have said: Had the fact that snuff was an important part of the

Changewater story compelled those in charge to curtail the brochure as "J. D." had planned it in the beginning? The answer was quickly in the negative; the local snuff tycoon had been one of the trustees of the Changewater church, so that was that. I really didn't expect a serious answer to my query: Was there ever a mythological connection between snuff, or some reasonable facsimile, and churches? In his "program notes" John Neel had written that the three-year pastorate of the Reverend Frederick C. Mooney, who served the Changewater congregation from 1895 to 1898, had been marked by two revivals. In the second, one of the converts was John Bowers, president of the American Snuff Company, he said, "which for years operated a snuff mill below Castner's store."

At that time I was unaware that Edson Castner was still there, as he had been for fifty-three years. When at last he loosened up for conversation in 1962, I did not know that the "red barn" across the bridge had been the snuff mill.

"While the matter is fresh in my mind," John Neel continued in the letter, he said, an hour after the arrival of mine, "I would like to know why a section of the ridge east of Changewater along the Musconetcong is known as Forge Hill. I understand that it took its name from a forge built in the mountain near the Changewater Methodist Church. I never have known the whole story. . . . I do not know where the tobacco was grown from which the snuff was made," "J. D." went on, responding to another of my questions. Yet I did find tobacco growing well in the garden of Mrs. Harry Snyder not long after that. John added that he thought he had heard somewhere that tobacco was grown at one time in Somerset County.

"The mill itself," he said, "was in a wooden building in Changewater." By that time I had found it, deep in the shadows of the ruined mill and the tombstone pylons of a trestle which once carried rumbling trains into Hampton Junction and from which tracks and ties were removed long ago. "As for the change of name, from Clearwater to Changewater,

I found *that* in a history of Spruce Run"—Sodom—"Lutheran Church. In my work for what was to have been a booklet I found an official document that gave the name as Changewater before the Revolution. . . ." Tom Watson in his *Gazetteer* makes two parts of the name—Change Water—but what the change was that turned Clearwater into Changewater is not known. In fact, I was told one day in the Changewater post office that it simply was not so.

I had asked John Neel, the encyclopedist, if he could tell me

Up the hill from the abandoned Changewater snuff factory, we surprised Mrs. Harry Snyder cultivating tobacco in her backyard. Snufftown—miles away—never had a snuff plant, but tannery workers went up the mountain to get their jugs filled on Saturday nights.

why, in Snufftown, they called and continue to call the tannery "the tan-bark" or "the tan-bark (mill)." It might be a localism, he thought. I know as well as you do that the tanning of leather in pioneer and recent ways calls for the tannic acid that comes from bark, and at this time I had begun to have my suspicions that George Walthers, or Walters, the Snufftown tanner, had his own secret methods, something that was not to be spelled out for me until later on.

By now a tanbark, spelled frequently without a hyphen, has become a word associated with horse shows and rodeos or even circuses. I have noted also that as far as Snufftown is concerned, the writers of an excellent little historical "journal," part of Hardyston Township's two hundredth anniversary in June, 1962—William Wurst, Richard Haycock, and Helen H. Wurst—seem to reiterate carefully a reference to "the tan-bark (mill)" just that way. I purchased a copy the day I talked briefly with Stockholm's Methodist parson when I was told that Mrs. Frank Purchas, of Lake Tamarack, might have a few left. I still was seeking at least a sneeze to link the snuff of Changewater and whatever it was that had given Snufftown its lingering name.

John Dixon Neel was unable to throw any light on the use of "tan-bark (mill)" in one connection and "tannery" in every other place that had one. "A couple of weeks ago," his letter went on, "my oldest son, William, visited me here from Washington, and while here he told me of having recently read a biography of a man named Daniel Morgan, born in New Hampton during the Revolutionary War." I recalled immediately the Daniel Morgan Association, formed as nearby as New Hampton (which actually is older than Hampton or Hampton Junction), and its efforts to pinpoint Daniel's birthplace.

"He was so interested," Dick Neel hurried on, "that he drove around New Hampton, trying to find out "if the homestead was still standing. He was told that 'the old Morgan place' was up on the mountain which I have referred to as Forge Hill." I have wagered that the book Dick's son had been reading was North Callahan's *Daniel Morgan, Ranger of the Revolution,* which says that "most of the evidence indicates that Morgan was born in Hunterdon County, New Jersey." Among the historians, sticklers for absolute proof have argued that because Daniel was born when his father was master of Durham Forge on the other side of the Delaware River, he might have been born there, too. I should think that it would matter most where his mother was at the time.

Even a casual glance at Charles S. Boyer's comment in *Early Forges and Furnaces in New Jersey* should arouse new thinking, as I thought I had told "J. D." long before. On my first visit John told me he had found a reference to "Jonathan's Forge." I surprised him by saying that I thought the full name might be Jonathan Robeson, sometimes spelled Robson and even Robinson, and I quoted Charlie: "A forge was located on Musconetcong Creek, about seventeen miles from its mouth, at a place that was later called Changewater, Warren County. It was erected by Jonathan Robeson soon after the building of Oxford Furnace," which, for lack of care, is falling gradually into complete ruin.

Oxford Furnace was closely associated with Changewater, or Jonathan's Forge, a fact I had come upon in persistent searching for Squire's Point, or Squire's Point Forge. I had found the path to it fenced off when last I went that way. I have not missed the fact that *Early Forges* would seem to put Jonathan's establishment in Warren, across from Hunterdon County. That, you will remember, is where Changewater still is, "post office-wise," but the forge in this instance was probably behind the church, although I have found no evidence of it. Usually, at New Hampton down the road, those who refer to where they think Daniel Morgan was born make only a gesture and say, "Up there on the mountain, that was the Morgan place. . . ."

And who was Daniel Morgan? Even the biographical sketches in *Generals of the Army of the Revolution*, a little book printed for sale at Mount Vernon in 1889, gives him almost three pages. He was "born in New Jersey of Welsh parentage," it says, "about 1736. His family having some interest in some Virginia lands, he went to that colony at seventeen years of age. When Braddock began his march against Fort Duquesne, Morgan joined the army as a teamster, and did good service at the rout of the English army at Monongahela, by bringing away the wounded. Upon returning from this disastrous campaign, he was appointed ensign in the colonial service and soon after was sent with important despatches to a distant fort. Surprised by the Indians, his two companions were instantly killed, while he received a rifle ball in the back of the neck, which shattered his jaw and passed through his left cheek, inflicting the only severe wound he received during his entire military career.

"Believing himself about to die, but determined that his scalp should not fall into the hands of his assailants, he clasped his arms around his horse's neck and spurred him forward. An Indian followed in hot pursuit; but finding Morgan's steed too swift for him, he threw his tomahawk, hoping to strike his victim. Morgan however escaped and reached the fort, but was lifted fainting from the saddle and was not restored to health for six months. In 1762, he obtained a grant of land near Winchester, Virginia, where he devoted himself to farming and stock-raising. Summoned again to military duty, he served during the Pontiac War, but from 1765 to 1775 led the life of a farmer, and acquired during this period much property. . . ." With the coming of the Revolution, Daniel again was ready to respond, and, what was more, recruits "flocked to his standard." At the head of a corps of riflemen destined to give brilliant service, he marched away to Washington's camp at Cambridge. Montgomery was already in Canada, and when Arnold was sent to co-operate with him,

Daniel Morgan eagerly sought service "in an enterprise so hazardous and yet so congenial. . . ."

"At the storming of Quebec," the narrative goes on, offering details which in large measure explain New Jersey's eagerness to claim Daniel Morgan as an overshadowed if not half-forgotten general, "Morgan and his men carried the first barrier, and could they have been reinforced, would no doubt have captured the city. Being opposed by overwhelming numbers, and their rifles being rendered almost useless by the fast-falling snow, after an obstinate resistance they were forced to surrender themselves prisoners-of-war. Morgan was offered the rank of colonel in the British army, but rejected the offer with scorn. Upon being exchanged, Congress gave him the same rank in the Continental army, and placed a rifle brigade of five hundred men under his command.

"For three years Morgan and his men rendered such valuable service that even English writers have borne testimony to their efficiency. In 1780, a severe attack of rheumatism compelled him to return home. On the 31st of October of the same year, Congress raised him to the rank of brigadier-general; and his health being somewhat restored, he joined General Greene, who had assumed command of the Southern army. Much of the success of the American arms at the South, during this campaign, must be attributed to General Morgan, but his old malady returning, in March, 1781, he was forced to resign. . . ." But "when Cornwallis invaded Virginia, Morgan once more joined the army, and Lafayette assigned to him the command of the cavalry. Upon the surrender at Yorktown, he retired once more to his home. . . ."

Even so, Daniel Morgan wasn't finished. In 1794 the duty of quelling the "Whiskey Insurrection" in Pennsylvania was entrusted to him, and subsequently he represented his district in Congress for two sessions. He died in Winchester on the sixth of July, 1802, and has been called "The hero of Quebec, of Saratoga, and of the Cowpens; the bravest among the brave, and the Ney of the West." So there you have General Morgan as he was and as he should be—all of which compels me to reflect on two things, perhaps three. First, it is through the dimly lit halls of folklore that the wanderer with curiosity and imagination arrives in the wider rooms of history, furnishing them well in the process; second, I have reached the conclusion that, at least in my own case, history should never emerge so dull as it was taught to me, and this has bred a determination, even an obstinacy, to do something about it; and, third, it is clear that something as far off the path as snuff, probably never made in a place called Snufftown, can lead to adventures anywhere in New Jersey.

Dick's eyesight was failing, he told me, and so for a while I sought to be both his eyes and ears. Long ago when we talked I had supposed that the "flouring mill" of the yellowing history books had become the long familiar ruins beside Changewater's bridge, six stories high, but "J. D." assured me that here had been a worsted mill "before the big fire left it in the condition in which you always have seen it." Up the hill and around the bend beyond the bridge in Changewater, I found the ruins of old "Swack," or "Swake" Church, called for a German Lutheran pastor named Swackhamer, much the same as they were when I first met John Dixon Neel. Perhaps they seemed more of a ruin than ever in contrast to the "rest area" provided on a cutout across the road to Newport and Woodglen. Obviously, there had been summer visitors for those who had "rested" had also trodden paths through the almost knee deep myrtle and the graveyard it hid.

Here, truly, is a resting place for many Lances, some Castners, and among others, Ziba Osmun, whose name I quickly recalled when later I talked to Miss Lottie Osmun, in Stewartsville. That was the day I went to the home of Mrs. Augusta Foss, who, gracious Mrs. Elizabeth Cool down the street had told me, had some memories of Pahaquarry to share. So, with Miss Osmun, in her late seventies, and Mrs. Sarah Williamson, about to be ninety, I was setting the wheels of memory in motion at an unexpected luncheon table. Miss Osmun never had heard of Ziba, whose little stone in the myrtle inside the broken stone fence at "Swake" Church carried this challenging inscription: "Erected by the people of Changewater to the memory of Ziba Osmun who departed this life July 22, 1887, aged 38 years, 10 months & 7 days." Edson Castner, in the country store at Changewater since 1906—a story all by itself —remembered that Ziba had been prying a boulder loose in a quarry nearby and it had rolled the wrong way and crushed him to death. Even though he was but a young man at the time, Edson said quietly and simply, "The whole town liked Ziba, so they gave him that stone."

I came back to Changewater as I awaited developments in another Snufftown, where, if snuff had not been made there, the name, even as Snuffletown, had become more of a mystery than ever over the years. I confess that until the last surprise denouement I still toyed with the idea that George Walther, or Walthers, the tanner, could have used the equipment of the old "tan-bark (mill)" to turn out snuff now and then. Years before I had called on Miss Sallie Walthers in Snufftown, and she had expressed ladylike annoyance that any town had been singled out for such a clinging name, inasmuch as "everybody took snuff in those days and thought nothing of it."

When I first saw Edson Castner's store, one of the last country stores remaining in the area, unspoiled and defiant in a shopping center age, I thought it had been closed. There was an obvious "for sale" sign as well as the usual State Police warning placard, but someone has told me that they were there when I first tried to talk with Edson, who at that time was almost as unfriendly as the tom turkey that strutted outside, in contrast to the warm friendliness he showed me on my later invasions and interruptions. "I thought the store had closed," I told Edson with appropriate apologies, "until I saw that geranium in the side window. There was always a light"—

a single old-fashioned bulb dangling from the ceiling on its own wire—"but I thought that was a night light to keep burglars out."

"Been here regular since 1906," Edson Castner protested, "and most people know it unless they're blind. Open seven days a week, this store is." "Sundays, too?" I inquired. "Sunday's my best day," Edson said.

I asked him about the aged tom turkey that used to object to the approach of almost everybody. "He died of old age several years ago," Edson said. "Fifteen years old, he was." The old familiar pot-bellied stove was in the midst of the room with two boys of the village, Richard Swift and Roger Wiley, unknowingly striking a pose familiar three or even four generations ago. No simulated flickers for Edson—there was a sure-enough wood fire going, for that autumn day was chill.

The bridge at Changewater, leading up the hill to Edson Castner's store (on the right). Though a contradiction of the times in appearance as well as in some of its staples, it does business seven days a week.

There was an old and faded photograph on the wall behind the ageless counter, taken in front of the store where there was a name-board over the porch reading, "Eugene Castner" and "General Store." "Relation of yours?" I asked. "Nope, not unless a forty-second cousin or something is a relation." Already he had told me that the Castners buried beside the crumbling walls of "Old Swake" did not "belong" to him. I asked Edson if he knew the names of the men in the picture, and he, disclosing that he was eighty, moments later, rattled them off as if the picture had been taken yesterday: Harry Banghart, Frank Rinehart, Eugene Castner (the erstwhile proprietor), "Eke" Stull, and Walter Hildebrant.

This is a country store as country stores used to be, not one rescued from oblivion and "glorified," and to me it was wonderful that those living in at least one area of northern New Jersey could see both kinds in close proximity—I know that Kirby Culver at the New Hampton Country Store will understand what I mean. He must know Edson, but I wonder if he ever examined carefully the stock on Edson's shelves over which hangs a sign left behind by a memory that newcomers cannot share. It reads: Fresh Copenhagen Snuff.

The cash register was an old model. Behind it I detected brand names I had all but forgotten, mixed with others that were up-to-date. Look through the doorway into the back room, and you'll see harnesses for sale. The stand-up desk where accounts were still being kept is close by the old counters. Here were, and perhaps still are, a disorganized assortment that began with socks, shoes, gloves, nuts and bolts, pipes, tobacco, razor blades, and ended with lanterns, assorted types of thread, stationery, suspenders, shovels for coal scuttles and the scuttles themselves, and even ammunition keeping them all company. Boys coming in for soft drinks were told to put their money on the counter and help themselves from the electric house refrigerator opposite.

"Where was the snuff mill?" I asked suddenly, even though

I had more than a vague idea by then. "Down the hill and across the bridge. Which way did you come?" I told the bespectacled Edson Castner, wearing a cap and sweater, almost, you might say, a man from another era, just like some of his wares, "Past the ruins of the 'Swack' Church."

"Then you passed it," Edson said. "Looks like an old red barn now. Nobody's in it. It was run by the Bowers Snuff and Tobacco Company for about twelve years—and they put out a good snuff, too. There were five partners: John W. Bowers, his two sons, LaFayette and John"—Edson pronounced it *LayFayette*—"and Stephen Blackwell and his son. Stephen went down on the 'Titanic.' " "Where did the tobacco come from?" I asked. "From the South, somewhere," Edson was quick to reply, laughing when I told him of tobacco growing in Mrs. Snyder's garden almost across the way.

"Why did it go out of business in Changewater?" I wanted to know. "It didn't—it was bought out," Edson said, his memory apparently as clear as crystal, and his replies coming in quickly spoken words. "It was the trust that did it." The trust? "The tobacco trust in New York. No tobacco, no snuff, you know. . . ." Here was added proof that there had been no connection between the "tan-bark" operations and snuff, if there was snuff, in the Snufftown of Sussex. "They—the trust —paid $250,000 for the Changewater business and promised jobs for the three younger men, LaFayette and young John Bowers, and Stephen Blackwell's boy."

That would seem to be the story of snuff in Changewater, except for a line or two of the always welcome comment of John Ehrhardt. "Quite by accident," he said, "my researches on water and flood control turned up a note in the state geologist's report on Changewater in 1890. It says, 'Changewater: Bowers Snuff and Tobacco Company, nine-foot-fall, thirty-five net horsepower, fifty gross horsepower.' This shows the plant was surely operating in 1889.

"There was a big upheaval in the snuff business in 1911,

When we talked to Edson Castner in his store at Changewater, he said that he had been there since 1906 and that he remembered the coming and going of the snuff mill. "The trusts took over its business, and the plant here was abandoned."

when the courts forced the Duke interests to divest themselves of some of their snuff holdings. Prior to this, the trade had almost sunk to one producer. As a result of this ruling, the George W. Helme Company in Helmetta (once called Railroad Mills, and Helme continues to make a brand of snuff called Railroad Mills) was pretty well on its way out, but when the trust was forced to get rid of some of its holdings, Helme acquired some of the Lorillard brands. Among the last producers of snuff are Helme, U. S. Tobacco Corporation (makers of Copenhagen snuff), and the American Snuff Company.

"No one would like to hear you say this—but snuff-making is like the offal utilization of the tobacco industry; the strong lower leaves, stems, and other items not usually acceptable in smoking tobacco, go into snuff."

Between Edson Castner, in his unforgettable little store, and John Dixon Neel, in his little log hideaway near Woodglen, still longing for someone who could restore "Old Swack" or "Swake," I was compelled to review what I had in my gradually growing bag on a snuffless Snufftown. In the process I retrieved a little book, dated like the New Jersey Midland Railroad, 1872, and titled *The Historical Directory of Sussex County*, compiled and edited by Edward A. Webb, whose address in those days seemed to be Andover. Among the paragraphs allotted to Hardyston Township and the following passages on Franklin, Hamburg, and Hardystoneville, Snufftown stands at the end of an impressive parade. "Snufftown," reads the directory, "is a village in the eastern portion of this township. The Midland Railroad passes through it. There are two hotels, two stores, and a Methodist Church here. This was built in 1826, and rebuilt in 1863. Rev. Joseph H. Timbrel, of Sparta, is the present pastor. The post office and district, a mile or so east of the village, is called Stockholm."

Well, now, I had known about Stockholm long before the new interstate highway began reaching its way around Netcong toward Columbia, its ultimate goal in New Jersey, but, strangely enough, Stockholm was not located on the map of Sussex that Edward Webb had provided in his directory, even though Snufftown was there and in spite of the fact that the Beers *Atlas* map declared Snufftown to be Stockholm Post Office. The Beers map offered other invitations, too, with the Canistear Reservoir to the northeast and with the New York and Midland Railroad coming down by then from Unionville, New York through Deckertown, now Sussex, to pick up a branch at McAfee's Valley.

More than ten years before that, by process of elimination, I had taken what turned out to be the right road to Snufftown, up the edge of Wawayanda Mountain to where, had I kept on going, I would have come eventually to Vernon. Long before Vernon, on the edge of a rocky hill, an old church appeared, a venerable building whose simplicity of line reflected an era of greater importance there, or, if not that, more devotion, less speed, entertainment of homespun simplicity, and surely less anxiety. Yes, the dates were exactly as they appeared in the old directory list—"The Methodist Church: Built, 1826. Rebuilt, 1863." But there was no name of Snufftown, or Snuffletown, and I supposed at the time that the church had assumed folds of the mantle of Stockholm.

There were (and are) two doors. When I first was there, the door on the right was open to a neighborhood commendably honest, and a giant key was in the oversize keyhole. I went in, tiptoeing as if I might be interrupting a service, some stranger in a moment of prayer, or even a tired angel. I always try to be prepared for these and other emergencies in such a place. The gallery, I found then, was concealed by what appeared at first to be wallboard but on closer examination turned out to be sheeting, carefully tucked in place at the top of two winding stairways. Outside there was evidence of preparation for Sunday services—a great pile of kindling chopped for use in the old Shaker stove, counterpart of another of similar design relegated to what then was a woodshed. By now a Sunday School building has been added and oil heat. Shakers developed this particular utility, the Shaker stove, achieving extreme efficiency by the burning of wood in the heating of pioneer buildings—churches, houses, and others.

On my return I remembered that it was across the road from the church that I had my first confirmation of the fact that this, indeed, was Snufftown. The man raking leaves said that his name was William L. Storms, and I asked him if he might be related to my old and much misunderstood friend, John C. Storms, over in Bergen County. William, who had become the township's building inspector by the time I went back, said frankly that he did not know. "There are many Stormses all around," he said, "but they all come from two families, one in New Jersey and the other in Pennsylvania. Snufftown? Snufftown was quite a place until the City of Newark took over much of the vicinity as part of its watershed."

"Quite a place it was," he repeated quickly, "for vacations or holidays," and I wondered what it would be like to send a post card to friends back home with the message, under a Snufftown postmark, "Having a good time; wish you were here." I rather think, from what I know now, that Stockholm was the postmark from the first, at least from the first day a train came through. "There were several hotels," William continued, putting aside his rake for a moment, "for summer holidays—they didn't call them vacations then. Among the most important was the Kincaid House, and besides that there was the Edsall House. The Midland Railroad came through originally for the mining business—some day, when there's more time perhaps, I can take you to what's left of the old Williams Mine. I can remember when the shaft was sixty feet straight down and when the ore was carted up to Vernon for shipment. I used to work for the hotels when I was a youngster. I drove the carriages for the people who came here."

The Methodist Church beside the Musconetcong at Changewater had John Bowers, president of the American Snuff Company, as one of its supporters.

Those were the people, I said, about whom we know too little, and Bill agreed. Then he recalled when there was a store on either side of the schoolhouse that was across the road from the church. An affable and friendly man, he told me that not far away was the knife factory, run by the Booths, sometimes recalled as brothers but perhaps more accurately as father and son. Down at the corner was what Bill called "the tan-bark," which, I always had thought, was a kind of cushion of bits of wood and shavings associated with circuses and ro-deos—my dictionary was of no help whatever here. Even the commendable *Souvenir Journal* used the term, "the old tan-bark (mill)," in 1962, and the photo caption for the building, still standing at that time, refers to it as "the old Bark Mill, Stockholm."

"Going north from the Kincaid Hotel and on the same side stood one of the most prosperous businesses," the anniversary booklet revealed. "It was the tannery and bark mill which was operated by Mr. George Walthers, whose beautiful home has been restored by Mr. and Mrs. Jack Rowett. Mr. Walthers came from Germany in 1825"—a fact noted on his impressive tombstone in the sloping graveyard of the Stockholm Methodist Church—"and in 1837 bought the tannery formerly owned by Joseph Fleming and carried on this business until his death January 21, 1887. The tannery was built about 1800 and was then owned by Mr. Todd. In those days, bark was ground into powder in the mill, different trees being used to produce different colors in leathers. Mr. Walthers was an expert tanner and dresser of leather. The old tan-bark (mill) is located on the upper part of the Pequannock and is much as it used to be except that the old water-wheel that was located in the stream is now a thing of the past. It is said that when Mr. Walthers died he took with him a secret formula for preserving hides. It is also said that until recently there was a dog hide there, over one hundred years old, that had been used to cushion the seat of a mowing machine, and, after that length of time of being exposed to the elements, was soft and pliable. . . ."

James P. Snell in his *History of Warren and Sussex Counties,* published in 1881, dismisses Snufftown in little more than four lines: "Another hamlet in the eastern portion of the township is known as Snufftown. The Midland Railroad passes through it, which affords its only claim to distinction." Be that as it may, both Stockholm and Snufftown are to be found on the outline map of the same work and, what is more, Snufftown is called an "enterprising village" in the biography of George *Walther,* which follows, with a facsimile signature to match but without an "s," even as Mr. Snell's spelling of Strait, as Hiram Strait, a Stockholm postmaster who died in 1901, spelled it, is given as *Stait.* George was born in Neaderstoelten, Germany, in 1801, and after extensive travels in his native country, he went to St. Petersburg, returned to Germany, and then sailed to America, landing in Boston.

George Walthers first went to Washington, D.C.; then to Frederick, Maryland, then to New York City, and then to New Orleans, all the while perfecting his leather trade before going to what clearly was Snufftown in 1837, a place called Snufftown when David Strait, a wheelwright and his father-in-law to be, removed from Milton in Morris County in 1831. Snufftown obviously was there long before George Walthers, of that I was convinced. "Since his residence in Snufftown," it was written while George Walther was still alive, "Mr. *Walther* has carried on the business of tanning and currying, and his tannery is one of the oldest establishments in that enterprising village. . . ."

All my notions of some strange alliance between churches and snuff, as well as the idea that equipment in a tannery could be used to turn out snuff of any sort, were faltering long before this. I managed, however, to learn a variety of only relatively important facts: that with the coming of the first train in 1872 the first "tourist trade" arrived; that by then there also was a station called Beaver Lake; that there once were four tracks and a siding where "stages" from the hotels met all trains, and that in addition to the Edsall House, across the way from Stockholm Station, there was not only the Kincaid Hotel but Hiram Utter's. Stockholm, like Newfoundland across the Morris County line, was clearly another early summer retreat, whether Snufftown was its alias or not.

Then I went to see Helen H. Wurst, one of the authors of the anniversary brochure, and Snufftown's walls as a snuff town came tumbling down as suddenly and surprisingly as anything I have encountered at the end of a long folklore trail. Mrs. Wurst told me: "*As far as we can ascertain, there never was a snuff mill in our area. Snufftown took its name from liquor sold from the top of the mountain. The men went there to have their jugs filled. A group of men frequented it and called it Snufftown when on their way to a carousal."*

Snufftown—so that was its derivation. What became of Tom Watson's preferred *Snuffletown?* Suddenly I could hear my grandmother speaking of Liverpool men on their way to the "pub" for a "snifter," and I wonder whenever I go to Change-water or Stockholm if they, too, snuffled when enjoying their snifters here.

Chapter V

FRENCHE'S "CASTLE" AND WATERLOO

Napoleon had reason to remember Waterloo—and so, I hope, will you. It is one of my favorite illustrations of the bread-upon-the-waters technique of folklore as related to the no-trials-and-so-no-errors ways of history. Waterloo Post Office, as it was noted by the Beers *Atlas* map, seemed to be down the wooded ridges of Alamuche Mountain, spelled with one "l," south of the Tamarack Swamp, and definitely in Sussex County almost on the line dividing East from West Jersey. As far as county and other lines go, it is almost like the Stockholm-Snufftown controversy.

No matter what various forces have done inadvertently to achieve Waterloo's comparative oblivion, there it remains on the long-abandoned stone-lined Morris Canal, parallel to the waters of the Musconetcong only yards away. So it could have remained except for what we found, what others remembered, and what still others felt impelled to comment upon. If you wish to drive through Waterloo now, you must turn from the road that comes up through Hackettstown; what is more, you will have to return the same way, for the upper end of the road through town has been cut off deliberately.

For me, Waterloo is east of Frenche's Pond and at the end of Jefferson Lake—the one a land of mystery in spite of the ever-extending Boy Scout Reservation and the other once a source of vast quantities of natural ice, with the large storage houses of the Mountain Ice Company along its shore. The old Morris Canal, once having established such inland ports as Port Murray, Port Colden, and Rockport on the way, flirts clandestinely with the road up from Hackettstown, so that discovering it is a game in itself.

In the beginning, many years ago, I went to Waterloo mostly to explore the dusty silences of the old Smith, later Cassedy's, Store, once vitally important to the canal itself, but much to my delight when I last passed that way, it had been reclaimed as a cozy little house. If you go up by way of Saxton Falls, which was not on the maps of the 1870's, you will pause, I know, to see a section of the Morris Canal, restored and maintained mostly as it used to be. I often have wished that the canal plane on the other side of the river could have been saved in much the same way. Because that was not possible, or expedient, early color post cards, made in Germany, and pioneer photographs now in the collection of the Rutgers University Library, must serve in their stead. In 1939 it was written that Waterloo "was a port of the abandoned Morris Canal . . . the towpath and lock remain in fair condition." The same record continues:

"Flush with the bank of the canal, so that no gangplank was needed from the deck of the boat to the floor of the shop, is the barnlike Smith's Store, the only retail shop in Waterloo. Here, in the large trading-room, newly painted and heated by a pot-belly stove in a place once given to mule trading and tall stories of adventure on the canal, are flour bins, counter, tea-chests, shelves, and harness racks, with a meager stock of modern, trade-marked package goods. A central pillar supporting the roof has been worn to a rounded base by the scuffling of numberless hobnailed boots that once trod the towpath beside the mule. . . ."

Perhaps the observer of those days missed the giant wheel with spindles that hoisted necessaries from the canal boats. For my part, I must take you up the other side of the road between Hackettstown and the state highway between Cranberry Lake and Stanhope, for here, at the time these adventures began, there was evidence of an old road. This, I found later on, was a road to Allamuchy, but unless changes have come since my last attempts were made, that traveler is truly intrepid who pushes through across the mountain from either end. Close by, as the Morris-Essex Boy Scouts learned long ago, is the body of water referred to variously as Frenchy's, Frenche's, or French's Pond. If, on those first journeys, I had come upon a copy of the *History of the Waterloo Methodist Church*, published in 1915 by the Reverend L. B. McMickle at Milford, Pennsylvania, I would have known that the ruined walls I had asked about, called part of Frenchy's Castle, once had been the ornate and curlicued home of James Frenche.

What the Boy Scouts (or those I first met) did not know

The Smith Store on the long-abandoned Morris Canal, as it appeared before private restorations of Waterloo began. A giant wheel with spindles hoisted necessaries from canal boats into the store.

in those days was just who Frenchy, as they spelled the name for me, truly was, or how to identify all that remained of the little kingdom of stone he had built and evidently had run with feudal glory. These lines had appeared in the WPA guidebook of 1939:

"Straight ahead on the road, which rejoins the macadam and then continues R. is French's Folly, an industrial dream. In ruins beside the brook is an old mill, built by James French, a native of Hoboken, who came to this vicinity in 1853 and left 50 years later. Some of the first Brussels carpet produced in America was made in the mill, which later manufactured fenders for barges. Its last use was as a drying and packing plant for medicinal herbs. Behind the mill, on a steep hill, are the remains of stone houses, roofless shells with gaping holes."

I wish the writer of this record had given the source, or sources, of his information, for it would have saved some of us considerable time. Answers to my first floundering questions were as hazily variable as were the spellings of the last name of James Frenche, himself, and so, for a time, I was compelled to forget the matter. One day I was a little startled in passing that way to find Dan Cottee, a Scout leader, and some of his minions exploring what they called "the ruins of the castle" and the other walls. They had not known that the ruins were there in summer, screened from the road as they were by the trees and undergrowth that concealed the whole side of the mountain, even as the climb began. On that day there was snow in the air, and on the next it came down in earnest, obscuring nearly everything not immediately beside the road. By now I must warn you that the last of the ruins have been pulled down because, I was told, their crags and crevices had been taken over by snakes.

Those who heard of my early Waterloo excursions and the journey among the "castle ruins" suddenly remembered evidences of the canal plane that climbed another ridge across the river. Word came from both John Ehrhardt, in Madison, and John B. Carey, in Cedar Grove, Essex County, almost the same day. John Carey, whose lifelong collections of Morris Canal memorabilia now have been turned over, thoughtfully enough, to the Rutgers University Library, wrote:

"I am sending you a snapshot of a place that I stumbled on. Two weeks ago I was riding around, looking for a likely spot to do some trout fishing, and I rode through the old canal town of Waterloo. On the road leading out to the main highway and on the way to Saxton Falls there is an old pond at the top of the mountain known as Frenchey's Pond. We had to park at the bottom and walk up in days gone by.

"This time I noticed roadscrapers and bulldozers parked there, so I investigated and found out that they are really building (or rebuilding) the road so it will go up to the Boy Scout camp. So I said to myself, 'I will have one last look at Frenchy's Pond.' I got out of my car and started up. On the way I noticed a path leading through the brush and trees, and this picture I am sending on to you is what I stumbled on. There are other ruins nearer the pond, further down at the other end, but I never knew of these. There must be a story back of all this."

There must be a story, I told John, and I would do my best to find out what it was. Months passed. John and some of the others concluded, perhaps, that I had forgotten all about Frenche's (or Frenchy's) Pond. But in the meanwhile, actually, I had heard of ghosts who haunted the ruins, hemmed in by tawny Indian grass and brambles, of members of families who argued that inquiries would not be welcomed, and of old men who spoke quite freely of what they didn't know. Then John Carey wrote to me again, this time enclosing a whole gallery of pictures, most of them clear enough to whet the imagination of any explorer. He said:

"Here's more on the Frenchy place. Two weeks ago I was up there on a Saturday afternoon. You will remember my telling you about the chimney that had me nettled, but now I have settled that—Mr. Ehrhardt enlightened me on this point. The chimney was built on top of the mountain for the factory, whatever it was. There is a tunnel that I crawled through from the chimney down, and this, I am told, eliminated the necessity of building a chimney. Imagine the inventive genius of a man who used a mountain for a smokestack.

"I cannot supply you with any more information about the place because nobody seems to know much about it. If Major Smith, a descendant of the Smiths who first ran the store on the canal were around, he might be able to fill in the gaps. However, he is not on hand, and no one in the village seems to know what that 'haunted place' is."

I decided to have another "go" at Frenche's Pond and Waterloo, although the ground was covered by a thin coating of ice. In the hotel in Hackettstown I asked the usual questions of the smiling woman at the desk, who said the names Frenche's Pond and Frenche's Castle were unknown to her. "Go ask the barkeep," she suggested, as if it were a dare, "he knows everything there is to be known about the countryside here." I followed instructions and interrupted a man scrubbing an already spotless table. "Could you tell me," I asked, "where Frenche's Pond is?" Perhaps, unintentionally, I made it sound as if my very life depended on the answer.

"You don't want to go there," I was told, and I wondered if I would hear some new ghost stories, or at least some of the older ones in a new dress. "It is awfully rough going this kind of weather," I was assured. I told the barkeep I would be careful. "But who," I asked, before I left, "was Frenchy, or Frenche—depending on how you spell it? Was that his real name? And what about those ruins up the mountain?"

The barman could tell me nothing. He had an old history at home, he said, but he was sure that Frenche wasn't mentioned in that. "Tell you what," he then suggested, "why don't you write to that fellow named Beck—he writes books and other things about New Jersey all the time. He ought to have some answers. Sure, that's the thing—write him a letter!"

By this time I wanted to laugh, but somehow I managed to hold myself to a smile. "I can hardly," I pointed out, "write a letter to myself. And, even if I did, I'd be right back where I started from. . . ." Before I left my good friend was doubled up in guffaws and hurrying off to tell others what had happened. "Boy," I heard him say, as a door closed, "did I just louse one up!"

Returning to the road up the mountain, the one someone had said was called Skunk Hollow Road by trappers years ago, Bill Augustine and I pushed on as far as the ice would allow. Sure enough, there near the crest was a long and lovely body of water trimmed with ice at the dark edges and surrounded by trees which even in winter did their best to hide it from the world outside. This, then, was Frenche's Pond. But where were the ruins? Where was "the church," as some had referred to part of the ruined walls, and where was what some of the reports had called another deserted "village"? The only buildings we had seen were part of the then new reservation of the Boy Scouts, and the shell of a house not far from where the reclaimed part of the Skunk Hollow Road starts climbing.

As usual, I went about seeking answers to the puzzle the hard way, like a plodding detective in an English mystery novel. Up the mountain meant up the mountain to me and beyond where bulldozers long ago had pushed back brush and stumps. Among the evidence of ancient trees I found an interlacing of old logging roads, eventually easing down to the main highway. Finally, I saw that a movement had detached itself from the shadows at the edge of the pond, and two youngsters appeared who said their names were Claude Bray and Robert Hanley. That this was a long time ago was proven the other day; when asking for Bob on the old road up from Waterloo, I was told by his mother that he was married, had a family of his own, and a shop as well, out on the highway near Cranberry Lake. When I met them first their address was Byram Township, not far from Stanhope.

From Claude and Bob, still in their gear for tending their traps, I confirmed the fact that this, certainly, was Frenche's (Frenchy's, to them) Pond, and here where their adventures spelled an occasional Waterloo for a mink, even the muskrats were proving elusive that year. Not that it made much difference, said Bob Hanley, who had come from Jersey City long enough before to have lost his "accent." "The market," he said, "is down."

Having disposed of the subject of ghosts, especially the local legend that has to do with the head of a man seen recurrently gliding along the tracks of the old Morris & Essex Railroad, we moved on. "Who was Frenchy, or French, or whatever the name was?" I asked. "Where are all those ruins of the village he is supposed to have built on the mountain?" Bob pointed confidently down the slope and then up the rise beyond the stream in the gesturing manner of an Indian. There, suddenly revealed by a fitful sun, was the skeleton ruin of what John Carey said had looked so much like a church.

By this time Dan Cottee and his Scouts had reappeared, only a handful of those who had been expected to explore the new camp grounds that morning. I have wondered ever since if they appreciated the "extra" thrown in for those lucky enough to respond. Soon all of us were scrambling among the broken walls of an establishment which in another day must have rivaled what remains of the old paper town, Harrisville, in Burlington County, where a coarse butcher's paper was stewed from marsh grass.

With all the dignity of a ruined monastery, the towered "castle" pointed its roofless "belfry" like a torn finger into the sky, I wrote on my return. There had been no fire. The roof rotted and then caved in many years before, a section at a time, leaving only the stone walls. Some of the rooms had been plastered, and so, using the inviting white surface, occasional visitors had penciled their names and addresses, perhaps without wondering whether this was a church or even a castle with all its battlements. Not until I saw the picture of the "residence of James Frenche, Waterloo, New Jersey," as it appeared in the historical account of the Waterloo Methodist Church, did I realize how quickly a house can be turned into a castle because there are a tower and all the ornate trim of a bygone age.

Beyond the towered ruin, the more concealed because its walls and lovely arched windows and doorways rose among the trees in the steep drop from the clearing (a lawn, no less, in the early 1900's) is what must have been an even more impressive structure, built of fitted stone perhaps carried painstakingly for many miles. From it led an old road, just discernible in the leaf mold of those days. If you will follow the road, as we were able to follow then, you will come upon the walls of a stone house—probably you cannot, by now—probably the oldest structure of all. When first we were there the mud that was used for mortar still lay in the chinks. Still further down, paralleling the fading road protected by stone walls from the lowland through which it passed, outlines of more stones revealed what, at first I thought, might have been a large barn.

The brick chimney of which both John Ehrhardt and John Carey had told me had no counterpart in anything of which I have written—although it may be under all the rest of the rubble by now. By this time the boys from Lake Parsippany were aroused, saying over and over again that those who had stayed behind because the weather wasn't just right would be sorry. They promised that when the troops began coming in, everything possible would be done to keep the ruined "city," as they freely spoke of it, just as we found it that day. Snakes, or the report of them, as I have told you, ended that dream. It was then that Bob Hanley, with sudden inspiration, mentioned the name of Walter Burge, and what follows is his story.

"Walter has been around here for years," Bob told me, "and he's working at our place today, helping build a new greenhouse." Claude added that perhaps if Walter Burge didn't remember enough, his grandfather, up at Panther Pond, might fill in a little. By the time we got there, Walter Burge had left off work on the greenhouse and was engaged in sawing wood in his own dooryard.

You know, it does something to you to meet men like Walter Burge. I suppose there are many who would pass his kind by as just another countryman, a man with a deep-lined face, quizzical eyes, and hands that are gifted enough for almost any routine. To many he may have been "that fellow up the road who used to be in the ice business—you know, when they cut ice out of the lake and stored it for the towns and cities." He was one of those men who in just a few moments made me feel that I had known them always, and whom I wished I could linger with as princes of the outdoors.

Walter told me quickly that he had come down from Great Meadows "Waterloo way" in 1894. "Frenchy," he went on, "as you have heard him called, was still here then. These were the days when we cut hundreds of tons of ice out-of-doors, and the big refrigeration plants were unheard of. I worked for the Mountain Ice Company—they had a twenty-thousand-ton icehouse, really a series of connecting houses—at Waterloo. I built the plant for them. Then they leased Jefferson Lake, and I built a thirty-five-thousand-ton house for them in there. They didn't give up until 1913. No matter what anybody says, the winters weren't what they had been, and, anyhow, modern ice plants were beginning to grow up all around.

"That dyke in the middle of the lake at Waterloo?" (I had wondered about that when we had wandered by that way in summer.) "I built that, too. That was to keep the current from going out into the lake and so making sure we had good steady water for ice. After the ice business gave up, I was a wheelwright and blacksmith for seven years, in a shop just down the

"Frenche's Castle," not far from Waterloo, was not a castle but the ornate residence of a man who made fenders for barges and tugboats. Its ruins conjured up some extraordinary stories.

road a piece. Then that gave up, too, but I can still prove that I'm a good carpenter. . . .

"Frenchy? That was what we called him. His name was James Frenche. That place you thought was a church was his house—his mansion, really. That's where he and his family lived, and it was really a headquarters for some lively times in those old days. You see, no matter what James Frenche was doing here, he traveled to and fro, back and forth, from Hoboken every day. He had a business there making barge and tug boat fenders."

That the padded timbers hung over the sides of river boats could be a business had not occurred to me, even when John Ehrhardt had revealed that such "fenders" were made, he thought, for canal barges at Waterloo. "That big spread of ruins just down from what people like to call 'the Castle'—that was a big sawmill. But before James Frenche was here it was a button factory.

"Don't know what Jim Frenche's notion was in building a tower on his house, but I know it was always said that he could see Waterloo Station on the Morris & Essex branch of the Lackawanna from there. Jim always had an idea of extending the road across the canal with a bridge, and you can still see the stone pillars he put up for it. Best he ever got, as far as I know, was a footbridge. And there was always the story that Frenchy was experimenting secretly with some kind of chemicals. I don't know as I ever heard what they were, and I learned not to ask questions. But those ruins up at the other end of the pond are all that remain of the chemical factory, if that is what it was. To them that know, that part of the lake's still called Chemical Pond.

"That new road, really a return of a very old one that went across to Allamuchy, throws you off a little. The building down at the bottom where it turns in—that was behind another bigger one that's now gone altogether. The help James Frenche employed lived there. It was quite an operation; Jim kept many hands busy; and he and his family lived in style." Careful not to break in as long as Walter Burge would talk, I had to ask him about the stone cabin that appeared to be very old, and he said that it was. "But I remember the Drake family that lived in that house," he said. "Like so much more, it's a heap of stones now, but it was a cozy little home before the 1890's were out.

"Yes, James Frenche was a great builder—and it's most peculiar that so many seem to remember so little about him. Even I never caught on to all I should have. He always intended to build a wagon road to Waterloo station, that I do know. And I'll tell you where the station is now. Cousin of mine bought it ten years ago,"—this was early in 1949—"and moved it up near the Netcong Circle where it's a bungalow. Willis Montania is the name—he still has the old station clock and the Waterloo signboard, they tell me. Ain't been up that way in a while.

"James French, or Frenchy—nobody's asked me about him in years, and I'm so glad you did. I like to remember, and there's so few, now, that gets me started. Frenchy had a boy, Harry, and a girl, Susan, I think. I remember them. I've heard tell Susan's still alive—in Canadensis, Pennsylvania, I think. Hasn't been down this way for years so far as I know." I remember writing a letter to Susan Frenche in Canadensis, but there was no reply; perhaps Frenche was not her name by then. "Ghosts? Only one I know of is the head some people say they see now and then along the empty railroad bed where the Morris & Essex trains used to take James Frenche up to Hoboken."

There, now, you have as much as there was after I had talked with John Carey and John Ehrhardt, then Bob Hanley and Claude Bray, who, that long ago, led me to Walter Burge. The odd reflection is that none of it came under the head of ancient history; Tom Gordon had nothing at all to say about any of it, naturally enough, in his Gazetteer of 1834, and the *Historical Collections* of 1844 pointed out only that Waterloo, "formerly called Andover Forge, is on the line of the Morris Canal and contains a forge, a store, a grist and saw mill, and about 15 dwellings." Of the area they added that the surface was "mountainous, rich in iron, and abounding in rare minerals." All this was over the dam even when James Frenche took over old walls and inserted new ideas.

Nor does the family name of Frenche appear from anything Charles Boyer has briefly written of the Waterloo Forge in his chapter on the Andover Iron Works. "Allen and Turner," he said, "after they had built the Andover Furnace, erected a forge on the Musconetcong Creek, at Waterloo, in 1763, where they worked up ore from the Rossville Mine, as well as pig iron from Andover Furnace. In 1770 the following advertisement appeared in the *Pennsylvania Gazette:*

"To be Lett also, a large FORGE, in excellent order, with 4 fires, and 2 hammers, in the County of Sussex, situate on Muscomiung River, about 7 miles from Andover Furnace, and 35 miles distant from New Brunswick and Elizabethtown Landings. Five thousand acres of well-timbered Land, part lying in the County of Morris, very convenient to the Forge, will be rented with it; also a Grist-mill, Saw-mill, commodious Houses for a Manager and Forgeman, and 70 tons of Pig-metal on the Bank, with more than a sufficiency of Coal to work it up. . . . The owners have six Negroe Slaves to hire out or sell, who are good forgemen, and understand the making and drawing of Iron well. . . ."

Waterloo, in a gazetteer of 1883, is called "a post village on the Musconetcong River and the Morris Canal, with a station (Morris co.) on the Morris & Essex Railroad; it has a large local trade, some shipping trade and several mills. Population, 200." Here, registering something more than mild surprise at the population estimate of the 1880's, I was inclined to rest my case—knowing full well that in matters such as this, no case is ever rested.

All that was the record of 1949 and 1950. I continued to ask questions along the Hackettstown-Waterloo Road, in and around Stephens State Park, at Saxton Falls, and, on one occasion I remember, as far off as up along Lubber's Run. Before the summer of 1954, the weather-worn copy of the history of the Waterloo Methodist Church came in, with "briefs," as the author called them, on the Methodist churches of nearby Lockwood and Stanhope. In his introduction, Parson McMickle, evidently publishing the history of the Waterloo church in 1915, six years after its fiftieth anniversary, has this to say:

"The picturesque and historic village of Waterloo is situated between Schooley's Mountain and the Allamuchy Ridge, on the banks of the Musconetcong River, about two miles below its junction with Lubber's Run. It would be interesting to know many things concerning its history: Of its Indian Village and Graveyard; of its white owners from the Jersey Companies and William Penn to the present; of its mines, forges, furnaces, mills, and stores, and the conditions which made possible a business of $75,000.00 a year; of the Mule Railroad; the Sussex, Morris and Essex Railroads, and the Morris Canal; of its activities during the Revolutionary and Civil Wars; of the slaves who were skilled forgemen and sold with the plants; of the names Andover, New Andover, Old Andover, Andover Forge, Andover Furnace, and Andover Forge Pond, and why so called; of its present lethargy and probable future; and of many other things; and especially of its sons and daughters who have made happy homes and reared good children, built Churches, became Educators, Judges, Senators, Bankers, Business Men, Railroad Men, Clerks, in fact filling many positions with honor, efficiency and credit to their native village, making a record of which anyone might be proud; to know about these things would be interesting to any native of Waterloo, but necessarily information concerning them must be omitted, as there is room for only a small part of its Religious activities in this booklet."

There is no indication here how Waterloo itself got its name. I have been told that it was a name dropped from the sky by the Delaware Lackawanna & Western, but the name of Waterloo was there in Revolutionary times, so that could not be true. I have a feeling that the name came, for one reason or another, from one of the early forge-masters. It is clear that much of Waterloo's story had drifted away even when Parson McMickle at last published his brochure, which has been most interesting to me because of its other pictures: the Lockwood Methodist Church, built in 1835 but abandoned apparently in the 1880's; the station at Waterloo when it was served by at least three tracks; the ruins of the Andover Forge at Waterloo, already a rocky heap at the turn of the century; the grist, plaster, and saw mills, tumbling into decay when I first saw them; the tavern, "starting point of the Stage Coach Route, Waterloo"; the Smith Store, in days when the name, A. L. Cassedy appeared over its door; the ice houses of the Mountain Ice Company and an accompanying scene of men and horses at work on the ice; the footbridge that led to the base of the Waterloo plane of the Morris Canal; the blacksmith shops at Old Andover and Waterloo; and, of course, the home of James Frenche, the very architecture of which, falling piecemeal into ruins of its own, gave rise to all the legends of a haunted castle. Most of the other likenesses are those of either the Smiths, for many a lifetime identified with Smith's Store on the Morris Canal, or their impressive houses, so that it is a wonder to me that still another Smithville did not emerge at one time or other. Perhaps the innate modesty of the Smiths is what kept me from getting more information on the scene. The remaining figures of this gallery include Basters, Almers, Grays, and other pioneers.

"John Smith," the introduction begins bravely among the Smith clan, "came from Schooley's Mountain and located at Old Andover Forge, near Waterloo. . . ." "Known as General John Smith, he was the progenitor of the Smith family, at Waterloo; Peter, Nathan, James, Joseph, Samuel and William being children, and Samuel T., Seymour R., Peter D., N. Augustus, Matilda A., and Caroline being grand-children. He was of German-French descent and started life at the 'bottom of the ladder.' . . ." Both Peter, son of John, and his bonneted wife seem to reveal a determined character if their photographs remain as evidence.

It was late in August, 1954, that there came two letters, one from P. Louis Smith, in Andover, and the other from Earl Wilson, in East Gary, Indiana—both the result of a curious circumstance. Five years or more after the first varied adventures in and around the land of Frenchy's Castle, I was asked to retell a few of the stories which, in my estimate, were the most unusual. I chose four or five that were peculiar to me because they presented riddles and therefore remained incomplete. I did this deliberately in the hope that someone somewhere might not have been "present" at the start and just might raise his or her hand on the second time around. This, I am happy to report, is exactly what happened.

Louis Smith, whom I hurried to see, was white-haired, proud of his ancestors, but especially delighted in the possession of the sword and gold bullion epaulets of his great-grandfather John Smith, a recruiting general in the Revolution. "What you have written was of unusual interest to me," said Louis, "and I'm as surprised as you are that history can be buried so quickly. I'm what you might call of the third generation of the founders of Waterloo, the later Nathan and Peter Smith, and one who knew the whole Waterloo area very well. Peter and Nathan pioneered there between 1826 and 1831, and shortly before that they purchased the six buildings, erected about 1790, that were to become the village of Waterloo. . . ."

These buildings, Louis said, all were of stone construction—the inn, remodeled in 1945; the store, the mill, two houses, and what has been called "the old homestead" for a long while. The latter, across the road from the mill, was a stable for cavalry of the British army, Louis went on. "That is, before Peter and Nathan remodeled it. Many an English penny has been unearthed in the garden out back that now is a lawn. You see, the first name for the village was Old Andover Forge, a name that must have drifted downstream a little from the newer Andover Forge, erected in 1815. The demands of the War of 1812 were fulfilled with iron millets or pigs from the original Andover Forge. About 1815 Allen and Turner, operating mines from Oxford to Hibernia, constructed the mill at what was to become Waterloo—ostensibly for a 'rope walk,' using the flax from Schooley's Mountain when they decided to make their own rope for their enterprises.

"An undershot wheel was installed, and by a crude mechanism hardwood cog teeth wheels drove a windlass at one end of the building with an anchor post at the other for the make-or-break stretching of the rope before using."

I was content to let Louis Smith talk, his eyes closed, his concern satisfied that my chair was as comfortable as his. "Now," he went on, with a sudden change of subject, "let me tell you about James Frenche and of Frenche's Pond or 'Castle,' all so quickly lost in the overgrowth of the years and the new construction of the Boy Scout Reservation there. A man named Humphreys constructed the brick building that came first—it was built for the manufacture of the first Brussels carpet in the United States. An Englishman, settling in the valley, was his manager on arrival in this country, and, later on, he was Humphreys' absorbentee of assets.

"Mr. Frenche had two daughters and two sons, one not exactly adopted but recognized among subsequent beneficiaries. The daughters' names were Susan—Mrs. Calkins, now ninety-five, active and visiting the old town each year—I'm

surprised you haven't heard from her. . . ." (This was in 1954.)
"Then there was Minnie, who died at the age of fifty. One son,
Harry, was an accomplished Sunday school teacher at Water-
loo between 1890 and 1895—he, too, is dead now. The father,
James, had been a Sunday school superintendent in a Hoboken
Church nearly twenty-five years. The adopted son, William,
who I think is still living, I seem to have lost track of."

All in all, there wasn't much that Louis Smith couldn't remember, given the opportunity of talking to one content to
take notes with as little interruption as possible. There were
moments, I remember, when I thought I must be listening to
a member of the cast of *Our Town*.

"It should not be overlooked," Louis went on, "that James
Frenche wrote all kinds of poetry, and a little book of it, if
it can be found nowhere else, may be in Mrs. Calkins' possession. . . ." I have tried recurrently to learn more of Mrs.
Calkins and what she might have added, especially with the
book as a new prod, but I got nowhere, and now I must presume that it is too late. It is odd, however, I remarked to Louis
Smith, that an earlier letter addressed to Susan Frenche in
Canadensis, Pennsylvania, did not at least come home to me.

"Mrs. Calkins' husband was a prominent Philadelphia attorney, " Louis told me. "Her son, who now is dead, had offices in
the Girard Trust Company's main office in Philadelphia. Oh,
well, I could go on like this for a long while. . . ." And he did,
showing me reverently the sword and heavy epaulets of General John Smith all over again, as well as the old coffee grinder
he had retrieved from the Smith Store in its heyday on the
Morris Canal, old photographs of the Canal and the Waterloo
plane I never had seen before, and a view of Waterloo station
in days when the old Sussex Railroad was still in evidence on
a parallel higher up.

The letter that came from Earl Wilson in East Gary was
something else again and, in many ways, in a class by itself.
It revealed among other things that many persons living out-

side the state were benefiting from a kind of neighborly clipping service by which the record of my researches was being mailed to former residents across the country. It also proved that the keys to many mysteries of folklore were in the hands of those who lived, and perhaps still live, further away than Stanhope. As far as Earl Wilson was concerned, this was the beginning of a long exchange of letters, in the first of which he said:

"Perhaps you will be surprised to hear from this section of the country. I hope you will excuse my bad writing and worse spelling, because my education was sadly limited and I am quite an old man now. However, I know exactly what you are telling us all in your folklore because I am one of the few still living who really knew and have seen much that you write about.

"I have a very dear friend in New Jersey who is kind and thoughtful enough to send me books and articles and anything else that you do—Schooley's Mountain, German Valley, now Long Valley, and so on. There are others that I now have, too, concerning Frenche's Pond, Smith's Store at Waterloo, and the old Morris Canal. Of these things I know, and I will say that your descriptions are very correct.

"I see where Walter Burge says he came to Waterloo in 1894. Well, I happen to have come there a year or two after that. I knew Walter quite well. By the way, I came there from Montana as a young carpenter. My apprenticeship had been finished, and I went there because I had a relative living in the state. My first work there was for the Morris Canal Co., doing repair and maintenance work on the locks and planes as a member of a regular crew. For a time I roomed at the home of a family of three—man, wife, and daughter. The man's name was Morris Bird—he was the lock-tender at the foot of the three-mile level, three miles west of Waterloo at the head of Guinea Hollow Dam.

"I also knew Jim Frenche and have talked with him many a

Young Bob Hanley was the young muskrat trapper who led me to Walter Burge at Waterloo. Walter had known the owner of "Frenche's Castle," and had worked for him. Apparently, James Frenche dabbled in a little of everything, from tugboat fenders to chemicals.

time. I also have been up to the pond and have seen the settlement there. You mentioned that it was all in ruins. Well, it was not so much of a ruin then. You also speak of the difficult road to get there when you first went looking. I can well appreciate that if you go up the south side of the mountain you may have difficulty. By now, you say, there have been changes."

I always have wished I could push on across Allemuchy Mountain to the village of the same name, either on foot or with the use of a Jeep. On the number of occasions that I have gone beyond the point where the very old trail had been cleared away and otherwise restored for the Boy Scout Reservation, I have been compelled to turn back by circumstances: the old road all but fades out; there are rocks and boulders on every hand reaching up from the thick carpet of dead leaves; and seeking out the hard ground of winter, I have found that drifts of snow linger here longer than in many other areas. Earl Wilson wrote that the way is easier from the other side of the mountain, but by now the terrain is private property. Earl also wrote of a footbridge "below Jim French's," but I had to assure him that it was gone and that much of the Morris Canal bed that he knew had been dry much of the year. He went on:

"Jim also had another bridge across the river south of the Canal—the Musconetcong, isn't it? Let me tell you that I put in some very cold days, cutting ice on the Waterloo Dam. I also cut ice on Jefferson Lake—Walter Burge spoke of that to you. I know all about the Smith Store and gristmill. You can see that what you have written has brought back pleasant memories, for I am old enough to remember a post office at many a place that does not have one now. I can remember one, for instance, at Pleasant Grove—I knew the Hunt, Hann, Heath, and Sipler families, and many others. I also remember the Dorincourt Hotel on Schooley's Mountain, where, you say, only the gateposts remain. I made several trips on the Morris

Canal—I know and can name every lock, plane, and level east of Hackettstown to Jersey City. And I can give you the length of each level from memory, but I sometimes wonder why I remember such things.

"I have seen some pretty fine engineering jobs in my travels around the world, but never have I seen anything like that accomplished in the Morris Canal, and it's a pity that more people didn't find out more about it until it began to disappear in fields and pastures. When I think that nearly one hundred and fifty years ago they built an amazing switchback across the mountains of New Jersey, it seems impossible—but it was there, sure enough, and I have tried many times to explain it to engineers. They cannot visualize it. . . .

"There are so many things that I could write about . . . such as when we went into the Jersey City basin and got a tug-boat to tow the hinged canal boats to New York's East River, unloading there and getting towed back. Also, we went to Staten Island and back, and that was quite a trip. When a big ship came in and we caught the big wash or swells, then we just put on life-preservers and hung on. There are few people living who realize that at one time the Morris Canal boats crossed the Delaware River between Easton and Phillipsburg, going into Lehigh Valley Canal from there, but they did so until the dam went out."

Last time I journeyed to the Jersey City basin of the Morris Canal, I found approaches to it long covered over with concrete, a small sign proclaiming that this was the East River end of the remarkable Morris Canal, and the basin itself a kind of marina for pleasure craft of varying shapes and sizes. Without the sign, almost as hard to find as are those who know the way to the basin, no one would guess that this was a terminus of a romantic and colorful crossing of all New Jersey. Earl Wilson continued:

"As I sit here, I have been thinking of a man I knew when I was in New Jersey. He was an old man then—his name was

William Black. He bought cordwood along the Morris Canal and boated it to such cities as Paterson, Newark, and sometimes even to New York. When I was in Alaska, perhaps about 1912 or 1913, I met a man who had known Mr. Black. He told me that he had died and that a book had been written about him. I wonder if you have ever heard of it."

I had not, and without a specific title my search was wobbly from the start. Once Earl Wilson asked me if I knew that there once was a "wonderful deer park" on Allamuchy Mountain, and I replied that I did not. However, he mentioned the name of Rutherford as the probable owner, and bells began ringing. There was a Rutherford on the road out of Hackettstown and the additional estate name on the mailbox was "Deer Park." Then I remembered the legend of red deer escaping from a deer park in a place called Aserdaten on the "slopes" of the Forked—two syllables, please—River Mountains, and there, too, the name of Rutherford, as well as Stuyvesant, was glibly spoken by old men of eighty or more. By now I have seen the rotted posts of the deer pen, and I have put down Aserdaten as the corruption of the name of a man, Asa Dayton, last described to me as traveling on foot into Toms River with a sack of corn on his back.

By 1957 Mr. and Mrs. W. Albert Banister were in residence in the "old homestead" of the Smiths, and I called on them, rewarded by seeing some of the interior of the house, some very old photographs of Waterloo as it used to be, and a store ledger kept by Peter Smith. Albert Banister told me that he was Peter's great-grandson. In Albert and Evelyn Banister are two of the gracious hosts that Waterloo, traditionally Old Andover, once knew.

I have had no word from P. Louis Smith, of Stanhope, in years. As for the letters of Earl Wilson, of East Gary, Indiana, they stopped with one in which Earl told me he would be going to a hospital for major surgery. I wrote to presumed members of the family, making inquiry at the address I always had used. There was no reply.

Chapter VI

"THE SCOURGE OF THE RAMAPOS"

I had been to Smith's Clove before. In fact, I remembered coming home one day to report on neighborhood arguments over the true meaning of the name. Too many, it seemed to me, were intent on using the Clove merely as the name of a brook. Others, clinging to the alternative Smith's Clove, insisted that more than a brook was involved and that this man Smith might warrant some further research.

Even when the late John Storms, of Park Ridge in Bergen County, mentioned "the Claudius Smith gang," I failed to snap to attention. We had been talking of something altogether different, the spelling of Hohokus, and John had been warning me not to spell the name of the town with hyphens, as in Ho-Ho-Kus. "Hohokus, as far as we know," he assured me, "was an Indian chief of local reputation, but we didn't spell it Ho-Ho-Kus around here until Ezra K. Bird, editor of the Hackensack *Republican*, insisted on printing it that way. Paramus?" he added quickly. "That's an Indian name, meaning the place of wild turkeys."

John had made passing reference to what he called "the Kiesege tragedy," and I made him spell the name for me. Then he said: "The Kieseges were German—a quiet farmer, his wife, and his daughter, who was fourteen. Two men from the Park Ridge area, members of the Claudius Smith gang on the Ramapo, associates of the Tories in these parts during the Revolution, went to the Kiesege farm, drove off the stock, and went into the house. Farmer Kiesege motioned to his wife to sneak out, and she and the girl attempted it. But a Tory, looking out the window, saw them skulking across the yard. He fired, and the girl was killed.

111

"When Captain Campbell of the militia's quarters in Tappan arrived, he found Kiesege's body locked in a cupboard—or what was left of it, for most of the farmhouse was burned. Mrs. Kiesege came toward him with the body of her daughter in her arms. The poor woman was a raving lunatic and had to be taken in charge while the soldiers buried the girl and her father in what had been their own dooryard. It's a gruesome Park Ridge story, but it's true and yet only a few know about it. . . ."

John Storms switched quickly to what he had found out about "the Baylor massacre," and I missed my chance to ask for something more about "the Claudius Smith gang," even a reference to *Claudius Smith, the Cowboy of the Ramapo Valley* escaped me temporarily. (Jim Ransom, in Westwood, had told me in his quiet way that it was that little book that launched his continuing quest for regional literature.) Thereafter, I seem to have noted occasional references to Claudius Smith, who presumably left his name and his mark on Smith's Clove, but for some reason I must have put aside what I heard as legends equally as tall as Claudius, if not taller. But, as I told Jim, the true meaning of "the Clove" as a name had thrown many of us off even as the name "cowboy" has deterred many who have not been able to associate a "cowboy" in the customary sense with the Ramapos, those mountains that reach across the New York-New Jersey border.

Then two questions came in at the same time: "Where can I find out about Claudius Smith, the Cowboy of the Ramapos?" and "Where can I get more specific information on 'The Cannonball Trail'?" I referred my inquirer to Jim Ransom, but I arranged to see him myself almost as soon, inasmuch as I suddenly recalled the title of the collector's item that had begun Jim's systematic book hunt. Jim is James M. Ransom—a breed of New York businessman, I often have thought, least associated with New Jersey history and folklore—who has centered on the half-forgotten mines of the Ramapos. While carrying on an everyday routine among municipal bonds in Wall Street, this young and enthusiastic family man has found time for off-hour research into the fading past of his county. Above all, my good friend is not one of those hide-bound historians who shun the ways of the folklorist as if they were those of an alien and careless transgressor.

As I had been embarrassed long enough by the recollection of having been in the Clove many times without realizing that, apart from being the village where Claudius Smith was born, it is an age-old cleavage in the mountains—still a passageway between two states—I went to Westwood. Much to my delight, I discovered that Jim Ransom knew more about Claudius, "Scourge of the Ramapos," than any man among my history-minded friends. In a flash he had spread before me an array of books either about Claudius Smith exclusively or in which Claudius was given more than scant recognition. The first child of this array, *Claudius Smith, the Cowboy of the Ramapo Valley,* had become part of a family—either histories of the New York-New Jersey area or little-known regional novels. Here are some of the titles: *Claudius: A Story Founded on Facts in Southern New York* by P. Demarest Johnson; *Cowboy of the Ramapos* by Marjorie Sherman Greene; *Near on Nature's Heart* by the Reverend E. P. Roe; *Claudius, the Cowboy of Ramapo Valley,* subtitled *A Story of Revolutionary Times in Southern New York* by the same P. Demarest Johnson; *Chronicles of Monroe in Olden Time* by the Reverend Daniel Niles Freeland, and the celebrated and equally hard-to-get *Outline History of Orange County* of Samuel W. Eager, Esq., with a Newburgh, New York, imprint of 1846–1847.

Don't let the New York names deceive you. There were such things as border wars, and there were times when parts of New York reached down into what is now New Jersey, even as there were days when parts of what now is New Jersey reached up into New York.

Now, then: Who was Claudius and what did he do that, in

the end, he should be hanged? Why, and almost more important, was he called a "cowboy," surely one of the earliest characters to be so styled? I will answer the first question first. Hazarding a guess, I would say that Claudius Smith, of Smith's Clove, made off with more than his share of cattle and that his romping through the Ramapos, from one secret hideaway to another and usually just a few steps ahead of the law and his would-be captors, served to build a nickname. However, although I know few real-life cowboys, I imagine that any one of them would, reasonably enough, resent comparison with Claudius.

The name is oddly misleading; it is as confusing as the one applied to those miscreants of the Revolution called "Refugees" in or near the Pine Barrens in the southern or central areas of the state. In days when the "Refugees," called "Pine Robbers" by Barber and Howe, were harassing citizens, stealing cattle, and making off with other plunder behind the lines in the Midlands and further south, Claudius and his "cowboys" were doing the same thing up north.

In *Forgotten Towns of Southern New Jersey*, I have given you the tale of Joe Mulliner, leader of a band of outlaws in Revolutionary days, whose lonely grave in a small clearing in the thickets not far from the Mullica River has been marked by those who have told and in some instances added to what is known. Joe, referred to as a kind of rough Robin Hood, even as Claudius was on occasion, was hanged in Burlington for crimes, primarily robberies, for which his gang was responsible. There are some who delight in reminding me that Joe Mulliner was never personally connected with a murder.

Claudius Smith was hanged in Goshen, New York, as you will see, and there is a strange parallel in the careers of Joe, the "Refugee" leader, and Claudius, the Cowboy. Down Jersey can claim the one, and Up Jersey, through which Claudius conducted his raids and had confederates in the Pascack "community," can claim the other.

This much as a preamble for the life, times, and adventures of an early American outlaw would suffice if it were not for those scoffers who seem to have an idea that Claudius was and remains an exclusive New York property. They would ignore the fact that the border between New York and New Jersey was never very certain for a long time; they, too, would minimize the statement of the late John Storms, who has said that Peter Ackner and William Welcher, both of Pascack, given a prominence equal to Park Ridge, sometimes spelled *Parkridge*, on the older maps through the 1870's, were among the associates of Claudius Smith; and finally, they would refuse to consult Eager's *Outline History*, in which he has given the following names as those of rascals who lived in the Pascack neighborhood and were known as aides of Smith: Benjamin Demarest, Tunis Helme, John Herring, Peter Ackner, Isaac Maybee, and Arie Ackerman. These are definitely named as harboring and consorting with the raiders of Claudius Smith, and at least two were associated in print with Pascack, a name with which Westwood has long been familiar. The fate of these men, named in confessions of those caught with or at about the same time as Claudius, is not as well defined as that of Claudius and his immediate lieutenants. The intimates, it is shown, were also found guilty and hanged.

"The inhabitants of Monroe, Cornwall, Bloominggrove and Goshen, and indeed all the southern part of the county (Orange)," wrote Samuel Eager on the first of several pages devoted to Claudius Smith, "suffered severely during the Revolution from a nest of traitors, Tories, and a species of robbers and midnight plunderers, called Cowboys. . . ." Northern Bergen County suffered similarly.

"The make(up) of the country furnished great facilities for such gangs of rogues to issue forth and prowl abroad during the night, commit all kinds of depredations, and then retreat in safety and hide themselves in the deep glens and inaccessible fastnesses of the mountains. Smith's Clove—west of the

Highlands"—naturally not to be confused with the Highlands fronting on New York Bay—"and along the valley of the Ramapo, nourished many infamous rascals of this description, who were guilty of all kinds of bad deeds, from theft to murder.

"Among these, and foremost in daring wickedness was the family of Claudius Smith, himself the leader—the oldest, greatest and most daring villain of the gang; and who, on the 22d day of January, 1779, in Goshen, expiated his bloody crimes on the gallows. Some of his associates in criminality were tried and convicted at the same time, and executed with their leader.

"This gang of felons was numerous," Eager goes on, "as appears from the convictions had at the time, from the confessions of some of them, taken in New Jersey, after the execution of Claudius, and from their written threats, which we place before the reader. The most notorious were Claudius Smith, his sons, Richard, James, and William; Edward Roblin, William Cole, John Mason, Mathew Dolson, John Ryan, Thomas Delamar, James Gordon, etc. The names of many others will be found in the paper submitted. . . ."

Sam Eager says that the family was of English origin and came to the New York-New Jersey borderline country from Long Island. He doesn't know just when that was. "It must have been many years before the war," he suggests, "for the family gave name to the Clove; and at that time," he adds, "the children of Claudius were grown up. . . ." Claudius is supposed to have been born in Brookhaven, Long Island.

Apparently gathering his lore from the older people of his day, even as I have tried to do in mine, the author first quotes a Mrs. Abigail Letts, "an aged lady" who said that the father of Claudius himself "was a bad man. . . ." Mrs. Letts told Eager that the elder Smith was "cross, self-willed, and abusive" and that before his death, being afflicted with loss of sight, used a cane to beat his wife and cause such disturbances that the neighbors had to intervene.

"He lived at McKnight's Mills near the residence of John

McGarrow, Esq.," Mrs. Letts further testified, and "on one occasion, when Claudius was secreted in the mountains, pursued and watched by the scouts who were after him, his father, who had been up to his place of secretion to carry some provisions to the gang, while returning was seen by the scouts, who fired upon him and killed his horse."

"We have heard it said," the author goes on carefully, "that Claudius was vicious from his youth, and that his mother, who was aware of the great tendency of his nature to the commission of crime, and knowing some of his evil deeds, on one occasion said to him, 'Claudius, you will die like a trooper's horse, with your shoes on. . . .'" As you will see, Claudius Smith remembered those words, even as he stood on the gallows with death minutes away.

Eager, in his history, is inclined to conclude that the father of Claudius was both privy to his son's thievery and also a fellow-conspirator. The first recorded act of law-breaking seems to have been the theft of a pair of wedges which had their owner's name stamped on them. "In order to disguise them and escape detection," runs the record, "his father assisted him to grind out the letters." There are indications here that at this time Claudius was perhaps of tender age—else why would he have needed help for so simple an act.

But what was this Cowboy like, physically? Sam Eager's *Outline* supplies the answer quickly enough. "Claudius Smith," he says, "was . . . a man of large stature and powerful nerve; of keen penetration; a man upon whom nature had bestowed abilities worthy to be exerted in a better cause.

"He conducted his expeditions with such cautiousness as scarcely ever to be suspected until in the very execution of them; and if a sudden descent was made upon them, by some bold stroke or wily maneuver he would successfully evade his pursuers and make his escape. Such of the aged as the author was able to persuade to talk in those early 1840's told many a tale of 'this noted man, some of which are doubtless true.'

"Smith's was a story of the most desperate character," the chronicler went on subsequently, "and his felonies, on every favorable opportunity, were committed as well on the property of the government as upon that of individuals. . . . Active and influential Whigs were the special objects of the hatred of Claudius Smith and for some particular cause, not now known, he threatened the lives of Nathaniel Strong, Colonel Jesse Woodhull, Samuel Strong, and Cole Curtis. . . ."

A peculiar argument seems to have gone on for some years as to whether a murder indictment was among those on which Claudius was ultimately tried, convicted, and finally executed, but it should be remembered by such particularists that in those days multiple robbery was also a capital offense. Samuel Eager's own mirror of the times, as well as the researches of other writers, indicate that at least in one instance Claudius did more than utter threats, although he seems to have enjoyed the provision of suspense for the murder specifically involved. He "took back his plan" against Colonel Woodhull, he wrote, because on one occasion and for good reasons the Colonel prevented his being shot down, "but," he added, "Major Strong was not so fortunate." I, too, must allow the matter to simmer there for just a moment.

Traveling through the erstwhile haunts of Claudius and his ruffians with Jim Ransom and looking up at the seemingly inaccessible heights of Mount Torne through the pass that was called the Clove, I was compelled to conclude that much of the countryside was as it always had been. Even the coming of the New York Thruway and the connections for the Garden State Parkway had failed to alter the setting as an heirloom of troop movements of long ago, of the rattle of early stage-coaches, and of the "bockeys"—these were mountain people who continued to weave baskets of oak splints and bring them down to sell in Ladentown, Rockland County, New York, and perhaps elsewhere. To Mount Torne clings a wonderful legend of George Washington, who, I reflected in this instance, must have been in top form to climb that high.

"From there he could see New York harbor, with glasses, of course," Jim Ransom told me, "and so keep posted on British activities there and in the area, first hand. Once when he was up there, he is said to have dropped his watch and it bounced down deep in a crevice. Presumably there was no way to retrieve it, and so, also presumably, it is still there. It must be," Jim added with one of his wry smiles, "for if you put your ear to the right crack, some say, you can still hear it ticking."

Near Suffern, when the light is right, you can look up at one ridge and discern what Jim told me is called Horse Stable Rock, so named since it was a lofty hiding place for no less than the Cowboy of the Ramapos. That was before there were cowboys of a different kind in the West or at least before they were so distinguished. There is no doubt that Horse Stable Rock was a favorite lookout, not only for Claudius Smith and his gang but also for the Indians, judging from the number of Indian artifacts that have been found there and not far away. Jim Ransom feels that Horse Stable Rock was a meeting place for Claudius and his raiders and a lookout for the others, and concludes that Smith and his men rarely exposed their position by daylight or went mountain-climbing at night.

"Some people still look upon Claudius as a kind of Robin Hood," Jim said one day as we looked down Smith's Clove from an elevation that commands a view of a panorama miles wide and from which a Japanese architect has added a modern motel without obvious intrusion. "Others call him 'The Cowboy'—but the best name of all, I'm sure, is 'The Scourge of the Ramapos.' Some of us prefer that name, I suppose, because it gives Claudius his proper setting, in the country where we are now."

There were two recurrent questions concerning Claudius Smith at the top of my list, even as there must have been on that of Samuel W. Eager's, hurrying about and asking ques-

Jim Ransom, of Westwood, an authority on forges and furnaces of the Ramapos, knew all about outlaw Claudius Smith, "Cowboy of the Ramapo Valley."

tions, as he prepared to write his *Outline History of Orange County*. Why had Colonel Jesse Woodhull, on an occasion memorable at least to Claudius, saved his life and in so doing also persuaded "the Cowboy" to "take back his plan" against the Colonel? If that "Major Strong was not so fortunate," was the Major the soldier who had been killed and was this the crime listed in the murder indictment against Claudius?

Here, I feel sure, are the answers, supplied in good time by the Eager text.

"Colonel Woodhull had a favorite and elegant mare which Claudius gave out he intended to steal. Knowing the desperate character of the man and his ability to accomplish what he purposed, Woodhull had her brought from the barn and put in his cellar, where she was kept for some weeks. Claudius, knowing the place of secretion, one evening hid himself in a barrack near the house and watching his opportunity, when the family went upstairs to tea, slipped in and took the mare. "He had not left the yard of the house before he was seen carrying off the animal in triumph. A gentleman at the table sprang up, seized his gun, and was about to shoot, but was prevented by Woodhull saying—'If you shoot and miss him, he will kill me'—and he, Claudius, escaped. . . ." Which report inspires two considerations—first, Claudius Smith was indeed clever to coax a strange mare out of the cellar while members of the family supped upstairs, and, second, Colonel Woodhull thought first of himself and then of his "favorite and elegant mare."

Major Nathaniel Strong was shot and killed on the night of October 6, 1778, and although this was a particularly cruel deed, according to all the accounts that Sam Eager summed up, there was no more than circumstantial evidence that Claudius and his gang were collectively involved. The Major was in bed, and the intruder, "being armed, entered the room with a pair of pistols and a gun. . . ." In bed or not, the Major was armed, too, and the invaders demanded that he put away his firearms "and he should have quarter. . . ." He put his gun in the corner and approached the door, through the broken panel of which he was fired upon and was struck down. "He expired without speaking a word," the account concludes.

It is apparent that the murder of Major Strong, no matter which of the villains accomplished it, capped the climax of a long and fearsome record. A contemporary writer said, "This new outrage filled the inhabitants with resentment and reached the ears of the executive." Governor Clinton, on October 31, pursuant to a motion of the Assembly, issued a proclamation offering a reward of $1,200 for the apprehension of Claudius Smith, and $600 for each of his sons, Richard and James Smith. This, in the end, had the desired effect. Meanwhile, how-

ever, there are at least two other stories you must hear, one of
which was destined to have a sequel when Claudius Smith was
on the gallows. It seems that there was another Captain Woodhull, not to be
confused with the Colonel but perhaps of the same family.
The Captain's house was at Oxford—I would like to think that
it was at Oxford Furnace, but that is far to the south, and so
I must conclude that this was Oxford across the long-disputed
New York line. "In the execution of their nefarious plans of
blood and murder," wrote our historian, "Claudius, with four
of his party, some of whom were his sons, in October, 1778,
late at night, came to the house of Captain Woodhull at Oxford, intending to rob the house and murder him; but fortunately he was away on duty.

"The object of their larceny was a set of silver. The door was
fastened and, not opened by Mrs. Woodhull, they broke it in.
She, suspecting who they were, and true to her nature, ever
full of quick expedients, and anticipating the intentions of the
robbers while they were breaking in, hid her valuable articles
of silver, etc., in the cradle, and then placed her child upon
them.

"During the time the rogues were searching the house, Mrs.
W. made herself very busy around the cradle, endeavoring to
quiet and still her child. The artifice succeeded to admiration, and they left without much spoils. . . ."

At this point I must ask if you know what a "hopple" is? To
be truthful, I didn't, until the account of what the robbers did
on leaving the Woodhull house sent me to the dictionary. As
the band made off, a horse belonging to one Luther Conklin
was spied, "hoppled" in the meadow. "They threw the hopples
away," the account reveals, "and several years after, when
ploughing up the meadow, they were found." A hopple? Oh,
yes. It's an apparatus that ties the legs of a horse, and so limits
him pretty much to the area in which his owner has left him.

Here is the incident which had its strange sequel at the

gallows where, I must say, Claudius Smith provided his own dramatic touch, born of a remembrance of a prophecy made many years before:

"Col. McClaughry was taken prisoner at the reduction of Fort Montgomery in October 1777; and while he remained so in New York, was deprived of many of the comforts he previously enjoyed. He wrote home to his wife to send him some money. She applied to Abimal Youngs for the loan of some hard money; but he declined, saying 'he had none.' Youngs was a notorious man of means, but of a miserly disposition, and did not like to lend his hard money to a woman whose husband was a prisoner. . . ."

It was soon noised about that Youngs had refused to loan the money.

"Mrs. McClaughry like a true Whig and a lady who loved her lord sold or pawned her shoe buckles and other female ornaments in New York, raised the money and gave it to the Colonel. It is said that this story came to the ears of Claudius Smith, who determined to punish him (Abimal Youngs) and through the instrumentality of his willing gang forcibly abstract the funds which he had refused to loan.

"The tradition is that they attacked his home one night, entered it and demanded his money, which he refused to give up or tell where it was secreted. Knowing that he had it somewhere about the premises, they took him out and tied him to the well pole, and then swung him up. After he had hung a moment, they let him down and again demanded his money, threatening to hang him outright if he did not tell. He still refused and clung to his money rather than to life. They hung him in this manner three times, and still he would not and did not tell. . . ." Then they let him go, much to his own surprise, I imagine, as well as theirs, but they went into the house "and, among other things, carried off some of his deeds, bonds, and other valuable papers. . . ."

This was one of the episodes, I suppose, which when multiplied, gave Claudius the reputation of a Robin Hood. Claudius Smith certainly was acting in behalf of a distraught woman who, he must have reasoned, should have been loaned money when she needed it by a man who had it. Beyond that, Claudius and his men could have hanged Abimal Youngs with the greatest of ease.

With a bounty on his head and smaller rewards offered for the capture of two of his sons, Claudius seems to have been more on the run than ever from that time on. "A number of persons banded together, headed by one Titus, a powerful man of much daring, and set out for the place of Smith's rendezvous, but the latter had gone to New York and Titus and his party followed. . . ."

Sam Eager was a commendably exacting historian, mostly folklorist, who made it his business to correct what he says was misinformation dispensed with "the best of intentions" by Judge William Bodle, whom he describes as "a gentleman of easy faith." The truth of the matter from this point on, he reported, was gleaned from a letter written by James Tusten, identified as the son of Colonel Tusten, "who was killed in the battle of the Minisink." The Judge had it that three indictments were found against Claudius Smith, one of them for the murder of Major Strong; he also made Titus the prime mover in the capture of "the Cowboy." Actually, James Tusten argued, Claudius was not tried for the murder of Strong "but for offenses entirely different."

Claudius Smith found New York full of British soldiers, no more friendly to him than were those from whom he had fled, and so he moved across to Long Island, where he took lodging at the home of a widow from whom he concealed his identity as much as he could. There a Major Brush caught sight of him after a boat trip across the Sound from Connecticut. He it was, Eager has written, who alerted Titus and two others, "and they worked out a plan to take the outlaw."

For one who had had so wild a life, leaving a trail of crime behind him that crossed and recrossed the New Jersey-New York border many times, if for no other reason than to make the most of appointed hideaways, the end was almost prosaic —at least as far as the capture was concerned. Claudius was in bed, as his landlady revealed without much hesitation, and there he was put in charge by candlelight. The outlaw made a try for his pistols, hidden under his pillow, but the attempt was that of a man half awake or even half-hearted. The Governor was notified, and Claudius was taken to Goshen, New York.

"He was confined to the Goshen jail," wrote James Tusten, "manacled, and chained to a ring in the floor, while the jail was closely guarded by parties of the inhabitants—for they were apprehensive that an attempt would be made to rescue him. . . ." An order was given to the guard to shoot Smith if an attack upon the prison was likely to succeed in his liberation. At length the date appointed for his execution, January 22, 1779, arrived, "and crowds flocked to see the exit of the man whose name had long spread terror through the country.

"Claudius," continues this detailed account, "was dressed in a suit of rich broadcloth with silver buttons, and with his large form and manly air, presented really a noble appearance. While walking to the place of execution he was observed to gaze intently towards the hills east of the town, to see (as was thought) if his comrades were not coming to his rescue; for he had harbored throughout, the idea that he should be preserved by some such interposition. None appeared, however, and he ascended the gallows with a firm step. Casting his eyes about, he bowed to several whom he knew in the crowd. . . ."

It was at this point that Abimal Youngs made his last, however belated, appearance in the melodrama that had been the life of "The Scourge of the Ramapos." Claudius, if he is to be complimented for anything at all, on the basis of the records, can be commended, surely, for his judgment of the man in an earlier instance, as well as for his immediate reaction to what must have been a pathetic and almost comic intrusion. "When Claudius was on the platform and just before he swung off," wrote Sam Eager, "Youngs made his way close to him and requested him to tell where his papers were, that they were of great use to him and worthless to anybody else. . . ." Claudius, in a last moment of dignity, was heard to reply, "Mr. Youngs, this is no time to talk about papers. Meet me in the next world and I will tell you all about them." The inference made by Claudius Smith was subtle, indeed: He had told Abimal Youngs that he, too, must go to Hell.

With only seconds left him and as the noose was being adjusted, Claudius allowed himself a twisted smile, as if he had suddenly remembered something. As he managed to kick off his shoes, only a few could have shared the recollection and perhaps only he listened down the halls of the years for the precise warning of his mother: "Claudius, you will die like a trooper's horse, with your shoes on."

"Not content to disgrace her and her memory of being the mother of such a villain," wrote Sam Eager long after, "by the cause and manner of his death; but to prove her a liar and false prophetess, and for that purpose publicly expressed, he threw off his shoes and was executed in his stockings. . . ." Jim Ransom told me that all who know anything at all about Claudius Smith remember this story about him. Sam Eager, who had checked it out and found it to be true, was so disturbed that he wrote, "History cannot produce an act evincing more infernal depravity, deep and ingrained, in the hour of death than that. It equalled," he added, "the conduct of the demon Nero who, to deliver himself from the troublesome control of his mother Agrippina, ordered her assassination, which was carried into quick execution. . . ."

"Thus died a man," the historian concluded, when he had recovered a little, "whose abilities, if rightly directed, would have raised him to eminence and greatness . . . it is believed that much of what he abstracted from the wealthy he bestowed upon the indigent." Thus also died, according to another source, a man whose skull was abnormally large. A skull was found long after, Jim Ransom told me, and from its size and other characteristics was adjudged to have been that of Claudius Smith, "Robin Hood" of two states to some, "Scourge of the Ramapos" to many more.

Chapter VII

"MEND 'EM," MENDOM, MENDEM, MENDHAM

In the beginning I was among those who doubted that the name of Mendham, a village and township in Morris County on the road east from Morristown to Chester, once Black River, could have come from anything as elemental as the retort of a man who said, "Never fear, I'll mend 'em!" But now that the at times considerably heated arguments have rumbled down the years and roads from Maplewood to Princeton to Roxiticus, now Ralston, then to Trenton and back to Brookside, I must declare myself on the side of the folklorists as opposed to those who cling to what some historians prefer to believe.

Here it must be said that two celebrated historians, no less than our good friends John W. Barber and Henry Howe, might easily be assumed to have led me astray, inasmuch as they accepted the declaration, "I'll mend 'em!," as good enough to be included in their *Historical Collections*—but this is not true. The error seems to have been in imputing the exclamation to Ebenezer Byram, an elder in the Hilltop Presbyterian Church in Mendham, whose white spire may be seen for miles, more clearly in winter, in that beautiful, rolling country.

I long have shared documentary proof that it was the Reverend Francis Peppard who made the spirited reply which gave a lasting named to Mendham in days before Mr. Peppard had become the dominie celebrated for introducing hymns to a congregation that wanted no music. Surely neither admirers of the Earl of Mendham nor the Indians, who had a word *mendom* meaning huckleberry or raspberry, were in-

128

volved, for all the respect I ever shall have for the erudition of
my friend, the late Charles Alpaugh Philhower. At the time of
my early doubting of the Barber-Howe explanation, I was still
sensitive, if memory serves, to the rebukes of those who be-
littled my easy acceptance of what old residents of Buckshutem told me in explaining the strange name of their town
as probably an Indian injunction, "There goes a buck, shoot
him!" By this time I know that Buckshutem is of Indian derivation and that there are other *buckshutems* in New Jersey, but
having seen Mendom spelled just that way on tombstones behind Hilltop Church and knowing well the frailties of pioneer
tombstone cutters in spelling words and even family names
the way they sounded, I still maintain that a few, at least,
forgot to cross their "o's."

I began my probing of the Mendham "mystery" and its
affiliated legends in the late 1930's. Then, long after in 1951,
came Helen Martha Wright's book on the history of the Hilltop Church. Variants began to emerge, at least more dra-
matically, early in 1952, and in subsequent years the Joseph
Hermans, who had come upon and lived among the unfolding
secrets of one of the oldest houses of what now is Montclair,
revealed that they had been criticized, to put it mildly, for
revealing Peppard family lore that disputed long-accepted
conclusions. From my notes I have discovered that this "campaign" against what must be the truth was still under way in
the spring of 1961.

Here is how the story developed.

When I came upon Helen Wright's book, I discovered that
she had begun her narrative with a description of a small log
meeting house at Rocksiticus, spelled that way although my
Roxiticus never had raised a Philhower Indian eyebrow. "The
settlement of Rocksiticus, now Ralston," she wrote, "was on
Indian Brook, a stream that flows into the North Branch of the
Raritan (River) near its source. . . ." The pioneer planters
who had settled here lost little time in building a house of

worship on a hill that overlooked one of the Minisink trails that led to the Indian council island in the Delaware. Across the adjoining hill was the village of Black River. In another direction the locality called "Rocksiticus" indicated that pioneers moved from there not far up the road to where two Colonial inns faced each other, even as they did when I last went that way.

One day as I stood beside the grave of Temperance Wick—Tempe to those who know the Wick house in nearby Jockey Hollow—I remember wishing that I could have asked her a question or two. Certainly, one would have concerned the legend of the horse she took to her bedroom—a story that one of the National Park caretakers did his best on one occasion to deflate in my presence. Another, I am sure, would have been to nail down the truth of Mendham's name, once and for all. A third would have concerned what really happened when lightning hit the spire of the Hilltop Church with such fatal consequences. Miss Wright made no fuss over Tempe at all and mentioned her father Henry only once as one of the signers of the contract for the building of the manse. I have noted, however, that the writers of a more recent guidebook, never as concerned with folklore, or what people say, as I have been, have cast considerable doubt on the horse that "climbed the stairs."

"Captain Henry Wick of the Colonial cavalry lived here," says the record, "but it was his daughter who made history for the farmhouse. One winter day, so the story goes, Miss Temperance Wick was returning on horseback after summoning a physician for her mother. Colonial troopers tried to commandeer her favorite white horse. 'Oh, surely,' Tempe is said to have remonstrated, 'you will let me ride him home first!' With that she brought down her whip on the horse's flanks and he took the hill at a gallop.

"At the farmhouse, the girl led the horse through the kitchen and into her bedroom. The soldiers came, searched the barn

and nearby woods, and left. Another version is that Tempe
rode her horse straight into the house without bothering to
dismount. Conceding the liberal dimensions of Colonial door-
frames and the delicate proportions of Miss Wick, the question
remains: Who opened the door—Tempe, or the horse?" Which
poses a pretty question—as does the narrative as it is told in
southern areas of the state. This time the legend has added a
stairway. However, if I must be technical, who is sure that
Tempe Wick was the possessor of "delicate proportions"?

It was at this point that, with mild disbelief, I quoted what
John W. Barber and Henry Howe had said: "The earliest
regular settlement in Mendham was on the North Branch of
the Raritan. As early as 1713 there were some few squatters'
cabins. At that time the land was taken up by the Wills family,
but they did not settle until many years later. The village of
Mendham is in the central part, 6½ miles SW of Morristown.
Among the first settlers in the vicinity were the Byram, Cary,
Thompson and Drake families. The gravestone of Ebenezer
Byram, which is now standing in the graveyard, records his
death August 9th, 1753, aged 61.

"When he came, the locality bore the Indian name, Roxiticus. The name of the tavern which he established was 'The
Black Horse,' from its sign. Tradition asserts the neighborhood
was rendered famous by the pranks of a wild crew of fellows
who lived there. Mr. Byram having been told the nature of the
society he had settled in, replied, 'I'll mend 'em'—an assertion
he carried out literally: hence the name, Mendham. . . ."

Paying no attention to any expressions of disbelief at the
time, if there were such, the authors hurried on to say that
Mendham in their day boasted "a Methodist and Presbyterian
church, an academy for males, and the 'Hill-top' Seminary for
females; several stores, two carriage establishments, and about
50 dwellings." A few lines further down in the same text it is
pointed out that Ralstonville and Water Street "are small collections of houses in the township—the first 1½ miles W and the

Members of the Hilltop Presbyterian Church at Mendham have many stories to tell about the parish's early days. Its third pastor, Dr. Francis Peppard, encountered strong opposition when he tried to introduce the membership to hymns.

last 3½ miles NE of Mendham." Which, it would seem to me, would indicate that Ralstonville or Ralston was in the area but not Rocksiticus or even Roxiticus at all. At this period neither John W. Barber nor Henry Howe, who merit a chapter all their own one of these days, considered that the expression, "I'll mend 'em!" was strange, indeed, for a tavern-keeper and, if true, might more easily have come from another.

Water Street has remained modestly elusive. It was never more so than on the day I brooded in the Hilltop Graveyard, where, for a time, members of the Phoenix family and others were compelled to take refuge in a separate enclosure because they made applejack. "The Phoenix burial plot," wrote Miss Wright, "is a memorial to the congregation's early struggle against the use of intoxicating liquors, if tradition is authentic. It is written in an historical account of the church that twenty-seven of its supporters had owned distilleries.

"The church records show that inebriety was a serious problem. The former account also states that when William Phoenix applied for a burial ground the congregation refused it, because he kept a bar in his inn. He then bought a large plot adjoining the churchyard and round it built the stone fence which remains, the only reminder of that early type of substantial enclosure. . . ."

However, if it was "Jersey Lightning" that some of the congregation feared, never dreaming of a day when the graveyard would be compelled to surround the Phoenixes and their kin, it was lightning of a different kind that left its mark in May, 1813. A reporter sent the following account to a contemporary newspaper, *The Palladium of Liberty:*

"A most distressing event occurred here yesterday. At the close of the morning service, there appeared a shower to be rising from the west, which prevented most of the congregation from leaving the church during the interval of public worship. About half past twelve o'clock the shower began with hail and rain; and about a quarter before one a stream of lightning was seen to descend from the cloud to the lightning rod on the church, and by the lightning rod down to within about eight feet of the ground (the lower part of the rod having been broken off and lost) the lightning there burst, and one part of it entered a window into a pew where several people were sitting, and struck the wife of Mr. John Drake, who expired instantly! Eight or ten others were injured, some of them very much. We hope, however, that they may all recover, but doubts are entertained. No injury was done to the house; and scarcely any trace of the lightning is to be seen on any part of it. . . ."

Historians of the area use this account to prove that it was the first Hilltop Church, and not the one left unscathed in the freak and tragic storm, that was destroyed by fire following a lightning bolt. Mrs. Drake's epitaph, which long ago became the dust of red sandstone, read, according to a clipping discovered in 1939: "Martha, wife of John Drake, was killed instantly by lightning as she sat in the Church on Sunday the 16th of May, 1813, aged 33 years, 6 months, and 24 days."

If you will take time to look through the records of Ralston and Mendham, you will soon come upon the names of Hanover and West Hanover. Madison's John Ehrhardt has reminded me that Morristown was known as West Hanover until 1739, at which time Morris County was formed. In 1740, West Hanover became Morris Town. "Those were days," John said, "when the County had three towns: Morris Town, Pequannock, and Hanover. 'Hanover Church' of 1718 was originally Whippanong Church," remembered in the name of Whippany, "and the first pastor was the Reverend Nathaniel Hubbell, a New Englander and Yale graduate. Land for 'Hanover Church' was given in 1718 by 'John Richards, of Whippanong, Schoolmaster.' A dominie who also was a medic was John Nutman (Edinburgh, M.D.; Yale, D.D.), and he served as pastor from 1733 to 1749."

Although the name of the Irishman who was to give Mendham its name had not entered his claim, I remembered, there on the hill where stones marked hidden chapters of the story, that many Scotch and Irish evangelists were in this very neighborhood—Hanover, Roxiticus, Basking Ridge, and the little villages around them—between 1717 and 1738 conducting revivals that left a deep impression. It was in 1726 that William Tennent established his Log College near the west bank of the Delaware River, the college that was Princeton-to-be. It was in that same year that Theodorus Frelinghuysen's co-worker went to New Brunswick as the first graduate of Log College.

Those were days when farmers were arriving in Perth Amboy and pushing inland through Hanover, Basking Ridge, Roxiticus, and further along the banks of the Raritan. Many undertook service in private homes until spring came rather than try the icy hills to Whippanong. When the weather was more suitable, travel was easier from Roxiticus and Drake's Clearing, then to Pitney's Clearing, from there to Smith's Grist Mill, and eventually to West Hanover. In some of the scattered records there is every indication that Water Street now is Brookside, and that conclusion, through the years, has gone uncontradicted.

I dare say that you have hurried through Roxiticus, or Rocksiticus, without knowing it—now that the heart of the neighborhood called Roxiticus is Ralston, the Ralstonville of old. I hope you will go back, for you will see what used to be the little one-story post office which, until the postmaster moved up the road, was the oldest in continuous use in the United States. Erected by John Ralston in 1775 as a store, its service as a post office began in 1792 and did not conclude until 1950, when the village historical society took it under its protective wing—ancient mailboxes, and all. Search for the key from W. W. Cordingly, a retired architect, led to Lawrence Thompson, in proud possession of the Thompson house in Ralston, which had been out of family possession only four years since 1714. It led further to the revelation that David Young, one of America's first astronomers, is buried beside the Hanover church with an impressive "Philom." This follows the family name and proclaims David to have been a man of great learning in his times. In this particular case David is remembered as one who prepared almanacs, and so far I have sought without result for more lore about him.

On those early journeyings which, although I did not know it, were in effect setting the stage for much more, I managed to amass a great miscellany of information. One was the story of the Reverend Fred W. Druckenmiller, then the pastor of the church at Union, once Connecticut Farms; he had been digging in the graveyard there, respectfully, of course, and had "come up" with a tombstone that long ago had vanished below the surface of the ground—the stone antedated the church by fifty years and indicated that Connecticut Farms and perhaps the church itself had been on a map somewhare as early as 1730. Another story is my own: I came upon something I never had seen before, a tombstone carefully carved to represent a coffin, on which were these lines:

> Here lies one bereaved of life,
> A tender mother and a loving wife;
> Kind to her relations and a faithful friend,
> Happy in her beginning and no doubt in her end.

Thus was Sarah, the wife of Joseph Cooper, to be remembered, the note of happiness clashing, somehow, with the stone on which these words were graven.

I think it was John Ehrhardt who told me that one of the pastors of the Hanover Church had been among the founders of the New Jersey Medical Society, indicating that the parsons of this era, perhaps concentrating on this area, were accustomed and equipped to attend the ills of the body as well as those of the soul. There must have been something especially comforting in the parochial call of a man who could be counted on to do all in his power to prolong life and then when all hope of that was gone, to prepare a soul for glory.

The Loughlin mill which, according to one of the guide-books, was making cider across from John Ralston's post office as recently as 1939, had become a charming house when I was there. At that time, John's house, up the tangled rise from the post office and store, long empty, had no occupants and no one in the neighborhood able or willing to tell its story which began, they said, in 1771.

Long, long ago there was an Indian village on the farm which, at least in the 1840's, belonged to Colonel J. W. Drake, on the side of a hill not far from the farmstead itself. "The houses were scattered continuously around the hill," says the record, and "Indian arrow heads, stones, and other relics have there been occasionally plowed up. In the winter of 1779–80, when the American headquarters were at Morristown, a portion of the army were barracked in rude log huts, in Mendham and Morris Townships. The headquarters of the officers, Colonel Robinson and Chevalier Massilon, a French officer, were at the dwelling now occupied by Colonel J. W. Drake, about a mile from the village of Mendham. On the breaking out of the mutiny in the Pennsylvania line the officers were extremely alarmed and, in one or two instances, ran from their camp barefooted in the snow 2 or 3 miles. Despairing of their country's cause, some of them wept. . . .

"When here, the soldiers lived miserably; broken down by diseases and want, they depredated upon the inhabitants, became filthy in their persons, and infested with vermin. When the sickness was at its height, no less than forty coffins were brought at one time, and piled against the barn of Mr. Drake, which, together with the church, was used as a hospital—the latter having been divested of its seats for that purpose. Callous and inured to the horrors that beset them, the soldiers, regardless of all, were seen playing cards upon the coffins containing the remains of their dead comrades. . . ."

I won't have to ask Tempe Wick about the hospital when and if I meet her, for there is a stone in the Hilltop Churchyard marking the graves of twenty-seven soldiers who died of smallpox in 1777. However, the picture remained a little cloudy at this phase, with the performance of Tempe's wonderful horse, the lightning that picked out poor Mrs. Drake because the lightning rod wasn't grounded, and even the celebrated Mr. Byram, whose chance remark gave a name to Mendham, to be etched in with greater clarity.

This was the moment for Sidney Doggett to make an appearance, writing two identical letters to Pennington and Flemington so as to be sure to find me. On each of the letters was an identical postscript: "In the Firestone Library of Princeton University I found a reference to the naming of Mendham—it was there that the statement was made that the village was named for Myndham in England." So here I had still another suggestion as to how the name, Mendham, came to be, although I have noted that Sidney Doggett at no time expressed his evaluation of the idea.

"In 1947," he told me, when I went to see him in Corey Lane, Mendham, "I was able to purchase one of the old historic landmarks here—the home of Dr. Ebenezer Blachley— and this is it. Dr. Blachley married Mary, Tempe Wick's sister, and settled down to practice medicine in the community and the countryside beyond. There were twelve children, four of whom became doctors, and the mysteries of medicine and 'physic' were both practiced and taught in this old house. Several young men who studied under the good doctor and one young man, E. S. Woodruff, married Mary Blachley and settled near the homestead. Dr. Blachley was one of the founders of the New Jersey Medical Society in 1766. . . ."

Immediately I recalled John Ehrhardt's statement, and this tied it down. Sidney Doggett said that as far as he could discover, the house had been built in 1740. "It wouldn't sur-

prise me," he added, "if John Carey, a master carpenter whom
Ebenezer Byram had brought from the Massachusetts Colony
to build the Black Horse Tavern and the Hilltop Church, had
a hand in building it. It has the clean, typical saltbox lines of
many New England houses. A map of Milledge, drawn in
1788, shows the house—in fact it is the only one in Mendham
designated by the name."

Mary Blachley's house was virtually a shambles when Sidney
Doggett found it. In almost every room and down in the basement, he soon discovered the past hidden away behind the
walls, back of new bricks, or under layers of paint. Peeling
away the intervening years for the secrets that might lie behind
them became a fascinating adventure—I sensed that as Sidney,
one of those men who make you feel at once that you have
known them through many a year, told me about it. Some
treasures were past mending, and that is why you may see a
cherry floor that not too long ago was a pile of boards in
Pennsylvania or a door that had to be designed according to
the lines of the Ford mansion in Morristown. It was delightful
to find in Sidney Doggett a man who could turn with ease
from the routines of a chemicals company to those of painting
in oils, playing architect, and returning an old house to its
rightful heritage.

From Miss Ella Mockridge, in Mendham, a former schoolteacher (as well as from many others) Sidney Doggett learned
that a man still living in Madison named Ferry once had
owned the house. Concluding that Mr. Ferry must be a very
old man, Sidney was amazed to find him, at the other end of
the telephone, the owner of a booming voice. Mr. Ferry said
he would be glad to drive over immediately and answer any
questions he could. The Ferrys had bought the house in 1887.
Armed with new facts from Mr. Ferry as to where old fire-
places were, how the house had the first bathroom in Mendham because Mr. Ferry piped water downhill from a spring
up the road, and how apples growing in an adjoining orchard

never really ripened till April if properly stored, the Doggetts had gone from room to room, questing and drafting, and restoring.

"Now I've come upon the legend," Sidney told me, "that Dr. Blachley, stopped by the curious or perhaps by a man who was tipsy, on his way home one night because he was carrying what seemed to be an odd bundle, actually was bringing home the body of a man who had been hanged. Who the man was, what his offense had been, or whether, indeed, he had hanged himself, we do not know." But, after all, I suggested, the young men who were studying under Dr. Blachley would be gathering in the clinic next day. . . .

The Doggetts of Mendham's Corey Lane (or should it really be Carey?) and the John Hermans, of Elmwood Avenue, in Maplewood, had this in common: the delight of discovery among the secrets of an old house. I would call theirs the oldest house in Maplewood except that I do not wish to cause another "battle" on a new front, in addition to the one Beatrice Herman inadvertently declared when she told me the story of the Reverend Francis Peppard. The first of several wonderful letters awaited me when I returned home, and so I am able to give you what amounts to personal testimony, word for word:

"My great love for good old Jersey history dates back some twenty-five years or more, I think, to my childhood days when I'd sit on a hassock at the foot of Grandma's rocking chair. Grandma had a small white box, and after carefully examining its contents, Grandma would lean back and softly rock. Even at a very tender age I sensed that the small box seemed to possess some sort of strange magic, for it made Grandma's eyes sparkle and look so happy, yet thoughtful, as she looked at me and seemed to see so far beyond me.

"As I grew older and understanding took the place of childish curiosity, I was permitted to look at, and even touch, six

Beatrice Herman, of Maplewood, great-great-granddaughter of the Reverend Francis Peppard, found it difficult to convince some historians when she spoke of the traditions handed down about her ancestor and his part in establishing Mendham's name.

silver monogrammed spoons. 'How can six old spoons seem to almost take Grandma out of this world,' I'd think, 'and transport her to into some beautiful, mysterious place?' And then one day Grandma said to me, 'Betty, of all my grandchildren you are the only one who loves to listen to my stories. Now I am going to tell you a true story—one that you must always remember, for some day it will be a part of our American history.' Out came the little box, and this is the story of which I later kept a written record:

"The spoons were once silver shoe buckles which my great-great-great-grandfather, the Reverend Francis Peppard, wore on his shoes while preaching in the old Hilltop Presbyterian Church of Rocksiticus, later Mendham. Mr. Peppard was born in Dublin, Ireland, in 1725. He had been educated for the priesthood and was soon to be ordained when he decided to sail for America and seek religious freedom. His parents objected so strongly that he sailed without their consent or knowledge and landed, penniless, in Perth Amboy. It was necessary to relinquish a huge fortune, and therefore he had no money for passage. His time was sold to Mr. Byram (Ebenezer, I believe) of Elizabeth, and Ebenezer, finding him well educated, employed him as a schoolteacher, reimbursing him himself later.

"Francis Peppard soon found his way to Basking Ridge, where he married Susan McCullom, daughter of a well-known Scotch family and relative of Jacob McCullom, a member of the old Legislature of New Jersey. It was here that he became friendly with the Reverend Samuel Kennedy, from whom he probably received his basic training for the Protestant ministry. In 1762 he was graduated from Princeton University and in 1764 he was ordained.

"Almost immediately he was installed as the third pastor of the Hilltop Church, then Rocksiticus. Mr. Peppard introduced the singing of hymns by note and received so much opposition that one devout member would go so far as to rise and leave the church as the singing began and return when the last note had died away. Strong opposition continued through his three years of service to the church, but he was determined to help educate the people to notes and books.

"Many of his friends from Basking Ridge would say, 'Why don't you give up trying to teach them?' He would reply, in his strong Irish brogue, 'Never ye mind, I'll mend 'em.' Now I know that this last line has been told and retold in many ways and forms, and it may be hard for you, and no doubt many others, to swallow. I swallowed it, and yes, even digested it, and let me tell you why.

"First of all, the oldest record of the church is found in an ancient worm-eaten book entitled 'Mendom Congregation Book.' It was written during the second year of Mr. Peppard's pastorate, and the spelling is M-E-N-D-O-M. Second, the Reverend James Carter said, in his historical address, 'When you remember that it was during the pastorate of the Reverend Francis Peppard that we find what appears to be the earliest indication of the change of name from Rocksiticus to Mendham, bear in mind also that during this pastorate we have come upon the oldest extended contribution to the history of the church.' Third, Francis Peppard was an Irishman, and, therefore, by force of habit, used many Irish expressions, of which 'I'll mend 'em' was typical. It was not meant to be slang, as some people may think, but was his way of saying, 'I'll reform them.' Fourth, I never have heard of any other minister of Mendham being opposed to his teaching.

"Since we all know that Francis Peppard had difficulties teaching the people to sing by note, he really had reason to say often, 'Never ye mind, I'll mend 'em.' Finally, these facts were told me by my grandmother, Clarissa Peppard Knight"—this was the great-great-great-grandmother of Beatrice Herman talking all the while—"and she obtained them from Francis Peppard, Jr., her grandfather, and son of the Reverend Francis Peppard. Clarissa Peppard was the principal and teacher of a one-room school in Bernardsville, and she never made a statement unless she was absolutely sure of its truth.

"Now every time I polish my silverware I rub tarnish from my silver spoon which Grandma gave me, and, as I gaze at it, I seem to see not a spoon but a shoe buckle walking through the streets of Mendham. Maybe some day I'll have a rocking chair, too, and slowly rock while I tell the same story to my grandchildren. And, as for a parson having to be a healer of the physical body as well as the soul, I have proof in the form of forty-eight prescriptions copied from Francis Peppard's note-book while preaching at Hackettstown."

Beatrice Herman appended to the above "A Cure for Ye Consumption," which, from the sound of it, would have cured anything with grim finality, far and beyond Francis Peppard's will to mend.

I replied to Beatrice Herman's letter, assuring her that I was properly contrite, that never again would I doubt the tallest folk tale brought my way. I assured her, too, that even as I had read what she had written so delightfully, I could hear the voice of my own grandmother, who although she was from Liverpool, used many Irish expressions, saying, "I'll mend ye!" Mrs. Herman thanked me for my confidence in her records of the name and lore of Mendham, but I warned her from the beginning and out of experience that when I reported her researches, she would be relegated to the lesser ranks of the folklorists, especially by those who had made up their minds and would never change them. Further, I asked if there was a silhouette or any description of the likeness of Francis Peppard.

"I'm sorry to tell you," she said one day when I went to see the long-hidden charm of her own house in Montclair, "that I know of none." She shared my feeling, she said, that there must be some in existence. Mary, daughter of Francis Peppard, was the oldest, and she remained in Bethlehem, Orange County, New York, where her father was pastor of the New Windsor Church. She married Reuben Clarke, of that congregation, and spent all her life there. Of her descendants, twelve were clergymen, one of whom was the Reverend Edgar W. Clarke. One grandson at one time was the president of the Singer Sewing Machine Company, I was told. "I don't doubt that some of these descendants have much material, but I don't know where to get in touch with them," Mrs. Herman admitted.

"I should very much like to know," she said, on one occasion, "when the spelling was changed from Mendom, as it was in the beginning, to Mendham. I believe that there is proof that it was Mendom as late as 1777, for the Reverend James Carter, in his historical address, said so"—and she showed me a copy. The passage read " 'The Revd. Thomas Lewis came from Long Island and settled among us till his death in August, 1777. His grave lies behind me, diagonally across the drive of Mr. Johnson, under the shadow of the church. The inscription reads: In Memory of Ye Reverend Thomas Lewis, Late Minister of ye Gospel in Mendom, who died August ye 20, 1777. . . .' "

Here, after another visit to Mendham, I reported another mystery to Mrs. Herman. The inscription she quoted showed that "late" was spelled "lete" and, further, that a copyreader with a chisel instead of a pencil disagreed with what seems to have been the original spelling, Mendom, belatedly crossing the "o" to make it an "e." Perhaps the first Mendom became Mendem, and that, in turn, gave way to Mendham. As you have seen, and as the Hermans were to see further, all sorts of stories were "arranged" to explain the emergence of Mendham.

"I wonder," mused Beatrice Herman one day when we were talking again, "what the historians, who claim that Mendham was probably named in 1749 for the Earl of Mendham, will have to say to the spelling on the Reverend Mr. Lewis's tombstone. I cannot believe that men as well educated as Francis Peppard or Thomas Lewis would not know how to spell the name of their town if, in deed, it had been named for the Earl of Mendham."

As recently as 1961 the controversy, much to my surprise, was still raging. I found that out only by chance inquiry the day I was so near the Herman house in Montclair that I felt I must pay a call. I doubt if Beatrice would have told me voluntarily. Modest from the first, she always thought I made too much of her quiet, persistent research, even as she looked upon the whole facet of what I have found to be a clue-hunt as fascinating as a detective story. "It's almost," she said, "as if I were being told in letters from so many who argue that they are experts in such matters that I could not possibly

Early tombstone cutters sometimes had trouble fitting copy, but their work was doubly complicated in Mendham, where the bereaved were of several minds about the spelling of the town's name.

remember what my grandmother had told me to keep firmly in my mind."

Not long after that there came a letter in which Beatrice Herman described what I feel certain is the last word and—for my part, inasmuch as I seem to have caused it all—an end of her embarrassment. She wrote:

"Now, after repeated trips to Trenton and a full day in the Mendham Town Hall, searching the original Town Minutes, I feel I have sufficient new bolstering support of my statements to you. One of the authorities has said, 'The reference to Mr. Byram's being in Mendham is a reminder that the Township of Mendham had been formed in March in that year, 1749.' I was further told that the town was really named in an Act of Legislature of the State in 1749. And, further, I was assured that Francis Peppard was not in Mendham in 1749.

"With these statements in mind, I seriously debated abandoning the subject—and I would have, if it had not been for you. After all, it had been claimed that the original will of Ebenezer Byram, dated 1749, listed the town as 'Mendham' and not 'Mendum' or 'Mendom.' It was also asserted with authority that the original spelling was Mendham in 1749. Then you spoke to me about the whole matter, and I awoke with an urgency to see Ebenezer Byram's will.

"My urge was rewarded, for the will, originally written in Bridgewater, Plymouth Colony, Massachusetts, in 1738, contained a codicil on the back page which read 'Mendum, Morris County, 1747–50.' Encouraged by this information, I searched the archives of Morris County for names of persons who were married or who had died in Mendham between the years 1749–1780. I found many records, however, in every case, up to 1775, in which the spelling of the town's name was either Mendum or Mendom. Insisting upon authentic proof even beyond the archives, I looked up the original documents. They were all spelled Mendum, and later, Mendom.

"Records on file in Princeton University state that Francis

Peppard was met by Ebenezer Byram when he (Francis) came to America in 1742. Mr. Byram, as we discovered long ago and as these records corroborated, found him well educated and hired him to teach school. Francis lived in Mendham from 1742 to 1752, when he married his second wife—he married first a daughter of Ebenezer Byram. This information was also found in records by Miss Nancy Davis, of Morristown, who spent twenty years on research.

"Minn's *History of Hackettstown* also says that Peppard lived first in Mendham, so some of my best friends have been, to say the least, misinformed. There remained one snag in the version my family believed in. This was the fact that I had been told that the town was named Mendham in an Act of the State Legislature. There was certainty, I was assured, that the spelling was Mendham at that time. So I returned to Trenton to look up the original source of that information.

"After much searching on the part of those in charge, I was surprised to find that this information had been filed as recently as 1935 and that the original source of the information was the Town Minutes of Mendham in the Brookside Town Hall. The Town Clerk there proved to be charming, intelligent, hospitable, and efficient. She graciously brought out all the old records for my inspection. They corresponded in every way with the original documents filed in Trenton. The spelling was first Mendum and then, a little later, Mendom. 'Mendham' does not appear until 1770. . . .

"At any rate there seems to be no record of an Act by the Legislature naming the town. Dozens of documents in Trenton, and pages of records in Brookside, prove, without a doubt, that the spelling for more than twenty years was Mendum. As I have said many times, I cannot believe that all the people were such poor spellers that no one one could spell the name of the town properly for twenty years! I do not want to criticize or discredit the research of others in any untoward way. However, the proof is there, and I doubt if anyone can come up with one more argument against it. All of which proves that you cannot ignore folklore, for, in this case, I thought that the original documents *might* disprove my story. Instead, they have upheld it."

Memo to Parson Peppard: What a lot of fuss you caused when, confronted by a congregation that disliked the infusion of hymns into the services of the Hilltop Church, Mendham—and, I have no doubt, in the face of other arguments, you replied, in the rich and beautiful brogue you couldn't help even if you had wanted to—"Never ye fear, I'll mend 'em!"

Chapter VIII

"SING UNTO THE LORD A NEW SONG"

Irish Francis Peppard, who gave Mendham its name, was by no means the only wilderness shepherd who wanted his flock to sing. There also was Welsh Jenkin David, who was to me little more than a name in the history of the old Honeywell Academy at Mount Hermon, beside Locust Lake and a little to the northeast of Hope. The name was enough, however, to elicit a full and colorful chapter from as far away as New Brunswick.

As the crow flies, even if this particular crow is as much in the mood for moving around as Jenkin David seems to have been, this, indeed, is a long flight—out of Warren County, over parts of Hunterdon and Somerset, and then across the Middlesex line. I know now that Elder Jenkin, as he was mostly called, produced his own music book, handwritten settings and all, and then called for a hymn. If, wherever he happened to be, there was sustained objection on the part of the faithful he merely packed up his voice and went elsewhere.

Our crow in flight would have seen something of Hope, Great Meadows, Rockport on the long-abandoned Morris Canal, Beattystown if not Pleasant Grove or Middle Valley, and then, I think, he would have skirted the First Watchung Mountain to the Raritan River. My own way was far more circuitous and almost inexplicable, and this is not because there are no direct roads angling down from Mount Hermon. I began in Blairstown; perhaps because I had heard that many earlier residents there had attended classes at the Honeywell Academy; perhaps because so many, like Miss Minnie Smith, had said that too many people assume that the history of

Blairstown began with John I. Blair; but probably because there was a kind of plot afoot to induce me to forget that an earlier name of Blairstown had been Gravel Hill.

The purpose remains obscure, but there is still every indication that what I had said at the start was the truth—that Blairstown first was Smith's Mills, then Butts' Bridge, and then Gravel Hill, all before John I. Blair deservedly became its namesake.

Behind all the name-changing there was, I feel certain, a quantity of name-calling, of a different variety, too. It was natural enough to name the cluster of houses Smith's Mills for the man who provided a means to grind grain for his neighbors from over a wide area, even though Mr. Smith's first name seems to have been lost in the shuffle. And it was just as logical to forget about Mr. Smith and his mills when Jacob Butts, of Ramsaysburg, came along and provided the first certain means of crossing the Paulins Kill, without the necessity of wet feet for man or beast. Even so, I am inclined to agree with those who imply that the name Gravel Hill was a step downward, no matter how high the hill or how plentiful the gravel.

Here, for the complainants, are words from the tattered history sent me by Somerville's Leon Guinaud: "The original name was Smith's Mills. Several years prior to the Revolutionary War a man of that name built a log gristmill and a sawmill on Blair Creek, a few feet above the present stone gristmill, the old dam being built upon the site of the substantial stone dam erected in 1903. Oak timbers of the old dam were found imbedded in the mud while excavating for the new. This old mill is mentioned in a road survey recorded at Newton, dated March 30, 1768, but it was probably built some years prior to that time.

"The road leading to these mills passed through where the John I. Blair (now John D. Vail) residence stands. To this gristmill the pioneers of Knowlton and Pahaquarry Townships brought their grain on pack horses, treading the intricate forest paths as the Indians had done many years before. This mill performed no other operation than grinding, the flour being bolted by hand to separate the bran. The rude sawmill was of the slow up-and-down type, but it answered the purpose of sawing the few boards the pioneers used in the construction of their log houses and for making the few pieces of furniture found in the homes of the early settlers. . . ."

I repeat these words from the text so that they will carry with them some of the authority which earlier summations seem to have lacked and because, among other reasons, this was the very area around which recurrent proposals for new state parks have been made. I remember that when I had made these observations, someone said that the implication was that the early settlers in New Jersey had next to no furniture and that, therefore, most of them must have been poverty-stricken. They were not rich, to be sure, but their lack of furnishings indicated that they built their houses and then only what they needed, which, I have said before, is a pretty good credo.

"Jacob Butts," the same record goes on, recalling the pioneer whose own spelling of the name is disputed in nearby Buttzville, "came from Ramsaysburg, Knowlton Township, buying of John Kunkle fifty-two acres of land on the south side of the Paulins Kill, which was conveyed by deed dated June 18, 1791, for which Butts paid $379.08. . . ." Let me say here what historians through the years have said of nearby Delaware, "formerly Ramsaysburg," because that name seems to be on the identical place where Delaware now appears, at least on the Finley map of 1833. That Ramsaysburg is not the Delaware of today is contended by no less than the Delaware postmistress, as you will see; she remembers when the John I. Blair "dinky" was in operation, helping students of Blair Academy who didn't mind waiting an hour for a connecting train.

"This land is now included in the farm of John D. Vail and

occupied by George W. Groupe," the frayed pages of the old history go on. "A little later he bought fifty-two acres on the opposite side of the Kill. These farms embraced all the land within the present limits of Blairstown. About 1795 Mr. Butts and his neighbors built a bridge across the Kill to connect the two tracts of land, and for the accommodation of people traveling the Hope Road. This was the first bridge to span the Kill and soon the name of the place was changed from Smith's Mills to Butts' Bridge. . . ."

The record could hardly be plainer. Even so, I am a little in doubt as to how names were changed, unless it was by familiar usage which is part, whether the historians like to admit it or not, of the processes of folklore. A man sets up mills, and people talk about Smith and his mills. Another man builds a bridge—and that is how it goes, as simple as that.

"Prior to his locating at Smith's Mills, Butts owned the present David Rinker farm," reads this old account, for which I have found no date, "and the Rinker farm seems to have been along the river below Delaware, and lived in the stone house now occupied by Mr. Rinker. After moving to Smith's Mills, he lived for a few years in a small house that stood near the site of the farmhouse now occupied by George W. Groupe. About 1800 he built a large log farmhouse nearly on the site of John I. Blair's residence, where Mr. Butts kept a tavern for several years in connection with farming. He was the father of M. Robert Butts, esq., for many years a prominent citizen of Northampton, Pennsylvania, and grandfather of John R. Butts, of Sarepta, New Jersey," which is down the Buttztown-Hope Road and, the last time I was there, had no one able to account for its name.

I delight in telling you some of these details because so many have worked up the tale that John I. Blair, one of the first millionaires of the country, came from "the big city," already a tycoon of sorts who found railroad connections impossible. The opposite is true: He went to the top in New Jersey.

Jacob Butts died about 1820, perhaps a little earlier than that, and James Ridgeway set up a tavern and kept it going after Jacob's death, at least until 1828. It was on August 25, 1825, a year after Warren County had been set off by itself, that a post office was established and given the name Gravel Hill. It would seem to me, parenthetically, that Smith's Mills, or Butts' Bridge, would have appeared with greater éclat on letters than Gravel Hill, but I began long ago to wonder at the peculiar functioning of postal minds. For instance, not too long ago, I could have taken you to a three-mile stretch of well-paved road in what used to be my parochial "beat" where there never had been rural delivery and where, at least at that time, there was no hope of any.

Please do not conclude that because John I. Blair was appointed the first postmaster he was the one who decided to hand his name on, as the developer of the village, once he was in the saddle. As a matter of fact, he was postmaster twenty-six years, during which time the name remained Gravel Hill. Before 1825, the nearest post office was at Marksboro, where every chance I get I look for evidence of the establishment or even the memory of the tombstone craftsman who signed his work, in the Swayze Cemetery below Hope, as "Tetzel in Hardwick."

"The compiler of this book," says the old record—and I truly wish I knew the author of these pages that leave many a question unanswered—"has discovered historical articles claiming that Mr. Blair was appointed postmaster at Butts' Bridge in 1819. This is an error for Mr. Blair did not come to Blairstown from Hope until 1821, then a boy of eighteen years. A letter from Washington says, 'There is no record of a post office being established at Butts' Bridge.'"

What probably happened in the intervening time is that John Blair, who was running a store in Butts' Bridge, later Gravel Hill, gathered up the mail at the nearest postal points, and then distributed it as he delivered orders for groceries. It was at a public meeting early in 1839 that Dr. John Albright, secretary, took note of a motion made by Matthias Vass to toss away the name Gravel Hill once and for all in favor of Blair's Town, and the motion being carried, that's the way it was spelled for a long while. "John I.," who certainly did not push for the change, would be content, I think, with the Blairstown of today, its hotel and shops of Gravel Hill days much as they used to be because the main highway from Columbia to Newton and Augusta curves around the village. To see Blairstown the traveler must make a business of it or at least turn off on the road that climbs up to Stillwater in Sussex.

Many have forgotten that few villages anywhere, and especially in this neighborhood, sprang into existence overnight. The growth of what became Blairstown was particularly slow. In 1850, it is recorded, there were only fifty houses, John Blair's store, a few mechanic shops, a carriage factory, two churches, and the first small stone structure that was to expand into the Blairstown Academy. In 1860 the population had remained static, but by then there were two stores. In 1870 a third store had been set up, and then, in 1877, when the Blairstown Railway came through, affairs began to move in earnest. It was between 1877 and 1888 that Blairstown virtually doubled in size. I remember coming upon that revelation in 1953, even as I mused on some slates missing from the roof of the railroad station, a depot in a subsequent age given over to the needs of a feed mill a few steps away. Make a note of the fact that a footbridge, built about 1850 or even earlier across the Kill, not far from the hotel, was followed by a counterpart, this time of iron, leading to what was, in the 1880's and after, a bustling station. This, I was told, was, as a leftover from an age that found it indispensable, one of the last of its kind to serve modern uses. You may also note here that John W. Barber and Henry Howe, making but slight contribution to this portion of the pattern, dismissed Blairstown in 1844 as a place with a tannery, "15 or 20 dwellings, 1 Methodist and

1 Presbyterian church," and an associate in the hills of Centreville, Walnut Valley, and Sodom, now Hainesburg. Across the single track from the idle Hainesburg station, I passed a large house of prosperous railroad days, as black as the growth behind it, while taking the rough road through to Polkville, just to see if I could make it. I could, and I kept on going to Delaware (*not* the Ramsaysburg of 1833), less than two minutes away.

A guidebook of 1939 goes into some of those gyrations of which I am repeatedly accused—however unjustly is for you to say. I don't think I ever wasted space by saying that at Paulina there was "a steam laundry, which washes the clothes and bedding of the students of Blair Academy" or that in Blairstown there were aspects of a Western town "with second-floor porches over many of the stores." I can remember such appendages in Philadelphia and Camden, and so, perhaps, can you; once they were the brightly painted trademark of the first grocery chains. I certainly never accepted assurances that the Paulins Kill recalls an Indian girl, Pauline, whose canoe hit a rock. A "kill" is a river or even a brook, and this one, I always have heard, recalls Paulin, the pioneer who named it.

Some ridicule is reserved by a few commentators for the old mill building on Main Street in Blairstown, virtually in the heart of a town hardly known to those who speed by on the concrete that now rims the town. I always have found the building which serves as a library and meeting place, definitely imposing, in spite of its solid, castle-like proportions. Perhaps it is true that John I. Blair made his first dollar selling sixteen muskrat skins and then progressed to flour mills, iron mills, and railroads, but it is more certain that he was a railroad king in his time and one of the nation's first millionaires and that he became one in New Jersey. Among other certainties is the fact that the mill with what some have called Gothic lines was erected about 1819 or 1820 by William Hankinson but remodeled in 1904, when the impressive arches were added. Today the mill has a substantial air all its own, defying anything short of dynamite.

The oldest part of the present hotel, as far as I have been able to find out, goes back to 1838, but from the time of the VanScoten brothers there have been so many managers that I have been warned a full page could be filled with their names. I always have been in search of stories of Jacksonburg, not to be confused with New Jersey's many Jacksonvilles. Beyond the certainty, however, that it had its own clover mill and the legend that there was a building that turned out spokes for wheels when its machinery wasn't busy making corn "licker"— something of a lost art, I should think—I have come away empty-handed. Maybe Miss Minnie Smith, or even Ben Hill, now that he has left Blairstown to live not far away, will have greater fortune.

One of the legends of the neighborhood I like best is that Walnut Valley was so named for the groves of black walnut trees which, in Revolutionary times, yielded gun stocks for the army. I have a feeling, however, that this may have come in the War of 1812—at least there is one variant that says so. I was reaching around, one day along Yard's Creek, when a chance query, without too much thought behind it, brought Mount Hermon and its Honeywell Academy into focus. I suppose I had asked where children of the pioneers of Butts' Mill (or Mills) went to school, and the answer was quick in coming: "Oh, many of them attended classes at the Honeywell Academy."

I had seen the Academy many times as I passed that way up the road along the Muddy Brook or down the little back-roads from the Paulins Kill—lonely, closed up tight and, with what I think was once yellow paint, gone brown. It was a joy to rediscover it, not long ago, in a new dress of white to match the church across the way, which has put it back in service.

The Honeywell Academy was the oldest "advanced school" in Warren and one of the oldest establishments of its kind in New Jersey. Actually it was founded, in 1798, with funds left for that purpose by John Honeywell, who died before it was in operation. It is known that he died at Green's Chapel which, old residents of the area have assured me, was an earlier name of Mount Hermon. In the light of what was to follow, it was fortunate that I filed my first report the way I did, even though I had no inkling of it at the time:

"It seems that John was a Baptist, but for some reason I'd like to know he was tossed out of his church. After providing

The Honeywell Academy, the oldest "advanced school" in Warren County and one of the oldest establishments of its kind in New Jersey, has been rescued and refurbished to serve the church across the road as a parish hall. Jenkin David, its first teacher, upset several congregations he served as pastor by insisting on music for their services.

by will for the support of his wife" with whom he had lived in the captivating little house behind the Academy, still pleasantly identified as the John Honeywell house, "and giving a few remembrances to kinfolk of the area in Knowlton Township, now Hope, he directed the whole of his real estate to be sold, the proceeds to be invested, and the annual income to be used in the establishment and support of the school 'to be kept at the Cross Roads leading from the Delaware, near Peter Wolf's, where I live. . . .

" 'My desire is,' he added, 'that the master who is to receive his pay out of my estate may be a man of civil conduct, and able to teach the boys and girls to read, cypher and so forth; and the mistress likewise to be of chaste behavior, able to teach the small girls to read, and the bigger to knit and sew and the like, so as to be a help to owners and children.' John Honeywell then named the Reverend Samuel Jones, of Pennepack; the Reverend Isaac Stelle, of Piscataway, and the Reverend Benjamin Miller, of Scotch Plains, to carry out his intentions. At once there was bickering, and one parson uncharitably (but perhaps accurately) remarked that the will had been written 'by one of our ministers who, it is hoped, is a better preacher than a writer of wills.' "

It was not until 1782 that Dr. Jones got around to calling on John Honeywell's widow, Rebecca. (I regret to say no descriptions have been found of her or her first husband John Honeywell.) Dr. Jones soon discovered, however, that no one seemed to be in any hurry to settle the estate. By the time the matter came up again Rebecca had remarried and reported that her new husband had spent a lot of her money and that only quick action would save enough to build what John had provided. Nevertheless, the school emerged.

I made a note ten years ago that the first Honeywell Academy was completed in 1803 "with the Reverend Jenkin David as first teacher." Of him it was written that he "secured as many scholars among the rich as he could get, who paid their tuition, but the poor were educated free." In 1832 the school had to be enlarged, and in 1834 a stone building called the John Honeywell House was erected as a house for the teacher or teachers, who until then boarded on farms not too far away. By then, it would seem to me, Jenkin David was no longer there, and the "stone building" well behind the school must have been a memorial at best. Jenkin David was the "Elder" of the Old School Baptists, I was still to learn, and was turned out, probably in more than one place because he wanted to "sing unto the Lord a new song."

Tom Clancy, who from the sound of his name may have been excommunicated by his own Church, for all I know, was the teacher who, in 1849, didn't like the name, Honeywell Academy—so, just like that, he changed it to the Mount Hermon Academy. The brown name-stone continued to recall the founder, however, even when the old building was taken down and replaced by one that was larger. The stone of the first Academy was salvaged and inserted in what I think was its original position to keep forever green the memory of a pioneer in methods of public education who without such a reminder and without the recollections of upstart folklorists, might otherwise be forgotten.

Folklore, casting its bread upon the waters, bestows favors on history sometimes beyond estimate, even in the calculations of historians themselves. In this instance, our metaphorical crow already had begun to fly over the first of four New Jersey counties—as an indication of distance but by no means an index of time; the journey from Mount Hermon, in Warren, to New Brunswick, in Middlesex, where Jenkin David lies buried in a graveyard once Baptist but now the property of a Hebrew congregation, could be made on foot in less than a week. Yet, it must be understood from the first that Elder David in leaving the Academy, its companion church across the road, his classes, and his congregation under cordial, if brittle, circumstances by no means emulated the crow in flight. It is amusing to reflect that the best of crows cannot sing and that Jenkin David's departure had much to do with his delight in singing. I had been reflecting on the parallels in the lives of Francis Peppard and Jenkin David as well as on characteristics that seemed diametrically opposed as I left the shaded hideaway of Green's Chapel one day in the undulating countryside of Passaic, Sussex, and Warren. Although it was late, I drifted by the Honeywell Academy in the hope of finding support for the lingering legend that Jenkin David and his wife Martha had ridden away, whether by coach or horse I do not know, in a clash of ideas over music in church and perhaps over the school as well. I had concluded that the Irishman Francis Peppard, who must have missed the music of the Mass, was a man determined to "mend" the ways of his Protestant followers, at least up to a point, and that Welshman Jenkin David, with music in his soul like most Welshmen, preferred to argue and then seek more tuneful pastures. I was never more thoroughly aware of the intense feeling of those who maintained that "the devil gets into a church by the choir loft."

Then came the letter of Mrs. David Serviss, who lived in New Brunswick all of fourteen months after I had written my report and in fancy watched Jenkin and Martha—I knew nothing of any children then—ride away toward Hope, old Moravian Town. Mrs. Serviss told me that Jenkin David was her great-great-grandfather and that she never would have known of his association with the Honeywell Academy except for what I had written. Inviting me to come and see her, she said: "A good friend has sent me what you seem to have written many months ago about a certain early school, Honeywell Academy, whose first teacher in 1803, you say, was Jenkin David. He was my great-great-grandfather, born in 1753 in Pembrokeshire, Wales. In 1794, he, with his family, a wife and five children, one of whom died on the way across the ocean and so was buried at sea, sailed from Liverpool, England,

and settled at Great Valley, Pennsylvania, near Valley Forge, preaching at the Baptist Church there. . . . Jenkin David's youngest daughters, Elizabeth and Esther, were born at Great Valley in 1795 and 1798."

Although it is a reflection mostly personal, I cannot help intruding at this point to tell you that I visited the Great Valley Baptist Church more than thirty years ago and that my guide was a cousin who came, of all places, from Liverpool. It is odd that my path should have crossed where Jenkin David had been when the name, even if it had been in evidence, would have meant nothing to me. It is quickly apparent that Jenkin David did not like Great Valley, but his letter of transfer to what was clearly Knowlton Township in Warren County in 1800 deftly concealed the reason.

"Among the old letters of Jenkin David's," Mrs. Serviss told me, "I found one that is most interesting. It reads:

" 'The Church of Jesus Christ, meeting in Cambria, Somerset County, State of *Penssulvania* under the denomination of particular Baptists.

" 'To the Church of Jesus Christ meeting at Knowlton or any other church of the same faith and order to whom this may concern, sendeth Christian salutation, grace, mercy, and peace be multiplied you through our Lord Jesus Christ, Amen.

" 'Beloved in the Lord: For as much as our Dear and Revd. Brother and Sister, by name Jenkin and Martha Davies, design by God's permission to come to the aforesaid place—

" 'This is to inform and testify unto you that the above named came up here the last spring with the intention of staying here and for that reason was received by us his old acquaintances and brethren.

" 'But this place did not suit his circumstances so he had no notion of staying here and for that reason was received by us as an occasional pastor and his wife as an occasional member and they have been here since that time. Mr. Davies preached and administered the ordinances with acceptance and he and

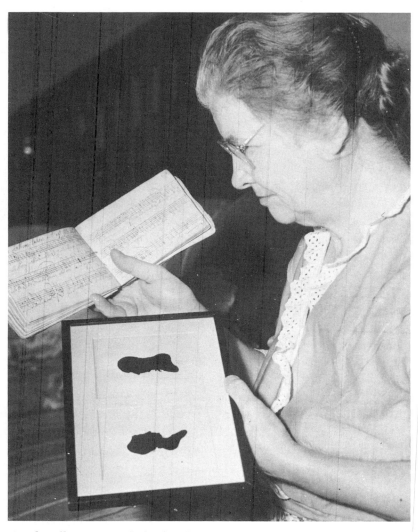

Family silhouettes and the hand-written music books of Primitive Baptist Elder Jenkin David, relics of his campaign to make his church services more tuneful, were found in New Brunswick in the possession of Mrs. David Serviss, a descendant.

his wife are in full Communion with us—therefore we commit them to your Christian Care, beseeching you to receive them in the Lord.

" 'So we commit you and them to the Lord and to the word of his grace which is able to build you and them up in the most holy faith. And may the God of Peace be with you all. Amen. This is the prayer of your Brethren. Signed before the Church, April 14, 1800. Theod. Rees, Deacon. David Rees. Evan Roberts. David Thomas. William Roberts.' "

The spelling, capitals, and all the rest were the same as in the original, Mrs. Serviss assured me, even to the misspelling of the name David as Davies. I have seen the name Jenkin David on his tombstone in the David plot, oddly enough at the end of the street on which Mrs. Serviss lives. Her treasures are locked away for safety's sake in a deposit box at her bank.

"When I saw what you had written about Knowlton and with it the name Jenkin David," Mrs. Serviss went on, "I was thrilled. I have been eager to learn more ever since. Between the years 1798 and 1805 much of interest could have happened. From 1805 to 1808 Jenkin David was pastor of the Baptist Church at Washington, now South River, and between 1808 and 1822 he preached at Cape May, returning to South River in 1822. He died there in 1834, and his wife Martha Evans is buried beside him in the old Baptist Cemetery on Livingston Avenue, here in New Brunswick. His last home was in Weston's Mills, not far away."

Mrs. Serviss showed me an old notebook that belonged to Jenkin David, in an array of old books he must have carried from place to place. One, most important to the legend that persists, was the hand-copied music book of which I have told you. George Wyckoff Cummins in his *History of Warren County*, published in 1911, said that Centreville, or Centerville, was Knowlton, I told Mrs. Serviss trying to be helpful. "Centerville, or Knowlton," he wrote, is "mainly noted for possessing the old Knowlton Presbyterian Church, which was built in

1802. The Knowlton Presbyterian Church was originally organized as the 'First English and German Congregation in Knowlton,' the first records of which are of the year, 1766. The church came under the care of the New Brunswick Presbytery in 1755." Clearly this church, strangely elusive in spite of all the signs that point ways to it, was not the one with which Jenkin David had any association.

"We were what is known as Primitive Baptists," Mrs. Serviss explained from a miscellany of books, clippings, and some silhouettes of Jenkin David and his wife Martha, "and down your way these are known as Old School Baptists." I told her that I knew the Old School Baptist Church in Hopewell, built in 1748. It replaced a church erected thirty-three years before that on quite another site, remembered in a very old scattering of gravestones almost in the dooryard of a farm high on a hill nearer Pennington. I say this mainly because a monument in memory of John Hart, a signer of the Declaration of Independence who died from hardships of the Revolution, has stood beside the church since 1865, while the legend has persisted that John was first buried up on the hill with his friends and not in Hopewell.

That Jenkin David was a Primitive or Old School Baptist would explain why Pastor David was more frequently called Elder Jenkin David, even on the framed obituary and eulogy that Mrs. Serviss with such great delight showed me. It was really a companion obituary, for that of Martha David was arranged beside that of Jenkin. The flowery phrases of these notices reveal that Elder Jenkin, born in Wales, was "called in early life from darkness to light and after baptism was united with the Ebenezer Baptist Church of his own land." This lately has made me wonder if Ebenezer, once a church but now a house, was named and served in the same Knowlton neighborhood by our departed friend. If I had known then where Ebenezer was, I would have shown Mrs. Serviss how to get there, just as I indicated the way to the Honeywell Academy.

After serving as a missionary in the Isle of Anglesey following his ordination in 1784, the clipping revealed, Jenkin David was instrumental in "gathering together" the Baptist Church of Beaumeris, perhaps called New Bridge later on, in Derbyshire. "We know," Mrs. Serviss supplemented here, still glowing over the new evidence which seemed to mean so much, "that he was in Great Valley, Pennsylvania, from 1794 to 1799, and that he did not leave Pennsylvania until about 1800. The dates of his work in Warren County have remained obscure until this new information gave me the inspiration to look for more. . . ." I told my new friend in New Brunswick that as I recalled it, Great Valley was within driving distance of St. David's, Pennsylvania.

Why after so many years at Cape May, from 1808 to 1822, one of the longest periods of service at one place in his career, did Jenkin David go back to South River? All kinds of things are possible: the Davids may have liked the sea more than the mountains; the Cape May congregation may have had less objection to music than those in other places; or perhaps when Elder Jenkin went back to South River, the flock may have recovered from a squabble over singing; or the pleasure of rejoining friends of long ago overcame them. Sight of the music book Jenkin used, stored away in the bank except when Mrs. Serviss wants to show it to visitors such as I, compelled me to conclude all over again that Jenkin David held to his rule of "love me, love my hymns," and when there was objection, off the David clan would go. Though the Primitive Baptists in general may have been opposed to anything on the musical side, so were the Quakers—and see what has happened. Having seen Jenkin David's silhouette, I can the more easily picture him, with his little book of hand-copied "bootlegged" music in hand, singing to his Lord even if it had to be solo.

How was the little music book saved? "You'd be surprised," Mrs. Serviss replied. "My father inherited what was supposed to be just an old chest from Jenkin David's son, Benjamin, when everything was being 'sold at vendue.' " In the book, in addition to the music, is a record of births and marriages and deaths as well as a carefully copied transcript of the marriage ceremony, pretty much as it is today. Benjamin David, who continued records in the yellowing pages, must have had a story all his own, for at seventy he married his first love after she had outlived two husbands.

Chapter IX

HOBOKEN TO ALEXANDRIA

For me the story of Hoboken begins with a great cleft in the Palisades, incredibly cut from the water level of the Hudson, continues through the colorful days of Castle Point from which Stevens Castle has now been removed, and then swings inland to Pittstown, in Hunterdon County. There the rural Colonial church of the Stevenses, St. Thomas's, Alexandria, has been reclaimed and restored, through a whole series of little miracles, to become one of the architectural show places of the region, reveling in the folklore of Colonial and later days.

I had brooded on the hurried lines that you will find yellowing in the record of John Barber and Henry Howe, written as they dashed about New Jersey in 1840, noting as well as they could the things they thought you and I should remember. They wrote: "Hoboken, supposedly anciently to be called Hoebuck, lies on the Hudson, one mile from New York, with which constant communication is had by ferryboats. It contains an Episcopal Church, and from fifty to seventy dwellings. The pleasant and shady retreats, delightfully situated at this place, on the banks of the river, long have made it a favorite resort. . . ."

Whereupon the authors of the *Historical Collections* hurried to Weehawken. In 1939 the population of Hoboken was estimated at beyond 59,000, conductors were being assailed for calling the city "Hobucken," and a "certain cosmopolitan atmosphere" still lingered "due largely to the presence of restaurants and cafes where the European culture had started them." This atmosphere still remains here and there, although Hoboken beer, whose fame began in 1642, is now unknown, even as the name *Hobocan Hackingh* meaning to the Indian "the land of the tobacco pipe," is but seldom remembered. "Very little occurred," says one authority, "to differentiate Hoboken from other towns in New Jersey before the coming of Col. John Stevens."

The Colonel was an inventor and financier. It was he who purchased the whole area, or most of it, that now is Hoboken when the land of William Bayard, Tory grandson of Samuel Bayard, was confiscated. In 1804 he mapped out "the New City of Hoboken" and began selling lots on the streets of New York City. In 1811 he set in motion the first scheduled steam ferry in the world, an operation ruled out legally in favor of Robert Fulton, who pressed his sole ferry rights on the Hudson. In 1824 Stevens' inventive genius quickly moved from boats to "Horses of Iron," and he turned out the first locomotive in the country, running it on a circular track on the grounds of his home in the city he had bought and built.

I had known all this in a general way. I knew that there had been an era of beer gardens, fireworks, mountebanks, and waxworks, as one writer described it. I knew that John Jacob Astor built a villa by the river and that when Washington Irving, William Cullen Bryant, Martin Van Buren, and other notables began dreaming of "holidays," they thought of Hoboken where baseball had its start in 1846, where the River Walk became as famous as seaside boards were to become later on, and where the body of Mary Rogers, found floating in the river near a retreat called Sybil's Cave, was said to have given Edgar Allan Poe material for "The Mystery of Marie Roget." Beyond all this, however, I wanted something new, a different approach through the legends and lore that so many insisted were buried forever under the debris of an era of change.

I must have said as much to John Ehrhardt in the days when he was living among the proof sheets of a weekly newspaper. For it certainly was John who told me that a Hoboken physician had deserted his native rounds to start a new life in the Madison that was Bottle Hill. At the time, the doctor's name, Rudolph Rabe, meant nothing to me. I had forgotten that I had met him years before at a medical meeting of homeopathic physicians in Trenton. I knew him the moment I saw him again when, I recall, he said he had no cure for a lapsing memory.

John had said that Dr. Rabe probably could recall the old Hoboken in a personal way. I found he could do much better than that. He quickly produced from his files a ten-page, blue-covered booklet written a few years before and printed in the shop of *The Jersey Observer*. Its title, I saw at once, was *The Hoboken of My Boyhood*, and I quickly gained permission to use as much as I wanted of it at any time. Although I must abridge some of the text, I would like what follows to stand as something of a memorial to the late Dr. Rabe, who grew up among the early Germans of Hoboken and who found time, in spite of a busy practice, to write down what life was like then. First, however, I must present the good doctor as I knew him. He was a wiry, seemingly ageless gentleman of the old school who liked to talk not only of Hoboken but of the Europe of old where he had traveled and studied. The walls of his office and the rooms beyond in his homey dwelling in Madison were resplendent with paintings from across the seas, and as I lingered on the few occasions we could fit together, I saw countless cupboards of sparkling European glass. The day I first saw the physician, he had just dismissed one patient and was awaiting another, but this did not prevent a few words of welcome and an autograph in his little book of Hoboken recollections.

"I seem to have writer's cramp," he wrote by way of salutation, "and that is one complaint that we doctors don't seem to have controlled very well. My earliest recollections go back to the old home on Seventh Street between Willow and Park Avenues, with its periodical inundations of the basement floor when, after a heavy rain, the water from the meadows backed up mercilessly into nearby houses; cooking had to be suspended and the family was compelled to migrate to the parlor floor, there to subsist on cold viands, hastily rescued from the rapidly rising flood.

"Later on we moved to Garden Street, near Tenth, with open lots opposite and an old stable in the center of this weed-infested waste; at the corner stood the grocery store of Christian Otten, as I remember the euphonic name; young Chris was one of our gang and upon one memorable occasion, during a game of 'Indian,' he realistically tomahawked me in dramatic fashion, for the red blood flowed freely over my blond hair, frightening my mother half out of her senses. It was a great day. . . .

"Still later we moved to Bloomfield Street, between Tenth and Eleventh, into a house built for my father by John Mc-Grane; the house still stands and is likely to become as old as Cheops. Eleventh Street then marked the boundary of the built-up part of Hoboken and into its wide expanse merrily jingled the bob-tailed horse-car, as it turned the corner at Washington Street on its way to the terminus of the line, ready for the return voyage. This turntable provided us boys with considerable exhilaration, whilst the single-manned car was a constant invitation to steal rides. In winter the horse-cars were filled with straw, to keep one's feet warm. . . .

"Above Eleventh Street were the Elysian Fields, proud in the majestic presence of magnificent oak trees, tulip, sycamore, and others. There were a few houses across the street from ours but for the most part vacant lots permitted an unobstructed view diagonally to the northeast, to the Hudson River, and 'Pop' Rodenburgh's Colonade Hotel which, like a baronial mansion of old, looked proudly out then on the broad, clear waters of the Hudson.

" 'Pop' possessed a fine herd of Jersey cows and many a glass of rich, creamy milk was sipped beneath the stately trees surrounding the hotel, where mothers and their small turbulent youngsters sat at the small wooden tables. Within the hotel was a long, mahogany bar, reflecting peace and good will from its highly polished rail at which the good burghers of the city quaffed Daniel Bermes' beer. . . .

"The old Twelfth Street dock jutted out into the swirling tides nearby and we kids, in the crabbing season, cast off our lines to catch the 'Jersey Blues' whose meat was of virgin whiteness, endowed with a flavor fit for Lucullus himself. Tending the crab lines kept us busily occupied, for at frequent intervals we hauled in each line very slowly and used the scoop net to advantage.

"Brick schooners from Haverstraw and other Hudson River towns often tied up at the Twelfth Street dock and we kids delighted in climbing the ratlines to the crosstrees high above the deck; half way between the Jersey and the New York shores lay anchored ice barges, waiting for the weekly tow to take them back to the upper Hudson, there to reload from the ugly-looking ice houses which disfigured the banks of the river. I well remember, on one occasion, a brick schooner, set deeply in the water and tacking across the river, crashed into an empty ice barge, the bowsprit ripping through the boarded sides as though through cardboard.

"Not far below the Colonade Hotel stood the ample pitched-roof brown wooden structure of the New Jersey Yacht Club on rising ground overlooking the river; about the place was the tang of the sea, mingled with an agreeable odor of pitch and tar; in the early spring all was feverish activity; hulls were being scraped down, others were undergoing their annual repainting and refurnishing. . . . On Sunday mornings during the summer the more secular minded could be seen getting under way for a sail up or down the river, the direction depending on the tide, for with its incoming, the catboats and sloops set their course for Fort Lee where, safely anchored, the doughty yachtsmen climbed the long and dusty hill to Burcheister's Hotel, among whose spacious rooms the bierstube, with real Teutonic 'Gemütlichkeit,' was an irresistible attraction for the thirsty tars.

"Or, if the tide was ebbing, the numerous white sails could be seen of a Sunday morning, headed for Pop Stillwell's on Gravesend Bay, later known as Bensonhurst. Jere Minehost Stillwell provided a lavish shore dinner, with clam fritters which these decadent standardized days know nothing about. . . . My father owned a twenty-six-foot South Bay converted cabin catboat, converted soon after purchase into a sloop rig; she was a good boat, seaworthy, comfortable, and safe. Old Captain Bill Curtin, of the sailmaking firm in South Street, was usually our skipper and a mighty good one he was.

"Sometimes young Frank Garland, an attorney, with his office in New York, took the helm; he, too, knew how to sail a boat and hold her close to the wind.

"German was spoken as freely as English and was understood in almost every Hoboken store, especially on Washington Street, with its wide expanse of roadway and its wide roomy sidewalks; with few exceptions the corners were occupied by friendly saloons, from whose swinging doors issued a delightful aroma of beer and pretzels; most of these havens of refuge were owned by Germans, although in the lower part of the city the Irish more often reigned. With few exceptions all were places of good order and decorum. . . ."

Dr. Rabe reached back through the years to recall some of the more celebrated saloon-keepers—Bernhard Hoellger heading the list with his establishment at Ninth and Washington Streets. "Society in Hoboken," he told me, "was predominantly German, and its activities were confined, for the most part, to the 'Deutcher Club' at Sixth and Hudson Streets, whose membership could boast the wealthiest and most influential of Hoboken's citizens."

"It was a privilege and honor to be invited to a ball or festival at the German Club," the booklet continued, "for here

German poetry and song held sway and 'Gemütlichkeit' prevailed; we youngsters were accustomed to beer and wine and knew the distinguishing characteristics of Rhine, Mosel, and other wines. 'Berncasteler Doktor' was no stranger to us and 'Liebfraumilch' provoked no ambiguous or unseemly remarks. Everybody drank, though slowly and with evident enjoyment and moderation; no one indulged secret drinking for hypocrisy played no part.

"In later years the purely American element of the city, no longer to be outdone, formed a club of its own, called the Columbia Club, and put up a seemly building at the northeast corner of Bloomfield Avenue and Eleventh Streets. Weekly dances were held, usually on Saturday nights and, as I recall these festivities, I seem to remember men in evening dress hurrying over to Duhrkoop's saloon, on Washington Street nearby.

"For us boys these early Hoboken days were golden indeed, happy hours of which we never tired and, when I chance to gaze upon the desolate Hoboken of today, bereft of its cozy saloons, its picturesque River Street and tidily kept German steamship piers, I cannot help but feel saddened by the wreckage of war and its Puritan fanaticism.

"I feel sorry for the boys of the present day who lived where, when I was a boy, there were camping expeditions on Saturdays. We used to take off to the Elysian Fields such articles of food as could be begged or even purloined from our mothers' pantries, including enough milk, flour, and eggs with which to fry, over a crackling fire, the most delicious German *pfanne-kuchen;* roasted sweet potatoes, as well as the ordinary common variety of 'Murphys' supplemented by Jersey chestnuts.

"At the old Bolivar House at which is now, I suppose, Seventeenth Street, were the headquarters of the shad fishermen, whose nets were hung out to dry, hung upon stout lines suspended between stout poles set firmly in the ground; frequently these nets were badly damaged by passing steamboats after they had been placed far out on the river for the night's catch. Fish were cheap, and, of course, absolutely fresh—fifty cents for a large shad was common. The river was clean and not, as it is today, an open sewer—bluefish, tomcods, striped and black bass abounded in the waters and it was not an uncommon sight to observe young swordfish swimming on an oncoming tide toward Guttenberg, where the old White Brewery, like an old castle, stood out like a friendly beacon.

"Down at Sybil's Cave on the River Walk, below Stevens Castle or Castle Stevens, was the angler's paradise, for here fishing was indulged with full relaxation . . . and in the winter, when in those days the ice cakes were plentiful, we played our own games of 'Eliza Crossing the Ice.' "

Dr. Rabe remembered the old volunteer fire company, replete with Dalmatian fire dog and Joe Cooke's speaking trumpet; baseball of the old "Jersey Blues" with Joe Dabin as the celebrated home run hitter; the drilling of the bluejackets and, on occasion, men from a Russian man-of-war, as well as the colorful traveling medicine shows which sold "Indian Sagua" at fifty cents a bottle. "Barnum and Bailey's circus," he told me once, "usually pitched its tents on the old Cricket Grounds at the foot of Eighth Street, although I remember Forepaugh's Circus encamped on the high ground beyond Eleventh Street and opposite the end of Bloomfield." I told Dr. Rabe that I could remember my own mother speaking of Forepaugh's Circus with as much reverence as is usually reserved in these latter days for Ringling's. The Doctor's narrative continues:

"No account of old Hoboken would be complete without mention of the German Schuetzen organizations—those colorful, picturesque assemblies which never failed to arouse the interest and admiration of the town. . . . [It was still the town of Hoboken, I think, and when it went beyond that, he went elsewhere as soon as he could—although he never discussed the point with me.] It was the custom, upon the death of a Schuetzen brother, to escort his remains, military fashion, as far as Eleventh and Washington Streets. As the medal-bedizened and usually portly Schuetzens came marching up Washington Street to the reverent strains of Chopin's *Funeral March*, we boys marched along.

"As the leader of the organization approached Eleventh Street, the command to halt was shouted; ranks were then broken and immediately reformed into two files, through which passed the cortege of the carriages, on its way to Flower Hill or some other cemetery. This final salute to the departed over, ranks were again broken and the parched members rushed into Duhrkoop's saloon, to be fittingly and adequately served; some entered Fred Schulken's place, a few doors below, remaining until the now unruffled drum beat. The 'assembly' lines were now reformed, banners unfurled to the breeze, the band struck up a stirring and lively march, *Ich hat ein Kameraden*, and the entire company, with renewed vigor and enlivened step, marched downtown again. . . ."

This, from what obviously was an eyewitness, is most valuable to the Hoboken record and, as far as that goes, most valuable for the New Jersey record. Then, perhaps from a surprising place, comes a commentary on the New Jersey mosquito, which, according to some published records, once was capable of picking up a horse on the mainland and depositing him miles at sea on Long Beach Island:

"In those days the mosquito problem was a real one, and every well-regulated household possessed its complement of mosquito nets for the beds, for without these, sleep would have been well nigh impossible. Since people sat out on the front stoops during the long summer evenings, it was necessary to burn punk-sticks in order to fight off these unwelcome and persistent pests. We boys gathered these punks in the form of ripe, brown cat-tails and then dried them in our mothers' ovens; they were also used on Fourth of July as lighters for our Chinese crackers and Roman candles.

"For days before any important election we gathered empty barrels, or, more correctly, stole them, so that the lives of our grocers were made miserable for days by our raiding expeditions and depredations. Election Night was always a glorious celebration, with many bonfires lighting the sky all over, hundreds of barrels and boxes being consigned to the devouring flames as they leaped high in the air, at times enlivened by the raids of rival gangs. . . .

"Well, life in old Hoboken in those glorious days was interesting and colorful. Lower Hudson Street, in the vicinity of Meyer's Hotel and Busch's Hotel, possessed a European, more particularly German atmosphere; people and personalities expressed themselves together, for the depressing era of standardization had not arrived.

"Old Hoboken," concluded Dr. Rabe, "is gone forever—except in memory. I have remembered only a few of the chapters that should be written down. The ghostly shadow of the old city seems at times to hover for a few brief moments over the subdued streets; the short re-candescence of the oldtime spirit, manifested during the more recent era of Christopher Morley's 'Seacoast of Bohemia' with its revival of lurid melodrama, has burned itself out in an agony of despair. But the memory of the old town will forever remain with some of us, until the last has departed from wherever we have wandered in this troubled world."

Dr. Rabe never would have admitted it to me, but I always have had this feeling: He moved away from Hoboken because all that he knew throughout the long years of growing up and his medical practice had begun long before to move away from him. He thought, no doubt, that he might as well steal away, too.

"Hoboken," says the *Universal Gazetteer* published in 1832, was at the time "a village of Bergen Co., N.J., on the Hudson, opposite New York, and noted as the spot where many duels have been fought." That is all there is as far as the authors, one Dr. Brookes and his reviser, John Marshall, Esq., were concerned. Hoboken, described in the even earlier *American Gazetteer* of Jedediah Morse, published in 1797, was given these descriptive words: "A tract of land in Bergen county, New-Jersey, situated on the W. bank of the Hudson, in the mountainous country between the town of Bergen and Fort Lee, about 7 miles above New-York City."

Celebrated for many worldly things, pioneers of the Stevens family also had a deeply spiritual side of their lives. Here is Hoboken's Church of the Holy Innocents, which they built.

There is no topical reference to Fort Lee, but Bergen is described as "the shire town of Bergen co., New Jersey . . . surrounded by water, except on the N.; the river Hudson separates it from New-York City, 3 miles distant; on the south a narrow channel lies between it and Staten I.; and on the W. it has the Hackensack R. The inhabitants are mostly descendants from the Dutch settlers. . . ."

So much for the gazetteers. To me Hoboken's story is a mixture of many aspects, some recalled by Dr. Rabe in contrasting the early German and Irish influences thrust from memory by the mixture of nationalities which cluster in cities across the land, and other aspects which I am sure did not occur at all to those I saw in 1955 when Hoboken was setting up its centennial. Even an absence of a year or two will make more than sadly evident the inevitable changes of time, especially along the waterfront across from New York.

Basically Hoboken's story must include great portions of the Stevens family saga, reaching into and beyond the Stevens Castle that used to be on the old Castle Point which, even in the 1950's, I had known was all but engulfed by an expanding Stevens Institute, now Stevens Institute of Technology. There was a great book, covered in soft red leather and a depository of rare photographs of the relationships and events in the history of the Stevens family. It has been kept for safety in the vault of the Church of the Holy Innocents, but not until it had been brought out and shown to me by John J. Heaney, the sacristan of the church, did I realize that the Stevenses have been and are at the heart of the Hoboken story.

Perhaps one of the best but often overlooked stories of Castle Point was written in the *Stevens Indicator* of July, 1911, by J. H. Cuntz, of the class of 1887. "Although Castle Point may have been seen by some of the early navigators who, it is claimed, entered the Hudson River during the sixteenth century," he wrote, "no record of it appears until the memorable voyage of Henry Hudson. After this daring navigator had ascended his river for one hundred and fifty miles, he returned towards its mouth, and, in consequence of an encounter with the Indians on Manhattan Island, anchored the 'Half Moon' in Weehawken Cove on October 2, 1609, where the serpentine rocks of the neighboring point made such an impression on Robert Juet, the mate. . . ."

Juet wrote in his log: "Within a while after, we got downe two leagues beyond that place, and anchored in the Bay, cleere from all danger of them on the other side of the river, where we saw a good piece of ground. . . ." The Hudson party had had, may I recall for you, a brush with the Manhattan Indians, and this explains Juet's reference to "them on the other side of the river." "Hard by it," the entry continued, "there was a Cliffe, that looked of the colour of white greene, as though it were either Copper, or Silver Myne: and I think it to be one of them, by the Trees that grow upon it. For they are all burned. . . ."

"From that date," said the writer in the forgotten issue of the Stevens monthly, "Castle Point has occupied a place in history." Although I am sure that I really do not have to refresh your memory on this observation, if you have seen the Palisades from one angle or another, Castle Point is that area of land high on Juet's rocky shelf, once topped by Stevens Castle itself and guarded by a wheeled cannon on the broad lawn. It must be remembered that Stevens Castle was the truly American headquarters of an early American family which remained so vital throughout succeeding generations.

The "Stevens Family Book" which the last time I was there, could still be seen by permission at the Church of the Holy Innocents, is a unique treasure. Its amplification of chapters in the family's way of life is virtually synonymous with all that Hoboken was and has been. It begins with pictures of St. Clement Danes, Westminster, England, for the first John Stevens was the son of Richard, of St. Clement's parish, and the direct ancestor of kindly Basil Stevens, of Montclair, who made the book a labor of love in his lifetime. The first John died in 1737, and although the big red book goes into details of the romance and marriage of Ann Campbell, among other such matters, I cannot hope to do justice to all the twigs of a proud family tree. This passage, however, is worth quoting: "Of John Stevens' children the eldest, Campbell, became a soldier, serving under Col. Peter Schuyler of the 'Old Jersey Blues.' Shreds of his letters tell how out of his own pocket he fed and clothed the troops on their embarkment at Newark for Albany on August 30, 1746. He won honorable mention in the French and Indian Wars. Lewis, another brother, was also a soldier, an officer in a British colonial regiment stationed in Antigua, St. Christopher, and elsewhere about the islands. After his military life he settled in Hunterdon County, where he had a large farm known as Cornwall. His home was known for its hospitality and he was known for his generosity, giving the land for quaint St. Thomas's Church, not far from Pittstown. . . ."

I quote this portion of the record for several reasons. First, here is proof positive that some of the graves around St. Thomas's are those of Lewis Stevens's French and Indian War associates, some of whom had joined him in the building of rude blockhouses up and down the Delaware River. The stones may not be on the actual graves, for it is known that at one time the earliest graves were leveled when across the road. On the other hand, my own feeling after years of association with the little church some of us overcame great obstacles to restore, is that this record of the ruthless ploughing lends credence to the fact that there *was* an even earlier church building. The road is the dividing line between Kingwood and Alexandria Townships in Hunterdon, so that St. Thomas's, Alexandria, as it stands today, once was St. Thomas's, Kingwood, with the names of Lord Stirling, John Stevens, James Parker, Francis McEven, Nathaniel Marston, Jacob Ludlow, and John Grandin solicited for ten pounds yearly for its support in the autumn of 1766. On December 4, 1768, John Grandin, on behalf of the church wardens, notified the donors that ten pounds was more than they wanted and that eight pounds would suffice in the future.

Although the text of what I have called the "Stevens Family Book" was carefully put together as a combination of text prepared from careful research and rare and irreplaceable photographs, the unpublished volume remains heavier on the picture side. The first John Stevens, as shown, bears a striking likeness to the younger William Penn. Reproductions follow showing the first land grant to the Stevenses in America by the hand of Queen Anne; the indenture that brought the first Stevens to these very shores, and the document by which the first John Stevens was appointed chancery clerk. Then the next pages take you to St. Peter's Church in Perth Amboy, where the first John was on the vestry when the charter was granted in July, 1718. The book must be seen to be truly appreciated.

Here, I think, I would have you remember that Hoboken is a place of "almosts" as well as accomplishments. "Hoboken came near seeing the capture of Benedict Arnold," wrote the alumnus narrator in 1911, "for 'Light Horse Harry' Lee, with three dragoons and three led horses, waited there many hours one night in 1780, hoping that Sergeant John Campe would succeed in his bold plan of kidnapping the traitor in New York, and bringing him across the river. But owing to a sudden change in Arnold's headquarters the plan miscarried. . . ."

Another "almost" was General von Steuben's attempt to live on the Bayard estate. After the war, Bayard's estate was confiscated by the state and ordered to be sold at public auction. That was when General von Steuben heard about it. Remembering well the site of what was later to become a large segment of Hoboken, then a truly woodsy, unspoiled retreat, he wrote Governor Livingston to ask if, in view of his services to the American cause, he could not buy the place before the public sale. The red tape and excuses of protocol, subsequently offered, became as ludicrous as the Governor's own views in the light of Hoboken's becoming an early resort. The Governor wrote that although he "scarcely knew a gentleman on the whole Continent our Assembly would take greater pleasure in obliging than Baron Steuben," actual withdrawal of the Bayard estate from public sale might set a bad precedent.

Governor Livingston then tried to warn the Baron of Hoboken's mosquitoes in a no doubt kindly but none the less silly let-down: "But if you was never on the spot yourself in the months of July, August, and September, and I thought myself at liberty to obtrude my advice upon you, I would say that considering how often you are exposed to the loss of blood in the way of your profession as a Soldier, I would dissuade you from putting it in the power of the Mosquitoes at Hoebuck to augment the effusion, for never did I set foot on a place where that troublesome and venomous little volatile, during those months, swarmed in greater abundance. . . ."

General von Steuben replied, and the inference is plain that the Governor's seemingly trifling tone, on top of the Assembly's stuffy legalities, had hurt. He withdrew his application, however, and accepted, for the sake of convention, a little house at what became River Edge. The General lost little time in selling it back to the families of John and Peter Zabriskie, who, as Tories, had lost their long, low, Dutch Colonial house by confiscation. There is no reference to mosquitoes here, but surely there could have been.

The auction of the Bayard estate took place on March 16, 1784, and Colonel John Stevens, always in love with the Hudson River, made the purchase for $90,000. After the purchase he built an imposing house on Castle Point, a family summer retreat from 1786 to 1814. Those were the days when the Colonel, husband of Rachel Cox, of Bloomsbury Court (now better known as the Trent House in Trenton) had a town house at Number 7 Broadway, New York City, opposite the

Bowling Green. From 1814 on he lived at Castle Point all-year-round in a mansion known as the Stevens Villa. This stood on the site of the celebrated Stevens Castle, which was removed for the expansion of Stevens Institute of Technology not long ago.

"A gentleman now living in Hoboken," says one account, written in 1911, "tells of a fine octagonal room on the southern side of the house, and of a music room, which was much in evidence while the mansion was occupied by Robert L. Stevens, who was a great lover of music. This house stood until 1853, when it gave way to the present Castle, which was erected by Robert L. Stevens. . . ." John Heaney, who pointed out the quotation to me, said that the "Sixth Street Gate," which I saw in those days, was one of the last leftovers of the Villa's day.

The great engineering achievements of Colonel John Stevens and his sons have been recounted so often that there is no need to dwell on them here. From the time of his purchase of the estate at Hoebuck, Colonel Stevens had been interested in the ferry running between its southeastern point and the lower part of New York. "After many vicissitudes," wrote Mr. Cuntz, "in the course of which the ferry was managed by various people, and the motive power changed from wind and oars to steam, he finally acquired complete control in 1821, and the ferry remained thenceforward in the family until a few years ago. . . ."

Many citizens of Hoboken, even today, may have forgotten the importance of the ferry in recalling the Stevens experiments with a locomotive, or a slightly unreasonable facsimile, operated on a circular track near the Castle. But listen to this —a fragment from the days of Hoboken, as a resort: "As many as 20,000 people would cross the ferry in a single day, to spend a few hours on the Green, along the River Walk, and in the Elysian Fields. There were delightful occupations and entertainments for all ages and classes. Among the popular attractions were 'aerial ways,' a circular railroad, and a primitive form of ferris wheel. Refreshments of all kinds were to be had at the '76 House' near the ferry, part of which was the only one of Colonel Bayard's buildings left, after the conflagration of 1780, at the 'Colonade,' a pavilion erected by Colonel Stevens in the Elysian Fields in 1830, and at many other places. . . ."

Remembering Dr. Rabe and his little book of reminiscences, written for his own pleasure and that of a few friends, I told John Heaney, at the time of Hoboken's celebration of the hundredth birthday of its emergence as an incorporated community—for Hoboken as *Hoebuck* was far older than that—that I wondered if many of the old Schuetzens were not marching in the parade. Later I was in some manner conscious of the unseen presence of kindly Dr. Rabe himself. I think my assumption of why he hurried off to Madison for those few years before he died were affirmed.

Everybody knew, he had said, that the first game of organized baseball was played on the Elysian Fields in Hoboken. "There is a state sign at the end of the street," he said, "but I wonder how many linger there long enough to read what happened when Hoboken's Knickerbock Giants played New York in 1846."

Last time I was there it was a relief to see that the Gatehouse, at the east end of Sixth Street, built of that greenish yellow stone called serpentine rock, was still there and that the apartment house, more imposing in its earlier days (days of Hetty Green's $19 per month flat there), was added proof that Hoboken was still Hoboken. Changes, drastic changes, had come elsewhere. Stevens Castle, with its familiar cannon at the door, was gone, and in its place stood a magnificent multi-story school building with a glass wall that faced New York. The Hof Brau Haus, where Christopher Morley used to bring his friends for German food and German music, was just another address in a neighborhood gone nondescript—Number 42 Second Street.

Bill Augustine and I found our way to what had been the River Walk, with a line of drab (and apparently unused) warehouses obscuring any possible view of the Hudson and the abandoned tracks of the old Hoboken Shore Railroad on the other side, at the base of a shaggy wall of yellow-green rock with its tendency to slide now and then offset by intrusions of concrete perhaps fifteen feet up.

The only discernible movement was that of a man and his dog in the distance followed oddly and at a respectful distance by a cat—dirty, delighted by any company at all, but clearly hungry for pickings which, along these silent wharves, obviously must be scant. For some reason we parked at one side, awaiting the walker's leisurely approach. As he came abreast of the car, I asked: "Have you any idea where the River Walk of the old days was?" "Why, this was it," he assured me, adding, "I've lived here all my life."

I stared and floundered a little, that I know. When I had recovered, I asked: "Did you ever hear of Sybil's Cave or Sybil's Spring?" The man with the dog turned and pointed in the general direction of the rocky wall across the narrow roadway, furrowed by rusted tracks. "That's easy," he said. "Right here is where they were." I had to regain a measure of calm all over again, for I had been told through the years that Sybil's Cave was somewhere under a new apartment building, and maybe, according to a new, privately printed book on springs, there never had been a Sybil's Spring. "It was quite a cave," the man was saying, for as quickly as that, we were old friends. "It was part of the old tunnel that came down through the rocks of old Stevens Castle. There was some who said that the tunnel was there even before the Castle was built. I played in it many's the day as a boy, running up and down the steps what were in the dark inside. And I've dipped many a cold drink of water from the spring, as well."

It was on the tip of my tongue to ask about Edgar Allan Poe and his "Mystery of Marie Roget." Historians had ar-

gued back and forth that the poem was based on newspaper
accounts of the discovery of the body of Mary Rogers, who
was found in the river somewhere beyond the closed warehouses, but I had to let that question pass. "What's your name?"
I asked, still amazed at my coming upon the one man in all
Hoboken who could supply so many answers. "Burke," he
replied, with the expected Hoboken pronunciation. "Do you
live around here?" I inquired. "Name's William Burke," he
said. "I live in the big apartment house at Twelfth and Washington. Used to be an eccentric old lady lived there—very
rich; they said her name was Hetty Green." After we had
shaken hands and exchanged confused pleasantries, he concluded, "Oh, yes, the cave. It began to tumble in, or maybe was
walked in, so they thought it might be dangerous to leave it
open that way. But I'll bet you the old spring is still flowing,
somewhere under all that rock."

We watched him walk away in the direction he had come,
completing a brief but remarkable exchange. It was almost as
if he had been sent to tell me what he knew at that precise
moment in that particular place. I doubt if I fully recovered
until we went back to the more familiar square of the Erie-
Lackawanna's Hoboken terminal of the Barclay Street ferry
with its statue of Sam Sloan, president of the Delaware, Lackawanna & Western Railroad Company for thirty-two years,
and the inevitable flock of pigeons. They appeared to be as
hungry as that stray and pitiful cat.

I would like to think that whatever had happened, is hap-
pening, or will happen in Hoboken, where the Stevenses always
will be remembered in so many ways, the little stone church
called St. Thomas's, Alexandria, not far from Pittstown in
Hunterdon County, will serve them equally as well, as a
memorial to the deeply devotional and spiritual phase of their
lives.

Even though the lack of heat has, at least for the moment,

precluded winter services, it is nevertheless a shrine linked to the Church of the Holy Innocents, Hoboken, opening at Rogationtide and closing with a Harvest Home service in the fall. This schedule is maintained through the guidance of Calvary Church, in Flemington, which with the assistance of lay readers helps the rector provide regular summer services once again. This church, "oldest in the present limits of the county" according to no less an historian than James P. Snell, is very close to me.

Calvary Church extended its interest in St. Thomas's in ways that included a long-gone generation of Stevenses. The late Lester W. Oliver, Jr., had been warden of St. Thomas's since the time that the Reverend E. Rupert Noel, an English priest, had held occasional services at Alexandria and had in-

St. Thomas's Church, Alexandria, founded in 1723, was an early rural church attended by the Stevenses of Hoboken. It was abandoned for long years at a time, but recently the building has been restored, and services are held there in summer and autumn. It is not far from Pittstown.

The interior of St. Thomas's is filled with the charm of antiquity. The window behind the altar contains panes of the original glass.

sisted on calling Lester "the Squire." He had been as disturbed as I by the desertion and emptiness of this beautiful little country church. The windows were boarded up—and for good reason in at least three instances of which I know—the plain glass window behind the altar which makes the view beyond a reredos at any season, the fanlight over the wide door, and the original panes at the rear of the nave. The cemetery with stones bearing the crudely cut names of Hunterdon pioneers had not been cared for in many a year. Two lines of graves form a kind of honor guard at the front; graves known to be those of Revolutionary soldiers bore tattered flags when I first saw them.

The name of Lewis Stevens, one of the earliest benefactors of the church during the days when his "Cornwall Farm" down the lane behind it, became part of my earliest association with St. Thomas's. Then a procession of virtually incredible events began—from persistent animals that ate their way through a new shingle roof to the neighboring firemen who willingly cleared the graveyard, cut the long, tawny growth of grass and weeds, and straightened the stones. Squire Oliver had consulted me after a young woman whose name I never knew said she wanted to be married there. She was warned that the church and its neglected setting would have to be put in order, and she said she would assist with that, financially. However, when she saw the interior for the first time and gazed upon the marble slab in the center aisle in front of the railed-in chancel, she quickly changed her mind about everything, and said that she did not wish "to be married over anyone's dead body." She had seen the tablet "memorative of Lewis Stevens, Esq., whose willing hands helped to raise these walls," and she concluded, as many of us did for a long while, that Lewis certainly had been buried there.

Years after, when I had obtained the approval of the late Basil Stevens, then of Montclair, I joined some of my friends in prying up the stone and crawling into every inch of the space between the cold, clammy earth and the flooring. We could find no trace of any burials at all.

In his letter to me Basil Stevens had said, "I am sure members of the family will be glad to have you remove the stone for the purpose mentioned, and in their behalf I will gladly consent to your doing so. It is my opinion, judging from an old letter, that the Hon. John Stevens II, an elder brother of Lewis, is also buried within the enclosure of the church. There is documentary evidence that Sarah Stevens, a sister of the Honorable John and Lewis, was buried *at* the church, but there is nothing to indicate whether she was interred within or outside the walls of the building. . . ." Even so, we found nothing but dust and hardened soil, with no fragments of coffins or of anything conclusive. However, anything could have happened during those years of abandonment, when, it has been written, sheep and cattle wandered in and out of the crumbled walls of St. Thomas's. Memories of the earlier log church across the road were fading out, with the help of an impatient farmer and his plow, almost as completely as did the old tombstones there.

On September 23, 1723, the Reverend John Talbot wrote to the Society for the Propagation of the Gospel in Foreign Parts, in England:

"I have been this month in Newton, Hopewell and Amwell preaching, and baptizing nineteen persons in one day. I visited several persons who were sick, who had come off their errors with Mr. George Keith; they were eighty years of age, and had never received the Sacrament of the Lord's Supper in their lives; but were loth to die without the benefit and comfort of it. So I was fain to come back to Burlington to get the elements; then returned to the mountains and did administer to their great satisfaction. They are preparing to build a church in the Spring, but when they will have a minister I cannot tell; but it is a solemn thing (as they say in New England) for the lost sheep to go astray in the wilderness; to be among wolves is worse; but for the sheep to be without a shepherd is the most deplorable case of all."

The ancient account in which these words appear goes on to say that the first church stood on the south side of the road that divides Alexandria and Kingwood townships, and thus "the church became known to us as St. Thomas's, Kingwood," a name it continued to bear until 1801. The old record continues:

"There is a tradition that whilst a regiment of Hessians were in the neighborhood an epidemic broke out amongst them and a very large number died, and were buried in the old burial ground around the church. In 1755, there was trouble with the Indians. A hatred of the whites had for years been growing in their hearts, as they saw themselves becoming more and more helpless under the encroachments of the settlers. During the winter of 1755–1756 marauding parties of French and Indians hung about the western border. To guard against their incursions a chain of blockhouses was erected along the mountain and at favorable points on the east bank of the Delaware. Governor Belcher dispatched troops from all parts of the Province to the defence of the Western frontier. It is probable that the soldiers said to be buried at Alexandria were some of those sent at this time, and for the purpose named.

"After the present church was erected the old burial ground was neglected, and buried beneath a growth of bushes and brambles. Some years ago, a neighboring farmer fenced the land, cleared it, leveled the graves, removed the stones, and annexed the old burial ground as a part of his farm. It is probable that the land was never deeded to the church. Probably, the only relic now extant of the old church and ground, in addition to the timbers of the church, is an old tombstone bearing the following inscription: 'S. C. Born S tem Ye 18 1748/Dyd Ianvary the 18 1749.'"

According to the same account written on stationery of the late Leslie W. Burdick, of Clinton, Hunterdon County, this old stone, obviously for a child, is in the church, but, actually, it is one of those propped outside the present church wall. Inasmuch as the present St. Thomas's was built in 1769, the hand-cut stone antedates it by twenty years. The first priest who assumed charge at Kingwood appears to have been the Reverend Andrew Morton, who also was serving Amwell. He is now remembered only in a small cemetery adjacent to the Amwell Academy above Ringoes, but his name continues in St. Andrew's Church at Amwell, which is in Lambertville. The old academy by this time is a well-ordered tavern, and the graves outside are commendably cared for. The time will come, I think, when a Rogationtide procession, not on foot of course, will begin in Lambertville, move out via one of New Jersey's more celebrated Old York Roads to Ringoes, once Ringo's, and conclude at St. Thomas's, Alexandria, once more than a township and an earlier place on the river, Frenchtown.

St. Thomas's has had its ups and downs, but through the restoration accomplished by Calvary Church, Flemington, and the Diocese of New Jersey, I must conclude permanency has been established after so many years of uncertainty, neglect, and forlorn isolation. The population that moved away will never come back, but a new congregation is growing in the area—alive to the traditions of the Stevenses and their country church as well as the riddles that remain unsolved. Why was the upstairs window at the back of the nave, which seats but fifty comfortably, filled in if there was no balcony? Was there once a balcony, small though it must have been? Architectural authorities tell me that there was. Meanwhile, the services go on amid a cloud of witnesses, however unseen or unheard.

Chapter X

BEYOND THE RIVER STYX

Last time we lingered in hills familiar to a certain notorious Tory named Moody—one Lieutenant (or Ensign) James L. Moody, his ghost, or a reasonable facsimile, was allegedly splashing about in the darksome pools of the Muckshaw Swamp in Sussex.

Now, with the name Bonnel (or Bonnell) still left to conjecture unless, or course, Bonnel was the name of the younger brother caught and hanged in Philadelphia, we must bring the Lieutenant to Morris County terrain—to Moody's Island. The island in Lake Hopatcong is one I used to visit when only carpenters and mechanics were around, sprucing up an amusement park for another summer—for it is this very island, or at least one of its neighbors, that took its name from the man whom they say used it as an occasional retreat.

I told you of Moody's raid near Sparta when after entering the home of Robert Ogden and taking off with valuable plate, the ensuing chase led the posse up and across the then uncertain New Jersey-New York line in country primarily inhabited by the "liners." These were ruffians of a long disputed region with whom, I imagine, Lieutenant Moody was much at home. He was long neglected by all but the little-known regional chroniclers; however, James P. Snell makes up for the omission this way:

"The following incident is related as having occurred at the tavern kept by Samuel Decker at an early day. On a certain evening a man was seen riding towards the upper end of the tavern stoop. The horse was a light sorrel in color, with a bald face. The knight [why he was called that I fail to understand] rode up the stoop, and made his horse step upon it. He then rode past the kitchen to the barroom door, then he turned and rode into the barroom, and was seen no more from the street. On entering, he advanced with his steed to the bar. Meanwhile, the barkeeper and proprietor was stooping down in the act of replenishing his bottle from the barrel, and, having his back turned, did not observe what was progressing. With a kind of neighing voice the knight from his horse called for a drink. The barkeeper looked up, and suddenly encountered the nose of the steed. He considered this as a challenge, and sprang through a side door to a wood-pile with the intention of grasping an axe with which to kill the horse. Some of his friends, deeming this unwise, detained him as he was returning with the weapon.

"The horse was with difficulty ejected from the house, when suddenly a band of pugilists poured from the barroom and swarmed upon the stoop. Oaths and imprecations arose, and clenched fists flew, till dark night drew a curtain over the turbulent scene. The design of this affray, as proved afterwards in court, was to provoke the tavernkeeper to kill the horse in the barroom, and then open up the animal, stuff the innkeeper into the cavity, and sew him up, leaving only the head protruding, after which they purposed using the bottles at will and departing in triumph.

"This outrage upon the common decencies of society was not originated by the denizens of Deckertown, but was the offspring of the fertile brains of what were called in those days *liners*. They dwelt upon the state line between New York and New Jersey, having doors opening into both States. These people were as wicked as the evil one wished them to be, and occasionally so much worse as to injure even the cause of the devil."

Lieutenant James Moody, Tory, spy, thief, and a recruiter for the King when it suited him, *must have had something*. Perhaps he was even the Revolutionary counterpart of a tavern balladier on off-evenings—and it matters little now whether names like Bertrand Island, Halsey Island, or Raccoon Island conceal an earlier name of Moody. Some say that Moody Island is still in the lake, although much smaller by this time; others argue that with the coming of the Morris Canal the waters rose and covered it up for all time. There was one occasion when Sussex folk, thinking they had the Tory encircled, lost him because a girl took a horse and rode mile after mile through the gloomy night to give him warning. Another ill-starred lass, identified with "Love Lane"—a ravine not too far out of Newton—was killed when her horse reared in fright as the Colonists closed in, losing Moody as they gave their attention to the hapless maiden. At another time the daughter of "Allemuchy," an Indian chieftain for whom the village is named, is said to have hanged herself after the raider held her prisoner overnight in one of his hideout caverns. Now even the Princess could be a likely ghost—although I know of no stories that connect her with either the Devil's Saddle or the Hopatcong Island called Moody.

As a matter of fact, I am not at all sure that the legend of the ghost of the Indian princess is not apocryphal, even as the name of the island may be, for some of the best maps of the area I know failed to point out Lieutenant Moody's namesake in the array of islands which identifies still another, called Willow Island. Bertrand Island is the one where, obviously for sufficient years, residents reminded post-Revolutionary settlers that Moody came that way and liked to hide there.

It is an uncontrived trick of stories handed down to transplant the most colorful legends from one place to another, and in this instance I firmly believe that Moody's Cave, which imagination at one time fitted up with Turkish carpets, a spinet piano, and even liveried servants, was part of a tall story grown taller. Say that to some and you will be told that such adornments were part not of the Muckshaw but of the

Hopatcong legend, for on whatever island it was Moody is supposed to have had a log house.

The ghost of James Moody, or whatever ghost it is, at least serves to introduce the region as it used to be to travelers who know it only as it is, and then only in summer. Nowhere in the writings of Gustav Kobbé, who went wandering when he was not commenting on musical concerts for the New York *Times,* are there more poetic passages than he lavishes on the lake called Hopatcong, in *Kobbé's Jersey Central,* published in 1890. There was good reason for this, for it seems the book was subsidized in part by the Central Railroad of New Jersey. With almost every railroad, and even trolley line, went at least one amusement park—one of the Central's was at Lake Hopatcong, "etched in silver, in the wooded slope of the New Jersey highlands. Hopatcong," said Gustav, "signifies 'Pipe Water,' a name descriptive of the lake before its waters were raised artificially for the purposes of the Morris Canal in 1832. . . .

"Since that time it has made islands of several promontories and entirely covered others, flowing far back into the recesses of the hills, and flooding the marsh which once divided it from Little Pond, with which it now forms a lake some seven miles long, and two miles in width at its broadest point. The main body of the lake is barely a mile wide at most but the coves on its western shore (the River Styx, Byram, and Henderson Coves) are deeply indented in the hills. . . ."

On the county maps of Sussex, Henderson Cove, Halsey Island, Bertrand Island, and the River Styx are still prominent in spite of all the summer incursions that have come, as well as many musical but meaningless development names. But you can now add Cow Tongue Point to your earlier list. The Morris Canal came up from Waterloo, turned south from Stanhope, and then reached its feeder up to Brooklyn, for once upon a time Hopatcong was as well-known as Brooklyn Pond; from there it went down to Shippenport and Port Morris before a venture even further south.

Long ago the name River Styx invited me in that direction, for I remember fondly an instructor in Latin who sometimes floored his classes with remarkable asides—such as snatches of *The Houseboat on the Styx* of John Kendrick Bangs. When translations were slow in coming, my now departed friend would rumble off into the "Song of the Frogs" by the shores of that mythical river dividing this world from the next; then, however reluctantly, we would be brought back to earth. Once the Styx flowed into a lake whose shores were crowded with Indians, the Nariticongs, instead of the hotels of early resort days and the newer bungalows or summer cottages in an era followed by modern designs.

Gustav Kobbé wrote in 1890: "Fish were plentiful in the lake and game abounded in the surrounding hills. The site of the principal (Indian) settlement is now submerged. It was near Halsey Island, which, before the damming of the lake, was connected with the mainland. The site was easily located by circular hearths of fire-blacked stones, from whose number it was judged that the village was formed of some fifty wigwams. The dead were buried on the extreme end of the promontory, now Halsey Island, where many of the remains have been dug up.

"Historians have also mentioned an Indian causeway of stone connecting Bertrand Island with the mainland, but no trace of it can now be found. . . ."

It is well to remember that in the midst of all the talk of reservoirs and even more reservoirs to come the old Indian villages were the first to go under water. Workmen who dug the Morris Canal are said to have exhumed, near the outlet of the lake, portions of an Indian skeleton with an arm bone that measured thirty-six inches, which, if it was in proportion to the rest of the body, indicated that the Hopatcong Valley housed a valley of Indian giants. The last Indians to have lived on these shores were followers of Chincopee, an aged warrior of the Nariticongs. Long after the Lenni Lenapes had emigrated from New Jersey, this Indian, stirred by memories of his youth, returned to pass his last days on earth among familiar scenes.

Said Gustav: "He erected a wigwam on what is now Chincopee Cove and occupied himself fishing and making baskets. But he was finally driven away by the white settlers. With what feelings must the last of the Nariticongs have turned his back upon the lake over whose waters his forefathers had glided in their little canoes long before a white man trod its shores. Silently he gathered his few belongings into a canoe, and paddled for the last time across the lake to which his race had given a name. Entering the River Styx and penetrating to its furthest recess, he vanished in the dark foliage of the mountain forest.

"The next morning a rift of smoke was seen curling above the trees on the side of the mountain bordering the Styx. It was observed at various times for about a week. Then a party was organized to reach the spot and effectually to drive away Chincopee from the neighborhood. But on the morning the party was to set out there was no smoke to guide it to the old Indian's camp.

"Nevertheless a start was made, and following the trail from the Styx into the woods they came, when half way up the mountain, suddenly upon the remains of a fire. Near it, torn and dead, his hand clasping his scalping knife, lay Chincopee. Not far from him, stretched on the ground, was the carcass of a huge bear. All about the spot was the evidence of the terrible conflict which had proved fatal to both. The wish of the last of the Nariticongs had been fulfilled. He had died on the hunting grounds of his forefathers. . . ."

I do not by any means agree with Gustav Kobbé's conclusion. I do, however, second his reporting that "some superstitious folk believe that his spirit still roams the mountains whose sombre slopes are reflected in the Styx, and sometimes, of a morning, when the mists are rising off the lake, they will point to the smoke of Chincopee's camp-fire curling up above the dark foliage." It is at least more likely that Chincopee's ghost is lurking about Hopatcong than it is that one of the Moodys has taken a fancy to the switchback on the island which, I have been told repeatedly, was named for James.

This is a land of Indian stories, no matter how much an era of speed and picture windows, split-levels, and gadgets ignores them. It is nevertheless probable that Chincopee's story is a variant of an older tale almost parallel to that of Quaquahela, a great sachem, who started to visit a distant tribe in the far south. At sundown he crossed from Pipe Water's town to Bonaparte's Landing and following the shore for a considerable distance, he drew up his canoe at what had been known as "L'Hommedieu Meadow." From there he set out for a lodge of his friend Comascomin, who lived on the banks of the Musconetcong, so closely packed with fishermen when the trout season opens these days that the unwary fish must be trampled to death. Gustav reported:

"He had gone but a short distance when he was attacked by a bear. Bruin being his totem, it was unlawful for him to kill the animal, and he started to return to his canoe; but the enraged beast prevented this, and a desperate hand-to-claw battle followed in which Quaquahela purchased victory with his life.

"A few days later the body of a huge bear was found, and beside it lay the club and totem and all the hunting gear of the chief. The red men searched for days for their sachem's body, but finding no trace of it, concluded that he had gone to the happy hunting-grounds. The next full moon, the clan saw on a side hill a mist ascending to the heavens, and wondered at the strange appearance. . . .

"That night their medicine man had a vision, and in it Quaquahela appeared and told him he had erected his spirit-lodge there, and would remain as long as the hills stood. Because of his sin in killing his totem, the bear, he was excluded from spiritland forever. He promised to accompany his clan in all their expeditions, and when he retired within his lodge, they would know it by seeing the smoke from his fire ascend to the tops of the trees. He also assured them that every time they would give a friendly whoop, he would answer. And to this day [wrote Gustav Kobbé more than seventy years ago] in damp or wet weather a thin vapor may be seen, rising in curling wreaths over the spot; and if a shout be given, the answer is heard as distinctly as if Quaquahela himself were replying. Thus the Indians accounted for the echo and vapor which add to the weirdness of the River Styx."

I must confide to you that I have tried the "friendly whoop" from the bridge that was long ago erected over the Styx, and for some reason I have heard no echo at all. Once a man in the distance who had been trying for trout and who, perhaps in consequence of my cry, tangled his line on the limb of a tree, gave me a long look of disgust and a few words that distance perhaps fortunately prevented me from hearing. On another occasion a local policeman concluded that I was either loco or possibly even subject to a charge of disturbing the peace for my shouting. It is just as well that I did not linger to explain that I was seeking a return call from Quaquahela or Chincopee—or even one of the Moodys.

The first white settlers were hunters who came to Hopatcong only occasionally—this, they say, was about 1775. Deer were plentiful in the neighborhood, and so they were hunted, at times driven into the water—this is a note from 1835 or thenabouts. It was shortly after that, however, that a severe winter exterminated most of the wild life of the region with the exception of animals used to hibernation, and it was not until the late eighties, which Kobbé described, that "the charms of Lake Hopatcong" became known to more than a few "of those choice spirits who penetrate into the very solitudes of the forests and mountains in their pursuit of nature's beauties." Pursuit of such beauties as I have seen in recent years around Hopatcong's shores would, I feel certain, lead to considerable trouble. Until the Central Railroad of New Jersey purchased and laid out the excursion grounds at Nolan's Point, an era in which the Hotel Breslin was built, "this lovely sheet of water" had not begun "to enjoy the measure of popularity it deserved," according to our Gustav. In the 1890's the Jersey Central carried fifty thousand persons every summer to Nolan's Point when amusement and picnic parks were operated by almost every transportation system worth the name. A reporter of this interval said: "There are a dancing pavilion, flying horses and swings, and at the large commodious float, boats without number. One can go fishing, rowing, sailing, or canoeing, or charter a steam launch and make a most attractive tour of the most attractive reaches of the lake. . . ."

This was the first suggestion ever made to me of a fleet actually referred to as "the Hopatcong Navy." My earliest excursions around the lake were in quest of a steamer someone said was rotting to pieces in one of the coves. Those to whom I addressed queries at the time replied with frowns or forms of astonishment that indicated I had better come up with better questions. I persisted in the idea, then, I recall, that the bones of more than one such vessel, dismissed readily under the name of "launch," were still there somewhere, unsung and unidentified. I will never know how close I was to being on the right track, for by the time I gathered up specific directions where to look there were only the blackened hulks of what may have been a mysterious fire.

Another contemporary wrote:

"The railroad furnishes the grounds and their appurtences free of charge, and the fee for the use of the boats is low. Parties of half a dozen or more can, for twenty-five cents each, make the tour of the lake in the steam launches, and boats can be had for twenty-five cents an hour. A hot dinner is served at noon at a charge of fifty cents. That Nolan's Point should have become the favorite inland resort for excursions in this section of the country is only the natural result of the beauty of its location, the amusement it affords, and the excellence of the railroad service.

"The company allows no liquor to be sold on the grounds. It seeks the patronage of respectable people only, and the excursioners at Nolan's Point, though they have no end of fun on their day's outing, are notably quiet and orderly. Hence they do not interfere at all with the comfort of private residents or of the guests of the various hotels. . . ."

Obviously trouble began when life became complicated and sources of fun were made more elaborate and expensive. For instance, board at the Nolan's Point Villa, said to have been the most comfortable of hotels, cost two dollars per day and from twelve to fourteen dollars per week. "There are postal and telegraph facilities at Nolan's Point," boasted the advertisements of the times, "and a telegraph and telephone office at the Villa, which also boasts modern sanitary appliances. Before the season opens, the manager, Mr. G. L. Bryant, can be addressed at High Bridge, New Jersey."

It was the Hotel Breslin, however, that gave Hopatcong its first big boom, for with it came a new atmosphere of wealth and fashion "in the wake of which," wrote Gustav Kobbé, tongue in cheek, "everything else follows." The hotel bragged of terraces, large flower beds, and intimate glimpses of a notable of the day identified merely as "Lotta, the actress." There were no charges for "looking" at Lotta, whoever she may have been, but rowboats from the Breslin cost all of six dollars per week, sailboats a dollar and a half an hour, and carriage with "double team" five dollars per morning. Those who were able to afford the Breslin and its extras lived in the day's lap of luxury.

"A beautiful drive is through Berkshire Valley," wrote Gustav, indicating that he had sampled the trip to and beyond a crossroads village that remains somewhat in a world apart. Another "pretty drive," he said, "is that to Dover." I often have wondered where the "fields of clover" were on that "ride to Dover." So ran the words of a popular song the memory of which, I suppose, betrays my age, even though I always like to think that there may have been some memory of a golden wedding day on Lake Hopatcong when, even at the Breslin, the best cost five dollars a day and twenty-eight dollars a week. Since then I have been back to see what they called Mount Harry and to view the site of Zuck's Lake View House or post office which, winter and summer, used to be called Rustic, New Jersey.

For the nonce, however, let us take a tour of Lake Hopatcong as Gustav would have had us take it, with as little delay as possible, taking care that ample skirts conceal all traces of ankles and that those little dinky straw hats which have made a comeback time and again, are firmly fastened to the topknot so that in a pinch or a clinch, double duty will be done. "We will start at the south end," he wrote, and so we follow.

"Where the lake narrows down toward Shippenport, it is not navigable for steam-launches, and, though the dredging of a channel through this part of Hopatcong has been under consideration for some time, the lake is still entered through a feeder of the Morris Canal. The little launch turns its way gently between the low banks of the feeder to the lock at Brooklyn, a little settlement which at one time gave the unromantic name of Brooklyn Pond to our lovely Hopatcong. . . ."

Gustav accidentally or deliberately made no reference to "Brooklyn Forge or Works or Hinchman's Forge," to which Charles S. Boyer devoted two full pages in his *New Jersey Forges and Furnaces.* "Brooklyn Forge," he said, "was located at the head of the Musconetcong Creek, at 'the uppermost falls near' the mouth of Lake Hopatcong. On June 5, 1764, Benjamin and Thomas Coe deeded 'one half of a certain forge with one fire' and one half of all their forge lands, water rights, etc., on the Musconetcong Creek to Garret Rapalje, an importer

of iron in New York. They expected in this conveyance that
sawmill which stood on the same dam. From this it is evident
that there was a forge there at that time. George Reading, in
1766, offered several parcels of land for sale, one of which, at
the 'Head of Little Pond,' was about six miles from 'a new
Iron-Works, erected by Garret Rapalje, of New York.' In January, 1768, Rapalje leased the works to Joseph and John Tuttle
for five years at an annual rental of 500 pounds, reserving the
right to build a furnace at one end of the dam. The Tuttles
were to deliver all the iron they made to the lessor in New
York at the market prices. These were fixed at first at 28
pounds per ton for refined iron and 24 pounds per ton for
'Whippany or bloomed iron.' The Tuttles, however, were not
able to operate the plant successfully and eventually made an
assignment. . . ." Gustav Kobbé went on quickly, referring
only to what remained of the Morris Canal feeder in his day:

"The passage through the lock is an interesting experience.
The lower gates are opened and the miniature steamer glides
into the lock, the gates closing behind it. It is now imprisoned
in a narrow passage. On either side are high dripping walls,
and in front and astern the closed gates. There is a sudden
roar of rushing, surging water. The launch lunges half forward,
half upward, the screw adding to the turmoil. The lunging
continues, the swashing, surging waters now lifting the launch
by the stern, now by the prow.

"The actions of those who have not been through the lock
before is a study. The babies cry: the women grab the nearest
man by the arm; the girls are prettily flustered; the men endeavor to appear calm; the passengers that have made the
passage before look amused; the only persons absolutely in-
different are the captain and the engineer.

"It is not easy to gain an idea of the length of Hopatcong, for
at every point the vista is limited to promontories and islands
whose shores overlap one another. . . ."

Gustav's record, by the way, boldly uses the same spelling

of the outlaw's first name that I first heard (one still accepted in many quarters)—Bonnel, not Bonnell. Furthermore, he places Moody not far from a promontory that seems to have been well-known, "Bishop's Rock, the boulder where Bonnel Moody concealed himself while Brandt, the Mohawk Chief, visited the Indian village opposite and induced the Nariticongs to take part in the massacre of the Minnisink."

The point beyond is (or was) worth the climb, too. It is Bonaparte's Landing, and the name, for the information of many a newcomer who argues to the contrary, was not pulled from the air. It seems that Joseph Bonaparte, ex-King of Naples and Spain, more familiar to old Murat Row in Bordentown, landed here while on a prospecting tour, a trip that took him as well to Budd Lake, once Budd's Pond. Joseph Bonaparte thought of settling at Budd's Pond, the record goes, "but during the negotiations he chanced to discover a caricature of his illustrious relative, belonging to the proprietor's daughter, which caused him to change his mind."

In 1950 I sought out Dr. Charles Gordon, who had been practicing in the Hopatcong neighborhood more than forty years, in tracking down the report that he knew where the "bones" of a forgotten steamer, which had sailed on the lake, were sinking deeper and deeper in the mud of an obscure cove. Dr. Gordon, who still was active in ministering to winter and summer residents alike, knew nothing of the wreck, he said, but he well remembered the Hopatcong steamers. "They were double-deckers, some of them," he said, "and some were paddle-wheelers. They ran for a long time, up and down the lake, after they were brought up through the Canal. You see, the lake wasn't dammed up the way it is now.

"I can remember the Canal when it was a going concern, with mules and horses and hay everywhere. You see, the lake was in two parts in the beginning. From Hurdtown was land. Up Woodport way was a second lake," said the doctor. Dr. Gordon had been a personal friend of Hudson Maxim, who developed smokeless powder not far from Farmingdale, in Monmouth County, and now lies buried at the end of his beloved Hopatcong. Dr. Gordon brought out two of Maxim's books—one of which I never had seen before, *The Science of Poetry*.

A horse-and-buggy doctor, the physician said that he often had resorted to horseback and sleighs in winter when high winds blew drifting snow from the lake and up the banks around Mount Arlington where Dr. Gordon lived when I saw him. The winter of 1950 had been comparatively mild elsewhere, but Hopatcong had had more than its share of snow, I was assured.

"Yes," he told me, "the old Jersey Central brought the first prosperity to the Hopatcong area, and when the era of small pleasures was over, an entirely new phase set in—and it was only natural. I like the lake," he added with what I knew was understatement. "Been here all my life. Born in Lower Berkshire. Came here to practice in 1910. Never got away, even when I should have, when the snow was four and five feet over the horses' heads." Ghosts? Dr. Gordon laughed. Obviously even country physicians are not medicine men who believe in such fables—if that is what they are.

Word went out that I was looking for the abandoned launches of the fleet of Lake Hopatcong, "the Hopatcong Navy." Oddly enough, the first response came from Washington, in Warren County. "I heard that you could not locate the remains of the old steamboats that plied the lake," said Charles S. Bergmann. "It may disconcert you when I tell you that you were so close that if you had shouted from the River Styx bridge, they surely would have heard you." I did not tell him that I had engaged in some shouting from the bridge for other reasons, with unexpected results.

"Here's how to get to the launches," Charles went on, with directions most specific. "Cross the River Styx bridge, bear right beyond the Bon Air Lodge on the Ithanell Road, and go to the end of that road. Then walk on the wood road towards the shore of the lake, on the Campbell property. There you will find the boats, what's left of them, as well as the steel rails which, I suppose, were used to pull them up on land in winter and then, at the end, once and for all. One boat is about thirty-five feet long and ten feet wide. Inasmuch as I spent my youth at and in Lake Hopatcong, I know the area well, and I hope I have been of some help."

Helpful though he meant to be, Charles Bergmann had not been over the River Styx for some little while—this I quickly discovered. Upon my return I told him that the rails were still there, just where he said they ought to be, and beside them were some rusted cables and wheels. Of the gallant craft that puffed around Lake Hopatcong in its days of an earlier elegance, there were but scatterings of charred timbers. I had come, I soon learned, two years too late.

This is how it happened, how one thing led to another, up from Davis Cove to "Sleepless Hollow," once the hideaway of the celebrated juggler and comedian Joe Cook. I will bore you with a few of the details just to prove that once you begin to let things happen, no magic formula is needed to dig the past from the present. The wood road Charles Bergmann had described had vanished, and in its place I found a new road under construction, with road-building equipment left handy for the resumption of work, once the week end was over. I saw the cove and a more modern landing on which an old iceboat of more wintry days had been held in hopeful readiness. There, obviously, were the rails of a marine railway.

Wheels were beside them, perhaps parts of a winch. Charred wood lay here and there, half covered by a rank growth brought by spring returning to the lowlands along the lake shore. I saw the story, or at least this chapter of it, ending as quickly as it had begun—and then, down the coarse stone of the new road, came a man. As it turned out, I could have

Those who frequent Lake Hopatcong, old Brooklyn Pond, in these latter days are startled to hear that there once was a Hopatcong Navy—its members enlisted from crews of the pleasure boats that plied the lake as well as workers on the Morris Canal.

found no better source of information if I had combed the coves for weeks. His name, he said pleasantly, was Fred Stocker. Asked what had become of the wrecks of the little launches that once were part of Hopatcong's life, he replied: "I burned them—two years ago." Then the owner of a variety of land packages in the vicinity, Fred told me that he had become a developer in spite of himself. "I decided early in my life that I would retire when my fiftieth birthday came," he explained, "on the theory that all the years after that are lived on borrowed time. In the gummed paper business for many years, we had closed a plant in Brooklyn to open a smaller place in Netcong when the war came. There were some routines the Government wanted me to undertake—and here I am. . . ."

Fred explained that he didn't live in Netcong, that his home was "here at Sleepless Hollow." This was a name that Joe Cook devised and that, Fred told me at the time, he thought would disappear eventually. I went back to Fred's first disclosure in spite of all this.

"Burned the launches?" I asked, obviously aghast. "Sure," he said. "They were falling apart. I was careful to salvage all the iron and stack it up. Then, one night, when I wasn't looking, somebody came in—must have been with a truck—and hauled it all away."

I mentioned Charles Bergmann's directions and how "the Campbell property" had been mentioned. "The Campbells are no youngsters any more," Fred said. "They still own that house out there, the one with the iceboat on the landing. They're among the few survivors of the elegant age along the lake— live over in Troy Hills now. They just spend summers here. See that summer place over there? That was theirs. You won't believe it, but it used to be the post office in Mount Arlington across the lake. They brought it here on the ice. Of course, it's fixed up to what it was then, but that's the way most things were brought over from the west shore. There were few roads.

The only way houses were built along the water was when materials for building were brought over the lake on the ice the winter before."

That, I think, is when Fred told the story of the black and white flags. He said that the launches—he called them "steamers"—on the lake were called "the black and white ships" in the days of their operation. "It all went by flags," he said. "If you wanted a black ship, you hoisted a black flag, and the right kind of craft came for you. If you wanted a white ship, a white flag would bring it over." "What was the difference?" I wanted to know. "The black flag," Fred said, "was for a small boat, a single-decker. If you hauled up a white flag, a double decker came over to the landing. The boats were important. They made connections with the trains on the other side or, if you made arrangements, they gave you a ride up and down the lake. The Jersey Central used to have tracks that followed the shore of Nolan's Point and then swung into Minisink and Morris County Junction.

Those were the excursion days of which Gustav Kobbé wrote and which always can be happily recalled by a glance at the maps in his little red-covered *Jersey Central.* Along Hopatcong, the Central's line is shown coming in through Hurd, now Hurdtown, passing Castle Rock Park, and swinging down below the Nolan's Point Villa. Only the railroad bed remained when I was there, an obvious hump of old cinders. As we walked to what used to be Joe Cook's villa, Fred Stocker talked of days long ago when there were "real winters" and "lots of iceboats" and "people who knew how to have a lot of fun in simpler ways." That was long before the Alamac Hotel, perhaps the most famous of them all, burned in Mount Arlington, before the German brewers and hatmakers who knew the lake gathered there and long before there were any crowds to speak of.

I was thinking of the two-dollars-a-day and twelve-dollars-a-week board at the sumptuous Nolan's Point Villa as Fred took me into the long glassed-in porch of the hideaway that had been Joe Cook's. At that time, Fred told me Joe was in an actor's home, memories of his days as a juggling comedian lost in other reflections, those of a man hopelessly crippled by arthritis. Joe built the house on a twenty-seven acre estate and then equipped it with all the delights that only a Joe Cook would devise, from a miniature golf course that would upset any professional to a game room and a miniature theater. Then, too, there was "Kelly's," one of two taverns that were part of the estate.

Kelly's provided a background for Joe Cook's crazy collection of relics and souvenirs, not the least of which was a piano autographed by world celebrities who, on arrival in these quarters, were given an electric needle with which to sign their names. What once was a barn was established by Joe himself as "Schultz's," a nineteenth hole which hid away, protected by locks and keys and barred windows, many of the prized steins and mugs that Joe didn't take away. His collection was so vast when he lived there that many were hung from the ceiling. "This was the Gessler barn, and Joe transformed it," Fred said. "Now some of the service clubs have outings up here, and we always drink a toast to Joe. . . ."

"See all those carvings?" Fred Stocker pointed to gnomes and elves of all sizes, here, there, and everywhere in all sorts of action—playing tennis, playing golf, hunting, fishing, and, on the walls of the lavatory, sailing boats *up the roads* and driving cars *across the lake.* "Joe said he was interested in a boy who 'whittled' and so he kept him busy here, 'whittling' all the time. And, by the way, you'll find Rip Van Winkle, life-size and apparently half asleep, out on the lawn." Of all that Joe Cook collected, he left more than seventy-five per cent at Sleepless Hollow, which those who spoke of it referred to as "Joe Cook's Crazy House."

Until I heard again from Earl Wilson, in East Gary, Indiana, there was no more on the lake at Hopatcong, no more on the little launches the wrecks of which Fred Stocker had destroyed, and no more from our gracious host of that bizarre, unplanned day of ten years ago. On leaving, I asked Fred, as a developer in spite of himself, if he knew who had imported the name Elba Avenue. He didn't. "It must have been somebody with a sense of humor like Joe Cook's," I suggested. "Don't forget, Bonaparte Landing isn't far away."

Earl Wilson had begun by remembering suddenly that he had made at least two trips on barges of the Morris Canal on Lake Hopatcong. He wrote:

"I guess you wonder how they were made, those trips to the lake. Now here is the procedure: We went up the feeder to Brooklyn Lock. At that point we put the mules in a stable where a man attended to the care of them for a few days. Then we took the boat through the lock to Brooklyn Pond, now Lake Hopatcong. At that time there was a pair of gates above the lock that separated the pond from the rest of the lake. William Black (who shipped along the Canal with cordwood from Hackettstown and Stanhope) had all the arrangements made, so there was a little boat, a kind of steam launch, either steam or perhaps naphtha or gasoline, that was waiting for us. The lock-tender opened the gates, and the little boat backed into the pond. We threw them a line, and they towed us up to Woodport where we got a load of wood.

"The next day the launch came back to Woodport and towed us back down to Brooklyn Lock, where we entered the Canal again, got our mules, and were off for our unloading place, either Paterson, or wherever Mr. Black had sold the wood . . . I wonder that no one told you of the excursion boats that docked at Landing at the foot of the lake. That wasn't fifty years ago or much more. When I was there, they had two double-deck pretty-good-size side-wheelers that docked there. These boats had a regular schedule. They would meet the trains or at least be at the dock when the trains got in at

Landing Station on the D. L. & W. The way up to the resort hotels further on up the lake was by boat. On Sundays and holidays these boats would get loaded with sight-seers and make trips up the lake and back . . . I guess I saw all this about seven years, around 1902."

On an August morning in 1956, I watched vacationists arriving from all directions, no longer the holiday-seekers of old, quickly vanishing in areas all around the lake, and Hopatcong was still a challenge for me. Only the Delaware Lackawanna and Western station below Landing was eloquently deserted by everything but a lingering freight train. By this time one end of the station itself, bearing an elegance which the present times seems over-anxious to bury, was a real estate office. From the list of stations still displayed, Minisink was as conspicuous by its absence as it had been familiar to Earl Wilson.

At last, after many fruitless inquiries along the way, I came upon two men cutting the long grass with scythes by the side of the road. I asked them about Minisink and Minisink station. One laborer replied that he never had heard of either. His companion all but interrupted him, laughing. Then he provided specific directions. A lean and sinewy man whose agility belied his age, said his name was Andrew Dingman, and I found out quickly enough that he was kin of the Dingmans of Dingman's Ferry. "Haven't been back there in a long while, and if I don't hurry up, from what I read in the papers, they'll have it under water before I get to it." Then, "Who would you be wanting to see in Minisink?" I showed him my letter from East Orange from a man who said he had been "born on the lake" and knew that Bill Gordon, of Minisink, would have answers for most of my Hopatcong questions. "There are Gordons down thataway," Andrew said, "but it's more than just a piece down the road. Minisink station's been a house, but from what I heard lately maybe it ain't no more."

Even so, Andrew Dingman can put himself down for all

time as the man who teamed up unknowingly with East Orange's Bill Gordon and Indiana's Earl Wilson to show the way to, what seems for me, the climax of all the golden days that Hopatcong has, unhappily, forgotten. Moments later, I was told at the inevitable gasoline station that the Gordons lived "three houses up the road, this side." I found the house, and there I found Bill Gordon, then eighty-eight, a man with a mustache and beetling brows and lines of laughter around his mouth and eyes. There were also Bill's daughter and other members of the family, and to them I am indebted for a glimpse at old photographs in a family album, showing men in uniforms that must have rivaled the "King's Navee" in its best-braided days. Thus I realized for the first time that I was speaking to the last survivor of the Hopatcong skippers, proud captains of the little fleet of steam launches. That is what they truly were, Bill said—the Hopatcong Navy kept busy in earlier days of commercial as well as pleasure craft, but rarely privately owned, on Brooklyn Pond. Here are some of the memories of the last of a group of six men and a commodore, resplendent in naval toggery that bore the name, emblazoned on the blouses in the picture I saw: "L. H. Steamboat Co."

"There were two lines of boats—the Black Line, painted black, was mostly identified with work from the Canal, while the White Line was strictly for travel on the lake itself. These boats had such names as the *Mystic Shrine*, the *G. L. Bryant*, the *Andrew Reasoner*, and the *Fanny*. Black or white, most were burned, either up the River Styx or at Bertrand Island.

"Cap'n Todd had a side-wheeler, and there were two others like it, one of which was called *The Lazy Moll*—she took five acres to turn around in. I ran one of the steamboats on the lake through twelve years. My brother, John R. Gordon, ran another. My boat was the *Andrew Reasoner*—she was fifty feet long. We took the canal boats wherever they wanted to go. Like as not, I'm the one who pulled the boat your friend Earl Wilson told you about.

"I can't understand why so many people forget to remember Minisink and Minisink station. Why, this mountain at the back of everything up here has been Minisink Mountain from the beginning . . . boats on the Black Line were taken from the water for the winter. The side-wheelers had to be left where they were, but the ice was cut from around them every day when winter came on. Those were real winters. More than three thousand people came here just to cut ice in days before modern refrigeration. There were ice plants all around the shores of the lake—at Nolan's Point, Callahan's, Hurdtown, and Donald Pond. Some boats went on running into November. My brother ran his boat until Election Day. Most of the steamers were hauled out or tied up when summer was over, but my brother John made the most of people who had to come here and travel up the lake so they could vote.

"The boats made three trips a day. I remember because I was finally argued into taking on a fourth trip—three trips up and back, I mean—then four. George W. Campbell, a Wall Street broker, owned the Black Line. The owner came to me one day and pointed out that none of the boats met the train getting in at 8:26. He asked me if I'd add an extra trip and meet those who arrived on that train for the various hotels. I objected at first, but when he offered ten dollars more a month —we were getting sixty dollars a month in those days—I agreed. I remember asking my engineer, Dan Hummer, if he minded. Dan never minded anything. He was always ready for an extra trip, anywhere, any time.

"When the excursionists arrived, we were more than busy. Sometimes, I tell you, more than five hundred people arrived all at the same time at the train end of the lake. That meant that all four boats were not enough—some, if not all, had to pull a loaded barge behind them. I can remember a lot of groups coming from far away on the train—among them were the Schuetzens, from Hoboken. They were German, at least by

Bill Gordon, of Minisink, who served in the Lake Hopatcong "Navee,"
shared his recollections of days aboard his boat the *Andrew Reasoner*.
On some summer mornings, he said, at least five hundred day excursionists would descend from the trains that stopped at the end of the lake.

heritage, you know, but I never knew any of those trippers, as we called them then, to get drunk. . . ."

Bill Gordon had closed his eyes quietly. Some days, his daughter told me, as if she had been reluctant to break in until then, he remembered more than on others. "It's funny," she added. "He says he can remember more and more things that happened, further and further back, on the days when the lake was, as he says it, 'fawg-bound.' Then, he says, there were other times when the mists off the lake were slowly climbing up the mountains. . . ."

When Bill Gordon opened his eyes, he squinted a little, almost as if he had forgotten that I was there. Obviously, this interlude of recollection was at an end, and I was content—or was I? "Mists climbing up the mountains"—I still brood on the phrase even on occasions since that talk with Bill, the last of the skippers of the Hopatcong Navy. If there is a fog hovering on the lake, at any time of the year, I listen for the sound of launches and the creaks of their paddle-wheels. If it is clear, and the weather sparkling cold, I look for wood smoke or even clouds in the making. Could not the mists sometimes be the smoke of a lonely Indian's fire? Could it not be that either Chincopee or Quaquahela, unknown to a modern generation of rush and rattle, are still up there, somewhere between the River Styx and Lubber's Run?

Chapter XI

TOBOGGANS AND WAMPUM

There is no essential reason for remembering New Jersey toboggans and the first New Jersey wampum in almost the same breath except that both involve adventures with pictures. One of these is certainly important because it offers proof positive of the existence of a toboggan slide not very long ago in the heart of what has become a labyrinth of almost everything called "the Oranges," sprawling up from Maplewood to Montclair in Essex County. The other is as memorable, because through a misunderstanding I assumed it to be a very early painting of New Jersey's first wampum factory, at Goffle in Passaic—and it wasn't.

The name of the late John C. Storms, of Park Ridge, in Bergen, is usually associated with the wampum made in New Jersey at the establishment of the much celebrated Campbells in John's home town, Park Ridge, once Pascack. After all, John had given much of his lifetime to the kind of research that produced one of his little books, *The Story of Wampum*, for which he was compiler, printer, binder, and salesman.

It was Jim Ransom, of Westwood, and Dr. Lewis M. Haggerty, of Hackensack, who pieced together the documented story of the plant in Passaic County. *My* error was in mistaking the painting of the Park Ridge operation for the one at Goffle in the midst of a conversation in which I was assured that Goffle, as a place and assuredly as a wampum factory, had effectively vanished from the face of the earth. Until then all I had seen were old photographs of the abandoned factory site and trading post at Park Ridge.

You may remember the Orange picture. Actually, it was an

219

engraving from the yellowing pages of the January, 1886, issue of *Harper's Magazine*—and I hope you will not misunderstand me. I am not inferring that you were thumbing your way through a copy in those days, but I thought that by some chance you just might have been one of those on whom I sprang the reproduction of the toboggan in operation asking, "Have you seen this?" I am sure some of those to whom I spoke considered it all a trap to make them reveal their age.

I had almost begun to feel that I had carried the picture through much of the Orang , almost from door to door. In reality what I had was a print—one of two I knew of—showing "the new toboggan slide at Orange, New Jersey" with an assortment of men and women, well-clothed against the winters "that used to be," poised for a plunge down the icy chute or ready to be drawn to the top by a horse. "Where *was* this slide?" I kept asking, adding always that "certainly someone must remember." Suddenly, and without warning, several remembered, not only the toboggan slide of the Oranges but also, as all folklore should be recalled, its story.

By 1939 the four Oranges—Orange, East Orange, West Orange, and South Orange—were on record as not resenting their title of "typical American suburbs," while residents themselves refine this distinction yet another stage by referring to the Oranges and Maplewood as "New York's most beautiful suburbs." At last an "R.F.D." man myself—"refugee from developments"—I can the better appreciate Mark Twain's roguish remark: "There's something I like about Newark. I think it's the suburbs."

Only a little more than a century ago, Tom Gordon in his *Gazetteer* was restricting his descriptions to Orange Township, Essex County, Orange, and South Orange, and in none of these was he too complimentary, however factual, in his estimates. "Orange t-ship," he wrote, was "bounded N.W. by Caldwell; N.E. by Bloomfield; E. and S.E. by Newark; S. by Union; S.W. by Springfield; and W. by Livingston. . . ."

Land on the west was "hilly; the First and Second Mountains crossing it here; elsewhere rolling; soil, red shale, generally well cultivated; area, about 14,000 acres. Orange, the post town," the record continued, "Camptown, Middleville and Jefferson villages, are towns of the township. . . ." The population in 1830 was 3,887.

Tom Gordon said that in his day Orange was "a straggling village . . . extending about 3 miles along the turnpike road, from Newark to Dover, and distant about 3 miles N.W. of the former. . . ." At this time the Dover that lies not far from Denville had not appeared and so was not even listed. Orange

This print from an 1886 issue of *Harper's Magazine* started me out on a search to find someone who remembered the Orange Toboggan. Dr. Francis J. E. Tetrault, from Quebec, and his uncle, Francis C. O'Reilly, were organizers of "The Toboggan Slide" on the side of "the Mountain" in what now is West Orange.

then had between "200 and 230 dwellings, many of them very neat and commodious. A large trade is carried on here in the manufacture of leather, shoes and hats," Tom Gordon added, with the fact that a "chalybeate spring near the town is much resorted to." South Orange, the only other Orange mentioned, was "on the turnpike road from Newark to Morristown, 5 miles W. of the first" and containing "about 30 dwellings, a tavern and a store, a paper mill and a Presbyterian church" in "lands around it" that were "also rich and well farmed."

John W. Barber and Henry Howe, preparing their historical studies only ten years later, seem to have spent more time in the Orange Cemetery than anywhere else, unless they had enlisted the help of one who preferred the copying of epitaphs to other researches. They mentioned the "Orange Mineral Spring" as "formerly a place of considerable resort"; they passingly noted the arrival of the Morris and Essex Railroad; and then, revealing that the population had dropped to 3,261, added a fat paragraph as well as an engraving describing the "laudable example" of the graveyard. There followed, even in the resort to fine type, the full text of the epitaphs of "Rev. Mr. Daniel Taylor," the Rev. Caleb Smith, Dr. John Condit, Dr. Isaac Pierson, the Rev. Asa Hillyer, and Amos Dodd. It was almost as if someone were selling cemetery lots—unless, of course, a descendant of one of those mentioned was a subscriber to *Historical Collections,* yet I have never heard that these historians worked that way.

I must admit that I appeared to Taylors, Smiths, Condits, Piersons, Hillyers, and Dodds, in my pat presentation of the magazine clipping on the Orange Toboggan, but I must also admit that I got exactly nowhere. At last, when I was almost ready to give up, there were letters. I don't know which came first, although it really doesn't matter now. Eventually I met all the writers, and each of them provided new strands in the forgotten saga of a time when wealthy New Yorkers built a toboggan slide down a steep Orange hill and erected a toboggan house at the bottom. The rise, when I last was there, was all but hidden by houses, with the promise of more houses to come. The old apple orchards and blackberry patches had vanished. The "clubhouse," however, was still there, only a few feet from where it originally was, concealing its identity in additions and coverings that made it a nondescript dwelling of many doors.

Let me introduce you first, then, to Mrs. Fred Haller, of East Orange, the daughter of the physician who was one of the toboggan club's organizers. I remember her as bright-eyed, merry in response, and as delighted as anyone I have met to recall the very scenes and activities I had been seeking so long in vain. She wrote me, quite simply, in a spidery hand:

"The questions you have asked, after talking to so many people, have taken me back to my childhood on Main Street, in Orange. I remember when the toboggan itself was stored in a room in our house, and we liked to play on and around it. My father, Dr. Francis J. E. Tetrault, and his uncle, were among the organizers of what they called 'The Toboggan Slide' on the side of the Mountain—that is how we spoke of it in West Orange—'The Mountain.'

"My father was a French-Canadian and, of course, used toboggans in his native Quebec. My father's uncle was Francis C. O'Reilly, who opened the road that is now Park Avenue, opposite Llewellyn Park, West Orange, and the houses he built for his workmen are still standing and occupied on the south side of Park Avenue near the Erie Railroad Crossing. [This letter came to me in 1952.]

". . . I remember the suits my father and mother wore while tobogganing. Father had a vivid red toboggan hat with a blue tassel, sort of a navy blue, and a red suit, with short trousers trimmed with blue. He wore hand-made red woolen stockings and arctics. My mother's suit, made by herself, was garnet wool, trimmed with light blue, with a hood to match, as well as a sash with fringe.

"After the slide was abandoned we children used the suits that were made for us, along with the hand-made stockings, for in those days we had plenty of snow. My father used a horse and sleigh on his customary rounds as a doctor. We also had snowshoes, which no one sees around here any more. Our house was on Main Street, opposite Ridge, next to St. Mark's Cemetery—a roadway there divides it from the Presbyterian Cemetery. One wouldn't believe it now, but we had a cistern in the back yard which supplied us with water in a kitchen where there was a pump. A well for drinking water, as well as a pail with a dipper, were in their places. A maid had to keep everything that was brass shined up all the time.

"We also had lamps—one that hung on the wall that was red, trimmed with colored stones I remember very well. That's because as I pulled it down to take the globe out one day the whole thing crashed and cut my hand. As my father was away in Canada at the time, I was rushed to the corner of High and Main Streets to Dr. John Bradshaw's office—this must have been around 1904 or 1905, or at least these things were familiar in our home until then. Strange, what you do remember and what you so easily forget as you grow older.

"I remember the old 'cable road' in West Orange, where many a family went on picnics. In the fall my father used to take me to 'The Mountain' and collect butternuts and chestnuts. There are none there now, and children who live in the vicinity don't know what chestnuts are unless they see the kind that's imported in one of the stores.

"My father used to have patients in what once was called St. Cloud on the Mountain, and I remember his having to go out at night or in the early morning with a lantern under his carriage. He usually took the hired man with him. He had a speaking tube above the doorbell which went up to his room any anyone, after ringing the bell, would whistle into the tube and arouse him. Nowadays it's not easy to get a doctor, and it is still sometimes strange to have one you don't know when we had one in the house all the time.

"I remember the Alonzo Stagg family when the Staggs lived on Valley Road, West Orange—yes, I mean Alonzo, the celebrated football coach—so few associate him with the Oranges any more. You might say the same for George H. Hartford, the founder of the A. & P. My chum was his granddaughter, and he and his wife were charming people, long well-known around here. On the corner of Bell and Main Streets there was a private school conducted by a Gertrude Smith—it was the home of her mother and father. I attended this school—it had just one room as the school, with the parlor a kind of annex. People don't even speak of parlors any more. She had a carpet on the floor that was a vivid turkey red, mixed with green, which I must admit I thought was awful even then.

"There were rugs on top of the carpet, and if any pupil did not stay on the rugs or dared to step on the grass outside, Miss Smith would give him or her a demerit. If you stayed on the rugs and off the grass for five days, you got a merit for each day with a picture card on which there was a verse for you to memorize at the end of the week. Oh, yes—there was another school, Miss Robinson's, where the post office is now.

"Bruger's candy store was where all the children around here loved to go—Mr. Bruger made all his own candy and ice cream, and for a penny you could buy enough to treat all the others. Some people say we always should look forward—but I like to think of things as they were in those days, even though people who live in the Oranges now won't believe them. Why, we even had chickens and *loved* them, along with the horse, the colt, the dog, the cat, and even the old barn. All of them were part of our lives.

"I could content myself with a Butterick *fash sheet,* as we called it then, cutting out all the paper dolls and coloring them and having a good time with my younger sisters. There were not so many different toys, then, you know—and some of the best, or the ones you liked best, were the ones you made yourself.

"We used to have political parades which were truly an occasion. I remember those which were held for Grover Cleveland and Benjamin Harrison. You know, there was a song that said something about Harrison in the White House with Baby McKee, whoever she was, on his knee. I wish I could remember it all. . . ."

And I wished she could, too. Reading through the final phrases again, it occurred to me that the ways of politicians and politics are mostly as they always were—without the torchlights, without as many parades, perhaps, and without the booming drums that frightened Sarah Tetrault Haller so much, until her doctor father bought her one of her own—but with the songs and cartoons that so frequently clash with good taste. Mrs. Haller suggested, even as she concluded, that I come to see her when I was in the vicinity, and I made it my business to be in the vicinity in a matter of days. As I told her as soon as we met, she had held a mirror to the ways of life in an area of New Jersey which probably has forgotten about them —cisterns, pumps, turkey red carpet and all. But the phrase that stayed with me was *All of them were part of our lives.* The very words told me that I must lose no time in seeing Mrs. Haller and those to whom she might lead me.

Mrs. Haller laughed until she all but cried when I told her of my journeys up and down the streets with the magazine picture of the Orange Toboggan in my hand. "All I knew about the Oranges before your letter came," I told her, with a wink denoting slight exaggeration, "was what a former Bishop of New Jersey is reported to have told the first Bishop of Newark; this was not long after the Diocese of Newark was cut from the southern end of the state, along the Musconetcong at the top of Hunterdon to a point between Newark and Elizabeth. 'Your diocese,' he is reported to have complained, 'took all the Oranges. We were given all the lemons.'" Although the story may be apocryphal, I often have wondered how such places as Bernardsville, or Basking Ridge, or Somerville, or even Princeton, for that matter, have reacted through the years to the lemon classification.

I have given you Mrs. Haller's picture of the toboggan of the Oranges just as she painted it for me, in that dainty handwriting which one sees so seldom any more. When I saw her, as well as her husband who had just returned from a veterans' hospital, she was as spirited as her words and talked of a hundred things, of her multiple collections—miniatures that fill a medicine cabinet that belonged to her father, doll house furniture that covered the top of the piano and of books of clippings that referred to anything of interest in her family from the days of 1884.

Shortly after that, Madeleine McHarg, of East Orange, told me her father had spoken often of the Orange Toboggan and that she had heard that a man who "still lived in Orange somewhere" had been what they called a "toboggan boy" on the old chute.

"My father," she told me, "was a changed man whenever he remembered days of the toboggan slide and we, when we were very small, visited the place where it had been. We took what was then called 'the Swamp Line Trolley,' which more or less paralleled Valley Road and then ran to South Orange. We used to get off somewhere in the vicinity of the Lackawanna Mountain station, and there my father showed us part of the slide, made of wood, which even then was rotting away near the foot of a steep hill. Now, of course, that section is all built up." That, I think, is almost an understatement: questions about the Orange Toboggan in the neighborhood produced expressions so eloquent that I wonder they didn't carry me off to the nearest hospital on their own.

"My father also claimed," Madeleine McHarg went on, "that the Swamp Line Trolley, complete with pot-bellied stove, was the original Toonerville Trolley—he was a former newspaper-man so perhaps he was right." I refrained from telling Madeleine that almost every old trolley line in New Jersey argued that it owned Toonerville's prototype. "The trolley rocked and swayed, meandering through back yards, reeking of smoke from the old stove. The motorman, known familiarly by his first name, delivered packages, inquired about the 'rheumatiz' of the old folks, and must have been quite a character."

I quickly reported on my conversations with Mrs. Haller and Mrs. McHarg, and what they had said was more than enough to produce more revelations. Perhaps the reference to the elusive "toboggan boy" had something to do with it. Whatever the reason, two men who had been boyhood friends and in 1952 were still that and neighbors as well, wrote colorful letters, each without the other's knowledge. That was why I was able

Orange Tobogganers dressed gaily for their trips down the slide. A lady's suit, made by herself, might be made of garnet wool, trimmed with light blue, with hood and sash.

to meet and talk with Joseph M. Brennan and Rudolph Richter the same day. There they were on Argyle Avenue, Orange, living across the street from each other, for all my wanderings with picture in hand. I reflected after coming home that there is nothing better than listening to a man recalling all the delights and wonders of his boyhood unless, of course, it is two men, old friends, sitting side by side as they reach into the shadows of the past. Joe said:

"I not only remember the Toboggan slide but I rode it many times. It was located not in Orange, actually, but in West Orange, just south of where Hazel Avenue is now. It started on the Orange Valley side of the First Mountain, just east of Hillside Avenue, and ended about a hundred yards west of Valley Road. The slide was internationally famous in its day and drew visitors from many states and Canada, too. The president of what they called the Essex County Toboggan Club was Oliver Sumner Teall, who was, if my memory serves, a stockbroker in New York who maintained a summer home in West Orange."

There was a slight pause, and I remember asking, almost as if I were afraid my words would break the spell: "Were you ever what they called a toboggan boy?" The kindly face of Joe Brennan, who, at seventy-eight, boasted a thick crop of graying hair as compared to the glistening bald pate of Rudy Richter, whom I was still to meet, broke into a broad grin. "Who told you that?" he asked. "I heard that one of the toboggan boys was still around," I explained, "and I figured it might be you or Rudolph Richter." "Do you know Rudy?" he asked. "Not yet," I explained. "It's just that he wrote me a note to come see him about the same day you did." That was when Joe Brennan laughed heartily and called Rudy Richter a rascal. "I had no idea he was going to write you," he said. That was when I proposed that Joe and I might make a surprise call.

Joe responded with delight, but before we had left his house on Argyle Avenue he told me something more. "Sure, I was a toboggan boy," he added, allowing his memories to go tumbling back through the years with a pleasure that was obvious. "I was employed as a toboggan boy, as they called us, by Dr. Jules Levy, an Orange dentist who was a member of the club. My duties consisted of pulling the toboggan up the hill after each trip down the slide. The boys walked down to the foot of the hill to pick up the toboggans, but when all of Dr. Levy's guests did not attend, I was permitted to ride down with the party. Having lived all of my seventy-eight years in the Orange Valley within a mile of the site of the slide, I am as familiar with the territory as it was then as I am with the way things are now."

On our way across the street I found myself hoping that I would be as vigorous and as hearty as Joe Brennan when, *Deo volente,* I am seventy-eight. Soft-spoken and filled with good humor, Joe said as we approached Rudy's door that he was "a mere youngster of sixty-seven."

When Rudolph Richter came to the door, I explained the situation and Joe Brennan stood behind me, laughing as usual. When we had settled ourselves in the warm comfortable house, Rudy said:

"Joe likes to josh me that he remembers more than I do—but that's not my fault. You see, I was born about four blocks from where the toboggan slide was. As a youngster I remember seeing it in action, although Joe Brennan thinks I don't. 'The Toboggan House' still is standing at the corner of Hazel Avenue and Valley Road—Valley Road runs the length of the foot of Orange Mountains and is only a block from Freeman Street; we'll have to go see the old place. It's a kind of apartment now.

"I remember standing at the foot of the slide and seeing the sleds come up the slight incline on the piles of straw that were placed there to slow them up. I remember seeing older boys"—at this point Rudy gave Joe a knowing look—"pulling and carrying the sleds back up the hill after the riders in their fancy clothes came speeding down. No one carried his own sled back when he could get someone else to do it for a few cents.

"And I remember, too, that the chute was made of wood, with sloping sides about a foot high. When there was not enough snow for the slide, water was sprinkled so that ice would form and coat the wooden trough. I remember the story, and have heard it many times, of the wife of a prominent physician who rode down the chute on her bicycle. She was the talk of the town, inasmuch as everybody knew her."

"She was fined for it, too," Joe Brennan cut in. "How long was the slide?" he repeated my question which almost had been lost. "Oh, about fifteen hundred feet, I guess."

Rudy Richter expressed the opinion that Joe Brennan had been chosen as a toboggan boy because of his size. "No," Joe replied to that, "I don't think so. I was just one of the boys standing around waiting for a job like that, the way boys used to stand around at the country clubs, and one of the members called to me. 'You there,' he said, 'you big fellow, carry up this sled.' And I did. As I told you, I sometimes rode the toboggans, but when I did I was told to sit up front where I could break the full cut of the wind.

"Come to think of it, 'The Toboggan House' had all kinds of other names. They even called it 'The Incubator' because, I suppose, it looked just like one, even before they began changing it. There were some who called it, for some reason, 'The House of All Nations.' They didn't use boys to carry the toboggans up all the time; after a while some horses were pressed into service. And, oh yes, there were little standpipes, like, built beside the chute, filled with water, so that when the snow began to go, water could be tossed in to freeze and make the slide just like glass. Fast? Sure it was. We figured sleds used to make the whole length in thirty seconds."

Reluctantly I left the companions of a lifetime still chat-

Orange Toboggan boys of old—Joe Brennan and Rudy Richter—matched memories of days when they hauled toboggans to the top of the chute.

tering about a variety of unrelated things, memories associated only because remembering the toboggan had brought them back. In fact, they were enjoying it all so obviously when I saw them last that I said my good-byes as unobtrusively as I could and all but tiptoed away. In the hall, as I went, I heard snatches of laughter over how men and women who rode the sleds liked to tumble out, all of a heap, at the bottom of the chute; the ways in which Dr. Levy persistently spurned patients who asked for painkillers; the ways boys of yesterday tunneled under fences to steal apples in the Oranges before caretakers sometimes snared them with long bull whips, intent on locking them in barns until after it was dark.

The Orange Toboggan had emerged with its regional stories which, although the neighborhood once had been known mainly as an early American center for the processing of leather and the making of headgear, were by this time more than talk through anyone's hat.

Quite naturally, until very late in 1962, the making of wampum, used by the Indians as ornamentation, jewelry, and money, was almost synonymous in New Jersey, at least in the associations of many of us, with Park Ridge and the late John C. Storms. That was why I asked Jim Ransom to join me and Charles Anderson, of the Pascack Historical Society, at its museum, a church when I saw it first. I wanted to see what John had collected there, particularly in the light of word of the uncovering of an even earlier wampum center at Goffle. Until then, I had not noticed the all but buried reference Tom Gordon had made to it in his *Gazetteer*. He wrote: "Goffle Brook rises in Franklin t-ship, Bergen co., about a mile and a half E. of Hohokus and flows by a southerly course of five miles through Saddle river t-ship, to the Passaic. It is a rapid, steady stream, giving motion to several cotton mills at Godwinsville. About 1½ miles above its mouth is a small hamlet called Goffle, containing 5 or 6 farm dwellings." Reading the surprise paragraph, I remembered how John Storms used to sputter like a squib when he saw Hohokus spelled Ho-Ho-Kus, as if the world would fall apart because of the variation.

Godwinsville was still on the Beers *Atlas* map of 1872, north of Paterson and Hawthorne and south of both Godwinsville and Wortendyke station. However, it was more than the name, Goffle, or even a place where wampum had been made, that summoned me northward. Even more odd was the fact that lies in the stray "clue" John W. Barber and Henry Howe inserted by appending paragraphs devoted to Bergen's Franklin Township, a very full explanation of the manufacture of "Wampum, or Indian money . . . to the present day (1844) made in this country. . . ." To John Storms—and to most of us—this meant the processes used in the making of wampum at Pascack, or Park Ridge.

John Storms was devoted to his artifacts and relics and all that he could learn about them in ways that were often unique. Through him, principally, the wampum machine of the Campbells was rescued and placed on view with a variety of other exhibits at Park Ridge. Through him, many learned much more of the region in which they lived than they would have through any other source—however overcredulous or naïve he may have been on occasion. A gentleman of the old school, he went back to work as a watchman long after he should have been working at all, to pay a debt saddled upon him when a friend defaulted on a note. I, for one, shall never forget him.

There is no reference, specifically, to Goffle in the *Historical Collections*. Many of us had been thrown off center because of that, I suppose, but further, by the place chosen for a most illuminating explanation of the methods of making wampum—under a description of Bergen's Franklin Township and its principal "localities," listed as Paramus, Hohokus, New Prospect, and Hopper's. This exposition followed immediately:

"*Wampum,* or Indian money, is to the present day made in this county, and sold to the Indian traders of the far west. It has been manufactured, by the females in this region, from very early times for the Indians; and as everything connected with this interesting race is destined, at no distant period, to exist only in history, we annex a description of the manufacture.

"The wampum is made from the thick and blue part of sea-clamshells. The process is simple, but requires a skill only attained by long practice. The intense hardness and brittleness of the material render it impossible to produce the article by machinery alone. It is done by wearing or grinding the shell. The first process is to split off the thin part with a light sharp hammer. Then it is clamped in the sawed crevice of a slender stick, held in both hands, and ground smooth on a grindstone, until formed into an eight-sided figure, of about an inch in length and nearly half an inch in diameter; when it is ready for boring. The shell then is inserted into another piece of wood, sawed similarly to the above, but fastened firmly to a bench of the size of a common stand. One part of the wood projects over the bench, at the end of which hangs a weight, causing the sawed orifice to close firmly upon the shell inserted on its under side, and to hold it firmly, as in a vise, ready for drilling. The drill is made from an untempered handsaw. The operator grinds the drill to a proper shape, and tempers it in the flame of a candle. A rude ring, with a groove on its circumference, is put on it; around which the operator (seated in front of the fastened shell) curls the string of a common hand-bow. The boring commences, by nicely adjusting the point of the drill to the center of the shell; while the other end is braced against a steel plate, on the breast of the operator. About every other sweep of the bow, the drill is dexterously drawn out, cleaned of the shelly particles by the thumb and finger, above which drops of water from a vessel fall down and cool the drill; which is still kept revolving, by use of the bow with the other hand, the same as though it were in the shell. This operation of boring is the most difficult of all, the peculiar motion of the drill rendering it hard for the breast; yet it is performed with a rapidity and grace interesting to witness. Peculiar care is observed, lest the shell burst from heat caused by friction. When bored half way, the wampum is reversed, and the same operation repeated. The next process is the finishing. A wire, about twelve inches long, is fastened at one end of the bench. Under and parallel to the wire is a grindstone, fluted on its circumference, hung a little out of the centre, so as to be turned with a treadle moved by the foot. The left hand grasps the end of the wire, on which are strung the wampum, and, as it were, wraps the beads around the fluted or hollow circumference of the grindstone. While the grindstone is revolving, the beads are held down on it, and turned around by a flat piece of wood held in the right hand, and by the grinding soon become round and smooth. From five to ten strings are a day's work for a female. They are sold to the country merchants for twelve and a half cents a string, always command cash, and constitute the support of many poor and worthy families."

There is no indication in this very complete account that a machine had been devised anywhere for even a part of the delicate operation, and if the Campbells or their antecedents had one going in Pascack, the Park Ridge of those days, some note, certainly, would have been made of it. At the same time, this is the first time I remember any record being made of many families being involved, at least in New Jersey.

"This collection of wampum," reads one of the attested statements Jim Ransom entrusted to me when the Goffle story became known, "was found after the excavation of the remains of a wampum factory in 1916 by Carl F. Schondorf. This wampum factory stood on the estate of Peter Meyer on Goffle Hill, Hawthorne, north of Paterson. This was an eight-acre farm. The wampum site on the farm lies about fifty feet this side of the Passaic boundary line and about three hundred yards west of Goffle Road on elevated ground.

"The wampum factory was operated by a Dutch family,

named Stoltz—a Mr. Johannes Stoltz or Stolts. According to the number of beds and clamshell fragments found on this site, it is probably one of the largest and oldest wampum manufacturing sites in New Jersey. The manufacture of wampum beads by the Stoltz family had been carried on for a great many years prior to the Revolution, perhaps from about 1700 to 1770, according to a letter now in the possession of Mr. Alfred Ronck, of Ramsey. This letter was the key to the finding of this wampum site. It was through this letter that the site was discovered.

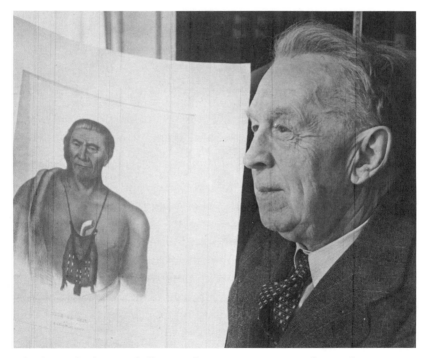

The late Charles A. Philhower, for many years a teacher and supervisor of schools in Westfield, was also celebrated as an authority on Indians in New Jersey, Indian artifacts, and New Jersey lore, especially that in the area of Sussex County. An avid collector of rare books, he gave much of his collection to Trenton State College and Rutgers University.

"About the year 1900 Mr. Ronck attended a 'vendoo' sale of furniture in the village of Suffern, New York. At this sale he purchased a dresser, and in the drawer of this table were found some old papers, one of which was a letter that had been sent to Mr. Johannes Stoltz. It was dated, I believe, 1768, Long Island. The letter read:

" 'I am sending you today 17 Wampum clamshells by'—there is a long blank here. 'They are picked shells. Your obedient servant (signed) C. Ackerson.' . . ." Jim Ransom showed me this letter.

It is apparent that the remainder of the detailed account was written by Carl F. Schondorf, who subsequently undertook the locating of the Goffle site and, after that, the careful excavations that were made. Referring to the modest but energetic Mr. Ackerson, he said:

"The person who carried these shells to the Stoltz cabin had to foot it all the way from Long Island to Goffle Hill, perhaps two days in the journey. North Paterson at that time was called 'Small Lots.' Afterward it became Hopperstown and now is Hawthorne. . . .

"Mr. Ronck knew that if he could find one of the descendants of the Stoltz family, he would be able to locate the wampum site, but it was not until about fifteen years later that an elderly man, John Hopper, came to light in Ramsey. Mr. Hopper then was ninety-three and in possession of a very good memory. He told Mr. Ronck he remembered the Stoltz family when he was a boy. He said his father bought the Stoltz farm and occupied it. He said that he remembered, when a boy of nine, his father ploughing along a stone wall and, after a rain shower, he went out and picked up thirty-five wampum beads.

"About a year ago," read Carl Schondorf's record, of which Jim Ransom had a copy, "in September, 1916, Mr. Ronck and I again visited Mr. Hopper at his grandchildren's farm in Ramsey. On this occasion he offered to drive (horse and rig) us to

Hawthorne and show us the spot where he found the beads eighty-five years before. Mr. Hopper was ninety-four and he still had a wonderful memory.

"The three of us started out, via horse and buggy. In about one hour's time this venerable old man took us to the exact spot where the discovery of wampum took place. He told the writer he remembered when his father took possession of the place—a log cabin or Indian hut had stood near the spot where the wampum was found. After Mr. Hopper took us to where the log cabin had stood, we began to dig and in less than ten minutes we had found evidence of the wampum factory. The next day I commenced excavations alone and worked on the site nearly every day for a period of two months, carefully excavating and sieving all the soil.

"Over a wagon load of clamshells came out and between five thousand and six thousand beads; seven hundred of these beads I turned over to Mr. Ronck for the Bergen County Historical Society. I worked and dug in an area twenty-five feet in diameter and about two feet deep. The whole aspect of the place appeared to be a shell-heap, the dumps of the sweepings of the factory. However, there must have been a log floor in the hut and the sweepings may have been forced through the crevices in the logs. I desire here to state that this is the first and the only wampum site of its kind discovered and excavated in New Jersey, New York, Pennsylvania, Connecticut, and the whole Atlantic Seaboard."

This statement covers, surely, considerable territory, and it continues: "This collection is very unique and is of great historical value. No museum in the world has anything like it. The collection is identified by the City of Paterson. It does great credit to our city and should be preserved permanently in the Paterson Museum.

"Wampum beads were made from the white, blue, and purple hearts of the clamshell, made into strings with native hemp and woven into belts, given to the whites to commemorate treaties. A great deal of the wampum was obtained by the Indians at trading posts. The same wampum beads often served serveral purposes, beads made into belts or other articles by the Indians were presented to the French and British in commendation of treaties and various agreements, and later when the officers wished to bestow something on the Indians, they had the beads restrung in wampum of a different form and gave them back again.

"The wampum made by Mr. Stoltz was traded at the Pascack trading post. . . . This was known as the John Jacob Astor Trading Post, located at Pascack (now Park Ridge), Bergen County, New Jersey. The trading post, originally an old blockhouse, was built in 1697 for defense against Indian raids, and later, at the time of the Revolution in 1777, was used as a fort by Colonel Ackerson, for protection against the British and Tories. It is claimed that John Jacob Astor laid the foundation of his great wealth through the wampum trade carried on at Pascack."

I had seen photographs of some of the buildings clustered in the operation of the Campbells at Park Ridge, tipped by hand into the little book that the late John Storms had put together all by himself titled, as I have told you, *The Story of Wampum*. One, I remembered, was a drawing of the wampum-making Campbell brothers—James, John, David, and Abram—at work at their cleverly devised machines in the "mill" at Pascack, a frame structure abandoned and falling apart in 1900. Re-reading his text, I am more certain than ever that John knew nothing of the operation on Goffle Hill, any more than did John Barber in the early 1800s. For, in another letter ostensibly written by Carl Schondorf and copied by Jim Ransom, it is stated, "The art in shell as practiced by the wampum-makers is not revealed in thrown-away specimens but in finished ones . . . delivered to the Indians by the traders. . . ." He had just said that there was nothing much to show where the excavations had been made, and he added, "I think

it was Mr. Barber who went to the Campbell's in about 1843
and visited the old wampum factory and his interesting story
of how wampum was made appears in his *Collections of New
Jersey*." I have given you this account, and the fact that John
Barber went to Pascack rather than Goffle would indicate that
the Goffle chapter had been closed even in his time.

"So I suppose," I remarked to Jim Ransom that day in Westwood and Park Ridge, "that with all the development that has
come to Bergen, there is even less to be found of the Goffle
wampum site now."

"Nothing at all," Jim replied. "You'd waste your time in going
over there."

And that was when he brought out, for the first time to my
knowledge, an ancient painting, with the remark that was
something like "Here's something I found *that you haven't
seen*." I concluded that this was all I or any of us ever would
see of where the Goffle wampum was made—and how wrong
I was. It was a painting, made by a contemporary artist, of
where Pascack wampum was manufactured by the Campbells
of Park Ridge, the Pascack of long ago.

Chapter XII

THE PUZZLE OF WANTAGE

I confess that I have been seeking, intermittently through the years, some completely convincing explanation of the name Wantage. The search began on a sunny day in Sussex County long ago when I wondered about a line on a variety of tombstones, *"Died in Wantage."* Once I was told that there was a stone on which an unwary stonecutter had run out of space so that the inscription became *"Died in Want."* I regret to tell you that I never have found it.

Wantage, in the minds of the majority, is a Sussex County township, described in 1844 as eleven miles long and seven miles across. However, on Sussex County maps as well as on those kept reasonably up to date by gasoline purveyors, it also is a place, maintaining about the same importance as Finley gave it on his map of 1834, howbeit in what seems to be a different location. Finley's Wantage was on the road up and out of Augusta. More modern charts have moved it not very far from the border of New York State. Arriving by careful calculations on the latter location, I was assured by an occupant of one of the three or four houses that this was Vernon. Vernon is a town and township at least five or six miles away, even as the most retarded crow would fly.

"This is Wantage," friendly people told me—in Colesville, in Beemerville, and even down in Pellettown, and at last I think I know why, even though Pellettown is across the line in Frankford Township. To many, Wantage never was a place but rather, a region. It was not until I talked with George Demarest in 1963 in a Sussex County blueberry patch, far from the blueberry country I knew, that I learned that Wantage

was a place and that once there had been a station there on the Lehigh and New England Railroad. "But by now," George added, "even the railroad is torn up."

It became a clue-hunt as fascinating as Ong's Hat had provided. "Was there a town called Wantage?" I asked. If there was not, why was its name continued on travel maps of today? Where did the name come from, in connection with either the Sussex township or the town? Was it, as the late Charles Alpaugh Philhower maintained, of Indian origin? Or was there, by some chance, a relationship between the Wantages in New Jersey and the Wantage in England from where, suddenly, I began receiving letters? The Indian theory conflicted with the fact that there was a Wantage, well established in Berkshire, England, in 400 A.D.

I turned to familiar pages and discovered, disconcertingly, that although Wantage was on the Finley map of the Gordon *Gazetteer* of 1834, and although Tom himself had devoted considerable space to Wantage, the township bounded on the north by the State of New York, there was no listing of a village of that name. John W. Barber and Henry Howe, in giving so much space to Wantage, again the township, ten years later that the publisher was compelled to resort to small type, found no room for even a chance reference to Wantage, the town. Deckertown, now Sussex; Beemersville, now Beemerville, and The Clove took all the honors.

It was on January 7, 1844, that the Reverend Peter Kanouse, speaking in the Second Presbyterian Church of Wantage, poured out a sermon which, I feel sure, used up about two hours and possibly three. I mention this for the benefit of those churchgoers who are heard in frequent complaint if the discourse of the parson of today goes beyond fifteen or twenty minutes. Beyond that, however, there is evidence that this sermon was as exhaustive as it was exhausting. The Reverend Peter called it *An Historical Sermon* on the title page of the printed version published within a year in New York and said further that it was designed "as a memorial to the inhabitants of Wantage," containing an account of the first emigrants, "their pedigree, dangers, deliverances, habits, religion, means of instruction, increase, improvements, and the present state of society among their descendants."

Peter's sermon makes up a small volume of some sixty-six pages, with almost as many remaining curiously blank. The parson, beginning with a text that uses up most of the Forty-eighth Psalm, offers no clue as to where the name Wantage came from, nor does he reveal that the Second Presbyterian Church in which he was preaching had absorbed the congregation of the Congregational Church of Wantage and Frankford, established in 1744 and known as "The Beemer Meeting-House," the very church in which he spoke.

It became obvious almost at once that the Wantage of which Parson Kanouse was speaking is still the township in Sussex, reaching up through the rolling country of the valley of the Clove River, even though he refers recurrently to it as a "town" in the New England way. Be that as it may, I must stress the fact that inquiries along the Sussex roadsides may bring you to at least three villages, as they did me, in which people, meaning to be helpful, tell you that they *are* in Wantage—a huddle of houses and other buildings beside an abandoned railroad right-of-way called Pellettown; Colesville, by now Coleville, and even Beemersville, now Beemerville. Belatedly, I have discovered that Wantage Township is what is meant and that if any of the maps I have seen were drawn with accuracy in their time, Wantage, the hamlet, has moved around as much as any of Dr. Philhower's Indians.

Most inhabitants of Pellettown said that this had been Pellettown as long as they knew, although far more recently a friend of Ben Hill wrote him at his home in Walnut Valley asking him to tell me why Pellettown was not on the Beers *Atlas* map. "When the railroad came through," an initialed

note read, "the farmers refused to sell any of their land unless they were given a station. This station was Ackerson, a
name still on the map, but most stops," I was assured, "were
made at the creamery crossing, and this became Pellettown
because the Pelletts ran the creamery. Until then the name
had been Papakating." Papakating is still the name of the river
(or creek) there, and Mamakating is the name of the valley
through which it flows, adding a warm "family touch" in a
land frequently frigid and filled with snow when the rest of
New Jersey is almost warm.

Sure enough, on many an older map Pellettown is as conspicuous by its absence as are Colesville, Clove Post Office,
Libertyville, and Lewisburg by their continued presence. Old
Deckertown became Sussex long ago, adding confusion when
the older name should have been retained to honor Peter
Decker, the first pioneer of Sussex to come over the Blue
Mountain in search of new sights and sounds in 1734. The
confusionists with their persistent fever for duplicating names
or providing meaningless substitutes are first cousins of the
demolitionists who feel a sense of instability in anything that
lasts. It is a paradox. Nowadays they must tear down and
bulldoze away before they build anything up.

"As to the time when the Township of Wantage began to
be inhabited by the whites," said Parson Kanouse before a
congregation which, I hope, had brought lunches along, "and
who the first families were that removed within our borders,
no precise account can be given. An approximation of the
truth is all that can be attempted. . . ." This, please remember, was something of an admission from a man whose family
name is remembered on a mountain not far away.

Some additional passages from a Port Jervis, New York,
letter that accompanied lines painstakingly copied from a
damaged copy of the *Historical Collections* and others from
the *Historical Directory of Sussex County*, published in 1878,
will be eventually woven into a pattern with a phrase or two

from a more recent guidebook's compilations. But now we must listen to Parson Peter.

"That there were no civilized men here more than one hundred and ten years ago I cannot affirm," he went on, "though it is extremely improbable that there were. An accident, however, related by one of our respectable citizens, Mr. Joel Crowell, will at least be a gratifying anecdote, and it may possibly reflect some light upon a lost date. Sixty-five years ago"—that would have taken the area back to the late 1700's—"Mr. Crowell cut a white oak tree of about two feet in diameter; and upon opening it, two distinct marks of an axe were found at the heart, made there when young, and probably by some straggling white man. The growth of the tree—say one hundred and forty layers or rings—and the time of the discovery by Mr. C. would carry us back not far from two hundred years, when the wounds were inflicted. As this date stretches far beyond any other well-ascertained period, when the first settlement of the town"—he meant township—"commenced, no reliance can be placed upon it. . . ." Which produces two questions: Why did the Parson bring it up, and, could it have been an Indian who slashed at the tree?

"One hundred years ago Peter Decker erected the first house in Deckertown," he went on. "About the same time, or soon after, some notices are found of other families. . . ." These were "a Mr. Winfield and a Mr. Cortwright, near the mountain, and a Mrs. Tisworth in the Clove. These families, it is probable, were the first that settled within our borders," said Peter, and judging from the number of grave markers bearing these names in the area, he was more than right. The parson picked up these and other disclosures from the diary of David Brainerd, pioneer missionary to the Indians, who had put the region down as "a desolate and hideous country." For David it was a land through which he wandered "over rocks and mountains, down hideous steeps, through swamps, and most dreadful and dangerous places. . . ."

The oldest inhabitants, Parson Peter concluded further on, came from somewhere over Kittatinny (Kittany) Mountain. Among these were the Middaughs, Cuddabachs, Westbrooks, Wilsons, and Adamses, who, the preacher declared, were surely in Wantage as early as there were families at Forks of the Delaware, later Carpenter's Point. Peter gave assurance that seventy years before the time in which he was speaking Deckertown was a place with but three houses, one more house than Wantage could claim if you depend on dots that presumably denote houses on the Finley map. Ten years earlier there had been a mere footpath, marked with blazed trees down from Unionville, New York. "And it is rumored," he added, "that a little previous to the last date, some few families from this region carried their grain, to be floured for family use, to the grist mill at Newburgh, a distance of forty miles at the least reckoning"—one way, of course.

By 1780 there were no more than seventy families in the "town" called Wantage. In the front ranks of these, Peter Kanouse put Wykers (Wykerstown is still on the road to Branchville), Beemers (Beemertown, or Beemerstown, with two graveyards to attest its age is down from the challenging slopes of Sunrise Mountain), Binks, Koykindalls, and Crowells. The second generation doubled the ranks, and the third more than tripled them, with Wintermutes sharing with Baxters, or Backsters, and the Coles (Colesville can still claim the charm of another world on the road from Sussex to High Point) rubbing friendly shoulders with the Rosencrantzes.

"The early emigrants," said the parson, "comprising the series of settlements alluded to, are, with few exceptions, either of Dutch or French origin, as their names sufficiently indicate." What of the Westbrooks, Wilsons, Adamses, Baxters, Crowells, and Coles? Parson Kanouse allows such a question to hang in the air as he points out that a few German families moved into Wantage directly from their native land. A few more had had their fill of salt air and spiritual fog around Plymouth and Cape

Cod and had hurried inland to the mountains, just as early shore dwellers were to do in a much later time when the first mass appearance of the clan called "summer people" made itself manifest. Undaunted, they crossed one rocky ridge after another, but the fusion of French, Dutch, German, and English stock merely served as a platform from which Peter Kanouse could sound off as a rabid partisan, and so I see no point in quoting him here.

However, after a reasonable skip, I must agree with Peter that all these pioneers had basic religious tenets sufficiently common to hold them together in a land that drove the fainthearted to drink, or at least back on their heels. If the parson ladled out as much church history as his little book, based on a sermon, would indicate, he was either displaying his own kind of erudition or seeking a way to put his flock to sleep before he aroused them with a picture of Wantage as a wicked land.

Under a sub-heading, "The Moral History of the Town," the preacher turned what he labeled "the blackest page in our history." I am quite sure no real estate man of the neighborhood, purveying what I must assure you before the floods come to make at least a watery border remains the most beautiful mountain country in all New Jersey, will give even one ear. For the Parson goes on:

"Commencing as early as the year, 1770, there was but little preaching in Wantage. . . . The town was regarded as missionary ground and, as such, it began to be occupied by the different denominations among us, but at such intervals of preaching as scarcely to give the Gospel any unfluence upon the community. . . . The Sabbath was desecrated by visiting, fishing, hunting, and other sports. . . ." Personally, I never have regarded visiting as one of the sports. "About fifty years ago commenced horse-racing, for which this region soon became notorious. To this was added gambling, and, soon after, drunkenness, counterfeiting, fighting, litigations, and many kindred vices, which spontaneously sprang up and flourished as in a hot-bed.

"Hitherto distilled liquors had been imported among us, in small quantities, from distant places, by private individuals, for medicinal purposes. But now the flood-gates were thrown open, and the fiery tide began to flow. At the close of the [Revolutionary] War, articles of merchandise were introduced, and with them strong drink was also introduced into the town. . . ." Township was meant once again as he went on:

"In 1783, three stores opened, and sold the liquid poison. And the number of stores continued, from this period, to increase with the population until, in 1833, there were thirteen stores" and "tavern-keeping" began. Taverns "were in like manner multiplied until there were, in one period, about one tavern for every two hundred and fifty souls in the township. . . ."

"A race soon appeared, as if the fabled Gorgon teeth had been sowed broadcast over the region—a Cycloptic race. Gambling, swearing, lying, cheating, horse-racing, balls, riots, and litigations (were) followed in their train by a company of duns, constables, and sheriffs; and as the fruits of the whole, bankruptcies, broken hearts, diseases, suicides, and premature deaths. Previous to the year, 1833, there had been, in the twelve taverns that existed in that period, thirty-five tavern-keepers, fifteen of whom became intemperate, and to thirty of them it had been an unprofitable business. . . ." I cannot help but wonder who kept Parson Kanouse's statistics and if they included the thought that some publicans imbibed most of their profits or that there were just too many taverns for likely customers, including transients, in the neighborhood.

Then, just as you begin to see Peter's hearers marching up a sawdust trail, at least by the next revival, the preacher does an about-face and admits bluntly that there *was* "a brighter side of the picture." This came, of course, "when the cause of temperance began to make a decided impression on the region."

Peter after a time revealed that there was an interval when you could have purchased the whole of the township for seven hundred dollars. "It is said that all the land in the Clove was once offered for thirty dollars," he said, and there the name, "The Clove," drops in again—a postal town as late as the 1870's.

Writing a commendable brochure, *The Clove and Its Valley,* at the house in which she was born on Clove Road, Staten Island, Dorothy Valentine Smith has pointed out that *Het Kloven* was the Dutch name for "the Cleft"; hence, the early Dutch of at least New Jersey and New York took it with them to designate natural ways of travel—and flight. This is true at the top of Bergen and Sussex Counties. I suppose this must be taken for granted in these New Jersey areas, for no one there ever thought it important enough to mention it on any of my regional journeys in the vicinity.

Mark you well that even in his time Peter Kanouse proclaimed that the Jerseyan dairy industry had its beginnings in Wantage. "The dairy business," he said, in a passage perhaps inserted after the sermon had been given in its original form, "now carried on to its present state, commenced in this town" —township—"about twenty or thirty years ago. . . ." Thereafter he waxes poetic, neatly mixing his metaphors, and returning among verbal roses and marble inscriptions, he let loose with some of the piousness that rivaled the peaks of his ringing phrases. But, for all that, Wantage remained a curious name, and so I show you quickly the directory for 1878 which, among many other things, underscores the emerging of Pellettown from Papakating, without the explanation offered by Ben Hill's friend in Newton.

"Wantage," says the directory, "is the largest township in the county. It is bounded north by Orange County, New York, south by Frankford, Lafayette and Hardyston, which are separated from it by the Wallkill, and west by Montague"—the latter but recently described to me as a region, more than a place, but even so likely to maintain a lonely height above the rising waters of the coming reservoirs. Concerning Clove Church, on the Clove Brook which once was the Deep Clove Brook, the directory says that in 1787 "a Reformed Dutch Church was organized and a church named Clove Church, from the valley in which it was built, the first pastor being the Reverend Elias Benschotten," which also has been spelled Ben Schotten and Benschooten. James P. Snell, writing in 1881, says that it was the Reverend Elias who organized the church under the Brunswick Classis—that is the Brunswick district governing body in 1788. In 1818 it became the First Presbyterian Church of Wantage, a name it still maintains in a shaded dell that reaches into the present from an ageless past.

It was from Master Snell that I learned something more of the background of Peter Kanouse. Peter succeeded the Reverend Edward Allen "as pastor of the Wantage Church, the mother of the three churches in that township—Wantage, Beemerville, and Deckertown. . . ." Here, too, there would seem to be the hint that Wantage was town as well as township, but I doubt if this is what was meant inasmuch as the station that was Wantage was miles away. Some have assured me, of course, that Wantage could have been a railroad name dropped there for convenience or to cope with some special argument, but here I must fall back on the location of Wantage, a village of at least three houses on Finley's map of 1834.

Learning his trade as a blacksmith, Peter worked first at a smithy in Rockaway, assisted the Reverend Barnabas King as an elder and then studied for the ministry. After ordination, he became so effective at Clove Church that he was called to be pastor of the Free Presbyterian Church in Newark, but he soon returned to the Second Presbyterian Church in Beemerville. As you might suspect, Peter's specialty was revivals,

This house, now in ruins, was used as a pioneer fort against Indian raiders in Sussex County. For a time a Boy Scout retreat, it was embellished with a fake totem pole, made of cement and gaily colored.

and it has been said that many a pioneer of the early West traced his "conversion" to the words of Peter Kanouse.

There are two cemeteries within sight of the Clove Church, one clearly the oldest and traditionally the site of the church when it was first on the other side of the road, guarded by an ancient oak along an old stone fence, and in comparison to the second site, smaller and less crowded. Not many yards away, down the hill towards Sussex, is what the New Jersey volume of the *American Guide Series* of 1939 called "an old, one-and-a-half-story stone and frame house, guarded by a frightening totem pole. This structure was one of the Minisink forts, built as a dwelling at the turn of the eighteenth century by a man named Titsworth, son of the founder of Port Jervis and later killed by the Indians. The place was eighty years old when Joseph Brant, the Indian chief from the Mohawk Valley, attacked it in 1781 with a band of Indians and British. It is known locally as Totem Pole; but the pole is probably not authentic. The old house today is a handicraft shop."

For all its history, or tradition, the old fort that became a house (or perhaps a house that also was a fort) had fallen into ruin beyond repair when I last traveled down the Deckertown Road. Only complete restoration would suffice, and it may be that Sussex County historians faced with the prospect of jeopardizing so many of their bronze markers have lost heart. The roof of the old fort, kept intact so long, had fallen in when I was there, and what was left of the stone walls held misshapen, glassless windows like staring eyes. Old timbers in the dooryard and on the rotted floor beside a hearth that had been narrowed down long ago, bore the marks of an adz. It seemed impossible that I had passed that way in the beginning to find the building intact, as fine an example of the pioneer's art of building as ever will be on New Jersey's own Indian frontier. Oddly enough, the spurious totem pole remained, not much of a guard, the contrasting colors of grimacing faces washed almost expressionless by years of weather—down to the basic putty gray of cement.

Recalling what Peter Kanouse had been before his pulpit years, I must include here one legend that concerns a pioneer blacksmith working in the Clove. When Indian marauders came, a Negro who was helping him, assisted him into the chimney over the bellows. As you must know, Indians rarely attacked colored men, and so the courageous helper stood his ground as the intruders prowled around the smithy. After hammering for a time on the anvil, one of the Indians began trying out the bellows, and the servant Pompey shouted, "Stop, stop, stop that *blawmock!*" Blaumock was Dutch for bellows. The Indians went away, and the smith, whose name was Etten, or probably Van Etten, came from hiding. The story goes that he thanked Pompey briefly and went back to work, just like that —although I doubt it.

The late Charles Alpaugh Philhower, who began his teaching near Bissel in Hunterdon County and who retired many years later as supervisor of schools in Westfield, Union County, had gained renown as an authority on Indians in New Jersey during the years between. My old friend who, I always have said, managed to find an Indian behind almost every tree in the state, if not an Indian meaning in almost every place name that bewildered me, used to write me regularly—and I miss his kindly correspondence. This time he said:

"Maybe I can give you some help on the origin of Wantage. Strange to say, it is of Indian origin, as I have known for many years past." There were rarely *if*'s or *and*'s or *but*'s with Charlie. He went on: "It is found at Hempstead, Long Island, where it was the name of an Indian village site at that place. William Beauchamp gives it in his *Place Names of New York,* Bulletin 108, Archaeology 12, Albany, 1907. There it is spelled Wantagh, of which Wantage is a variant. The local pronunciation in Sussex is *Wan*-tage, with a broad 'a,' but in Indian it is Wan-tag, which, according to Indian usage, gives equal stress to each syllable. The Indian name Wantag has been anglicized, making the hard 'g' a soft 'g.'

"The Indians of Long Island and New England began to move to the westward immediately on the advent of the paleface from the east. This movement was greatly heightened during the Mohegan Pequot war with the white men of New England, and the fleeing Indians found sanctuary with the Indians of New Jersey for a time.

"When they moved on to the westward, they left behind with whites who took over land from them New England names such as Pequacock at Lake Hopatcong, Pequannock River, Weequahic, which is a variant of Weequeswick and comes from Connecticut, as well as others. It was left by the

Raritans' name for the Indian village on the site of the old Waverly Fair Grounds on Newark Bay, just south of Weequahick Lake. This is the result of Colonial contacts of the white man and the Indian. The many Indian names are memorials of a noble race."

I have a whole sheaf of correspondence from Dr. Philhower of which some day I hope to make something more permanent than a packet of letters in a folder. I want to do that because there are those who would minimize my friend's knowledge of the Indians of New Jersey, in spite of the state's distribution not long after his death, of a pamphlet by that precise name made up of some of Dr. Philhower's articles. But I must tell you that he did not convince me, completely, in his solution of the name Wantage, either in connection with the township or the elusive and even wandering village in Sussex. Perhaps in this I am too persistent. I had begun to think it must be something like that when D. Nelson Raynor, a newspaperman nearly all his life and an officer of the Minisink Valley Historical Society, told me that he was a native of Long Island and that Wantagh there had been established in his time.

"I am a Long Islander by birth," he said, "having been born at Freeport—Raynortown until 1853—which is about four miles from Wantagh, near Seaford, and I remember when Wantagh was started and became a hamlet on the way to the beaches. It sounds like a Long Island Indian name, somewhat, but I don't recall ever hearing its derivation. The same goes for Wantage in Sussex—I don't remember seeing or hearing of any records as to why it was so named. . . ." This was after I could go back to Charlie Philhower. When Nelson Raynor revealed this, he had been in a position to look into such matters as recording secretary of the historical group in the midst of the mystery, or at least close by, as he was the editor of the *Union-Gazette* in Port Jervis thirty-eight years of the seventy-one he had been part of the profession.

In a letter, he wrote: "I often have wondered where Wantage

(the village) was, as there seemed to be nothing tangible like a settlement and I am still in the dark. But it is like Montague is now. If you came here and asked where Montague was, we could say, just beyond the state line at Tri-States, and about ten miles long. There never was any tangible village of Montague, and it sprawls, actually, all along the River Road and on the Clove Road, a delightful section of rest and peacefulness. It is all on high ground and is about all of the New Jersey side of the Delaware River which won't be flooded by the big dam. The lake at this end will be too shallow for many purposes and will not be taken over for recreation purposes—I hope.

"In our Historical Society rooms I almost accidentally picked up a nearly worn-out history of New Jersey. The first pages were missing, so I can't tell you whose it is. I don't believe you know of it or you would have had Wantage at your fingertips."

I quickly recognized the text, painstakingly copied, as that which appears on the concluding pages of the Barber and Howe *Historical Collections*. When I had expressed my gratitude to my friend in Port Jervis, assuring him that he would have recognized it, too, if the title and earlier pages had not been missing, I told him that quite by chance he had focused my attention on a name that was instantly familiar. Remember the schoolmaster of Log Gaol who, continuing his letters to friends in the South concerning the true identity of the Old Pig Drover, had gone off to teach at the school of the Reverend Clarkson Dunn in Deckertown—William Rankin? Remember that strange letter he wrote, explaining that he would not be able "to attend at Johnsonburg on the present occasion?" The occasion was *merely* the Johnsonburg send-off of Samuel Fulton, the achievement of a goal, the end of a crusade of many years as far as Mr. Rankin was concerned, restoring Samuel to the bosom of his family in his proper identity. I rarely have come upon such humility, such modesty. It was as if William

Rankin were saying, "God knows what I have done—let it go at that."

But it is no less than John W. Barber and Henry Howe who say, in 1844, that the "annexed items, relating to this section of the country," were furnished by William Rankin, the principal of the high-school at Deckertown:

"In the latter part of the 17th century, some Huguenots, or French Protestants, had been exiled to Holland, emigrated to America, and passing up the Hudson river, settled at the mouth of the Wallkill River, near the present site of Kingston. In after years, individuals from this settlement, which was composed of French and Hollanders, in their explorations passed down the Mamakating valley to the Delaware River, and formed a settlement at the mouth of the Navisink. About the year 1740, a man by the name of Peter Decker, a Hollander by descent, passed over the Kittany or Blue Mountain, from the Navisink settlement, in pursuit of good land on which to settle. He descended into the valley, now the town of Wantage, and selecting the place where Deckertown now stands, built a house, probably the first white man's abode in the township. This house stood near the site of the tavern of the present Horace Vibbert, Esq. This Peter Decker, the original pioneer of Wantage, was grandfather to the resent Bowdewine Decker, Esq., of the Clove, and was the predecessor of almost all the large and respectable collection of people of that name now in the township. A short time after Decker, two other individuals of the Navisink settlement also crossed the Blue Mountain in pursuit of tillable land; these were by the name of Winfield and Cortwright. After making diligent search throughout the Wantage valley, they could find, as they supposed, but little land fit for cultivation, exhibiting an instance of the Hollanders' error in judging of the quality of land in a county differing in aspect from [their] own. It seemed these Low Dutch people, on first coming to this country, thought no land worth cultivating but level flats. Winfield selected a spot of about 11 acres on the farm now owned by Thomas I. Ludlam, Esq. This he supposed might be worth clearing for the purpose of growing wheat and corn. Cortwright found 5 acres nearer the mountain, which he thought might pay the labor of cultivation. From this time emigration continued to be made into this valley, and additions to the infant settlement.

"In the year 1770 a few Baptist families from the New England states settled where Hamburg now is, and built the first houses. They were of the names of Hart, Marsh and Southworth. They selected one of their number, a Mr. Marsh, to be their preacher, and thus laid the foundation for the first Baptist church in the county. In 1777, the Rev. Nicholas Cox, from Philadelphia, became the preacher in this Baptist church. Two houses of worship had now been erected, one in Hamburg, and the other at Augusta. In about 1782, the house at Hamburg was taken down and rebuilt on the site where the present Baptist Church now stands. . . .

"During the French and Indian war, a Mr. Crowell, yet living in this township, being about 88 years old, remembers that, when a child, his father was called out in defence of the settlement against the Indians, who were lurking through this then thinly populated region, for the purpose of massacring helpless and unprotected families. His mother was left alone with some small children; in the dark night, as they were preparing to go to bed, suddenly the dog broke out with that peculiar and terrific kind of barking which was but too well-known by the settlers to be caused by the scent of Indians. This venerable old man yet distinctly remembers that moment of thrilling interest, when his mother, 'turning pale as a cloth' (as he expresses it), earnestly urged him, a small boy, to run out into the woods and hide, that he might save his life, for she could not escape with her infant children, but must remain in the house and be murdered with them; but the little boy, refusing to go, clung round his mother's neck in floods of tears, declaring that he would die with her. The Indians, however, through cowardice, or for some other reason, did not approach the house. . . ."

At another time "when the Indians were known to be prowling through the woods with hostile intentions, a settler in the town of Wantage, being in need of provision for his family, ventured into the forest in pursuit of game with his gun and dog. He unfortunately lost his knowledge of courses, and wandered into the woods, until he lost his way and night came on. He crept into a large hollow tree, with his gun and dog. When all were about prepared to go to sleep, the dog became suddenly agitated, and broke forth in violent barking. The man well knew that this unguarded conduct of his fellow-lodger would betray their retreat to all Indians within a mile around. To cut the throat of the dog would be the only effectual barrier to his dangerous indiscretions. But then this would be dishonorable, and not very just; for, although the barking was ill-timed, he knew it was certainly well meant. So he resorted to expostulations and entreaties with the dog, and to hold his mouth shut. At length all became pretty quiet again. Many anxious hours had now passed away in listening to every rustling motion of the surrounding bramble—when suddenly again the dog's every nerve quivered; and as he uttered a loud bark and growl, a most terrific snort of a horse echoed through the gloomy woods. This sent a most thrilling panic through the very souls of the old oak's trembling tenants; for the Indians were known frequently to travel through the forest on horseback. All was fearful expectation and watchful anxiety, till day-break brought relief by exhibiting several horses feeding at a distance on the natural grass of the woods, and enabling the lost wanderers, during the course of the day, to find their way safely home. . . ."

This was William Rankin's contribution to the record of Wantage, made presumably about 1843 or 1844, certainly no earlier than 1840. To it are appended "additional particulars" which include Neapos, Consauls, Winfields, Vananwigens, Wildrichs, Westfalls, Westbrooks, Jobes, Shumars, Deckers, Vanaukens, Fitzworths, and Meddaughs.

I continued to meet and talk with those who, when they said, "We have lived in Wantage nearly all our lives," meant Wantage, the township, no matter where they happened to be in that region of Sussex. I remember reading the impressive epitaph on an even more elaborate stone on the grave of "Doct. Berret Havens" in the old cemetery at Clove, down from Clove Church and across the way, which revealed that he had been born at Sag Harbor, Long Island, and had "settled in Wantage, where he lived a life of industry and integrity; and at his death left a liberal bequest to the Clove Church." But it was not until June, 1960, that I gained anything further, even though I discovered two more cemeteries, one of which bore the name "Wantage Cemetery" on its iron gate—the more memorable because a doorknob had been attached *on the inside*. This was the cemetery to which I returned posthaste after receipt of letters from England postmarked "Wantage, Berks."

These letters were from Sister Penelope, of the Community of St. Mary the Virgin, in a convent of the Church of England in Berkshire. A mere thank you for my review of a book Sister had written, it marked the beginning of a new hunt. I wanted to know something more of the Wantage in England, and Sister Penelope wanted more about the Wantage in New Jersey, especially when I asked her about the old family names and added that there was a Berkshire Valley. It was not too far to the east from Lake Hopatcong. It could not have accommodated an overflow of excursionists or very busy summers when there was little provision for last minute reservations or sudden changes of mind.

When I first wrote to Sister Penelope, she responded with a packet of material. There was an array of picture post cards, one of which showed the market place of the other Wantage, now lined with parking privileges all around and dominated by a statue of King Alfred. Others showed "the Avenue," virtually a leafy hallway through gnarled and ancient trees; SS. Peter and Paul's Parish Church, both interior and exterior, and, of course, the Convent of St. Mary, itself, a sprawling but impressive establishment which serves as the mother house of a community of religious which has branch houses, schools, homes for women, and retreats for the aged in England, India, and South Africa.

Here are some of the pertinent passages in Sister's letters: "I don't know the meaning of the name Wantage, but it is indubitably Saxon. You find it spelled variously in ancient sources as Waneting, Wanating, Wantingh, and so on. A place in the area called Wanting is said to mean 'Brian's Fee'—'fee'

The name and even the location of Wantage are puzzling. Some, like the late Dr. Charles A. Philhower, defend an Indian derivation, as found in Wantagh. Others argue that the name is for Wantage in England. Here is one Wantage cemetery that I found.

in this context means 'inherited estate.' The one great certain thing about our Wantage is that King Alfred the Great was born here in 849. We are passing proud to have his statue in the Market Place.

"I wonder if the inhabitants of the Wantage in New Jersey ever have read the historical novel, *Alfred the King* by Patry Williams. If not, I'm sure they would enjoy it. I wonder, too, if they have any records of who it was that gave their place that name—presumably someone from Wantage here—but who and when? This Wantage is a new countrytown, as we say— the population has increased a lot since the Atomic Research Station started at Harwell.

"Oh yes—some of the names of the old Wantage district families are Kent, Belcher, Seymour, and Bedford. Stamp and Clement used to be, but I am not sure that there are any left now. There was an old monastic foundation here affiliated with the Abbey of Bec in Normandy. . . ."

I thanked Sister by return airmail, telling her that without knowing it she had assigned me to seek out the oldest burial places in Wantage Township once again. However, thus far after repeated new invasions I have found no Kents, Belchers, Seymours, or Bedfords. This does not necessarily prove any- thing at this point. The earliest graves in Sussex were marked with fieldstones, many without initials and, beyond that, fre- quently in obscure family plots. Now I have despatched a list of names, in contrast with those of the pioneer Dutch and early Germans, to Sister Penelope: Nancy Compton, who owned the first mill in Beemerville; William Cole, for whom Coleville or Colesville was named; Levi Deavenport or Davenport; West- brooks; Winfields; Cortrights or Courtwrights; Westfalls; and Fitzworths (although I have been assured that Fitzworth is a misspelling of Titsworth or Tietsworth).

Returning to the Wantage still indicated on today's travel maps, I found matters much as they had been years before, but with no one now to say that this was Vernon. The single track of the Lehigh and New England Railroad, once the New Jersey Midland, had been taken up and the ties tossed aside in the ditches that had run originally beside the rails. The right of way was etched by snow, and an area where a station could have been was empty. The road, virtually private for the owners of the huddle of houses, was precisely half a mile in from the way up Pochuck Mountain to Glenwood, and beyond the houses there was nothing more. A gate had been erected across the roadbed.

At the Pellettown that once was Papakating the ties had been thrown clear in much the same way along the old right of way, except for the sections where removal would have interrupted traffic on the road up from Newton to Sussex. Suddenly I was startled, and then haunted, by the observation that *this* Wantage, where a station on the Lehigh and New England had been, was not the Wantage indicated by Finley's map of 1834 or even the travel maps of recent years. Finley's Wantage was on the road up and out of Augusta. More modern charts had apparently moved it not very far from the New Jersey-New York border. Were the map-makers at fault? How could a town, or village, or hamlet, be moved around like that, no matter what the source and meaning of its name?

I was thrown off completely one day when I was casually thumbing through the pages of Part VII of the *Industries of New Jersey*, covering Morris, Hunterdon, Warren, and Sussex Counties. The accompanying list of cities, towns, and post offices of New Jersey, a gazetteer of 1883, included these two lines: "Wantage (Sussex co.), a hamlet 1 mile n. of Deckertown." This indicated that there was always a village or hamlet called Wantage in addition to the township, but that it certainly "got around"—perhaps with the help of those who make maps, or those who set up and name railroad stations, or those who have liked the sound of the name, no matter what its history.

Chapter XIII

BEYOND GREAT-GRANDFATHER

You might put it this way: I have discovered my great-grandfather. More than that, although he may not know it, he led me to Alexander Hamilton, the "Great Duel," and finally set me to wandering up the Palisades. This, I will admit, is a strange admission from one who has protested to so many that folklore is one thing and family trees are another; for rarely, if ever, do the two combine. The lore of the folk develops, of course, as history is handed down from one generation to another, but personalities involved sometimes become confused as to their own importance and that of the tales they tell.

The rule has its variants here, as you will see, because my great-grandfather, Abraham Clark, became a part of Jerseyan folklore in only an accidental way. Even so, he plunged me into the fading memories of other days along the west shore of the Hudson River, as well as on other journeys that by no means could have been planned. Later on, I was to wonder if they ever would end or if all the secrets between Constable's Point and Sneden's Landing (over the New York line but still atop the Palisades), would come into the light again. The memorable story of Great-Grandfather Abraham provided both clues and urgent invitations.

Almost as far back as I can remember, I connect the story with my maternal grandmother, a diminutive but regal lady from Liverpool, England. Her father, she used to say, was a Cunarder, and she said it in such a way as to imply that he was a man of rank aboard one of the older ships. There came the night, appropriately stormy, when "Nan," as we all called her, was one of those in the family summoned to a rain-sloshed window by an eerie scratching sound. It was as if frozen fingers were drumming on the glass.

The little group which, I think, must have included my Aunt Annie, grandmother's sister, pulled aside the draperies drawn to shut out the lightning of the storm, to behold, etched by the flashes, a hand extended from a sleeve which wore the familiar braid. There was no mistaking the sight for what it was, we always were assured, even though the hand did not seem to be attached beyond the sleeve to anything in particular. The fingers drummed on the window again and then vanished.

Shortly after that, official word came that the father of the brood and sire of my grandmother—Abraham Clark—would not be returning home. That is how I remember it, even though later revelations may seem to clash with some of the details. I remember as well a portrait, somewhere in one of the albums that have vanished in the mists that shroud intervals in the life of every family, and from this a careful likeness was made in crayon. This, I feel sure, was Abraham Clark, his round face fringed with whiskers and his impressive head indicating that every inch of all the rest was a sailor-man. I am not sure by now where either the original or the copy is, but I do know that the adventure, which raised the curtain on the Hudson's water front in New Jersey, once more important and better known to ancestors of present-day New Yorkers, is over.

I also remember the story that Abraham Clark never was taken home and that he was buried in the Cunard Line's American port of those days, Jersey City. This fragment of information had been at odds for years with the conclusion that Abraham was "lost at sea." When I finally found the grave, or at least the name on a memorial stone, I concluded that perhaps "Abra'm" had not been "lost at sea" at all but died aboard ship close enough to shore, or even somewhere in port, so that burial on land was possible. So, between in-quiries less personal, I began looking for the "Cunard Plot," as I was told it was called, in one of the older cemeteries—although I don't know even now why I should have started in one of the oldest of them all.

I will spare you the details of the piecemeal inquiry. You will say that I could have obtained information at the Cunard Line's offices in New York or even abroad, but I must tell you that the most persistent questions in almost every direction bore no fruit. On one occasion after being passed from one department to another the would-be informant at the other end of the telephone line expressed surprise and bewilderment that there was a Cunard graveyard anywhere.

The simplest method is often the one that lies neglected but well within reach, so I began calling the cemeteries listed in Jersey City. Some of those I called first were profuse in their doubts of there being any such thing as a Cunard Plot; one, I am quite sure, considered that I might be inquiring of the kind of plot associated with sabotage—who ever heard of sabotage in a cemetery? At last, when I put through a call to one listed in the proverbial yellow pages as Greenville but also as the Jersey City Cemetery, a helpful voice responded that there *certainly was* a Cunard Plot, but that it wasn't theirs. "It's in the Bayview cemetery across the way," I was assured. "Overlooks the Statue of Liberty."

And so I found it at last in my own peculiar way—peculiar because, first, I do most things the hard way, or so I am told; second, because the phantom of my great-grandfather and the name of Jersey City associated with it had remained locked away in cobwebs at the back of my mind; and third, because the obvious questions in the obvious places at the beginning had provided nothing helpful at all. The most surprising reflection was that I had passed within sight of the shaft bearing my great-grandfather's name with others many times without suspecting, during preceding years. For the Cunard Plot looks down on (or did when last I looked) the tracks of the Jersey Central and the Baltimore & Ohio. However, I hope that I may be forgiven because, from a speeding train, one cemetery appears much like any other.

Bill Augustine and I found the plot with a shaft in its midst bearing names and dates reaching back to the 1850's. There were several individual stones supplied, their inscriptions revealed, by shipmates of the seafaring men they honored. However, the one that was most impressive and on which I found the inscription "Abraham Clark, October 25, 1878," with many others like it, provoked a lingering reflection: Inasmuch as the man in the cemetery office had said that the Cunard Plot contained fourteen graves and inasmuch as the shaft itself listed well over thirty names, was Great-Grandfather Abraham "lost at sea," had he died on land, or was he here merely remembered, as some of the others, on the stone?

The cards in the office revealed no more than names and dates. Frequently I have tried to learn more from the company's offices in New York, and promises have been made, but after a while I began to wonder if my motive or even my sanity were not being questioned—so I gave up. Meanwhile, this end of the riddle, a fragment of an old wives' tale involving the tapping of ghostly fingers on a window pane, supplied a renewal of the urge to try and see the land of the Palisades as it had been through changing times.

It will seem in all of this that I have put the cart before the horse, and perhaps I have, but I must tell you that in seeking out great-grandfather's grave I journeyed up and down the Palisades, knowing full well that I would have to come back many, many times. Before it was over we had ventured into every ancient graveyard in sight, beginning with that of the church at Ridgefield, as it had become—a church that you will recognize at once, even from a distance, if you have not been traveling too fast along the upper reaches of the Jersey Turnpike. The church and its spire, as well as the village, lie plainly etched against the Palisades ridge that with jumbled houses on its back, hides the Hudson River and the New York skyline behind it. This, if you will venture across the Newark meadows, is the English Neighborhood Reformed Church, which I admitted from the beginning was a most unlikely place for great-grandfather, or even a Cunard Plot, to be.

It is clear that Ridgefield long ago was the English Neighborhood, but even chance reference to it is minimized in these later days because modern developments have followed natural trends to hem it in on every side. The mists and smogs of the flats as well as the hovering smoke of industry combine with the frequent purple shadows of the lower Palisades to push isolation toward obscurity. Once in the churchyard, I was met by a kindly caretaker who gave me material from which came a mixed background that sounded anything but English. Be that as it may, just the name English Neighborhood Reformed Church should be enough to entice you, too, over that far. Once there, you will learn that this is where there happens to be the earliest record of this particular ecclesiastical (or should I say, religious?) organization, going back to November 18, 1768. Here it is, officially: "As Mr. Moore has conveyed to us, the underwritten trustees, one acre of land, on purpose that we should erect a church on it, agreeable to the Reformed Church of Holland, established by the National Synod of Dort. . . . What the document discloses, over such names as Abraham Montany, Stephen Bourdette, John Day, Michael Moore, and John Moore, is that there was an agreement that the church now actually building in the neighborhood would be conformed to the doctrine, discipline and worship established in the United Provinces, by the National Synod aforesaid."

There was further promise under the same date and over the same signatures that there would be engaged "such ministers, elders, deacons, and members" as "shall be called and appointed in this church." This first building stood, according to the map made for General Washington by Robert Erskine, the Surveyor General, at what is now the northeast corner of

Grand Avenue and Hillside Street in Leonia, a quarter of a mile from the Fort Lee Road. However, it is written further, "Of the character of the ministry of the first Dominie there is no record." It was a period preceding the Revolutionary War. The record I found at the old church read:

"In the Dutch Church the debate between the Coetus and Conferente was taking place. The Coetus were anxious to have an independent Dutch Church in America. The Conferente wanted to remain true to the Dutch Church in Holland. This debate was peacefully settled under the leadership of Dr. John Livingston in 1771. The Dutch Church became independent.

"Is it any wonder that when the Revolutionary War broke out, of forty-four ministers in the Dutch Church only three were Tories and sympathetic toward England? Thus our Church had one of the three Tory ministers. He fled to New York, took his records with him for safe-keeping, and preached in New York, keeping the Church intact, with no break in the pastorate of the Dutch in New York City. The Church (in English Neighborhood) was without a pastor for sixteen years, having only an occasional service as the neighboring ministers were able to supply. . . ."

However, at this point I was concerned mainly with finding the oldest cemetery in the vicinity, and without the slightest idea that after we had found the Cunard Plot I would be compelled to push on and on, both to the south and to the north, from the Kill Van Kull to Sneden's Landing and the Palisades Park that is New York's own. All to whom I spoke insisted that this one plot, beside the old church of the English Neighborhood, was it. It was, I admitted, in a kind of world apart, even more than most cemeteries are, filled with the added comfortable feeling of watching the world go by in the distance but with no urgent need to be a part of its frantic disposition to go elsewhere. It was here, I think, that it came to me that Great-Grandfather Abraham, if his grave were in the vicinity at all, would not necessarily have been laid away in the oldest, or one of the oldest, graveyards. It was here, certainly, that someone said that a few calls to numbers in the yellow pages might eliminate the need for miles and miles of wandering. At that I'm glad I didn't hear the suggestion when first it was made.

Edging along the land across Newark Bay, easing over from country remembered by too many only for the dip and roar of airplanes, the penetrating and lingering smells of oils and gas under refinement, I found myself approaching again the long-proclaimed site of the Hamilton-Burr duel. The New Jersey Turnpike joined long ago in setting up, with a mixture of extensions, tunnels, bridges, and other devices, in a way that was not repeated by the Garden State Parkway, new means of escape from a whole far-reaching region which many will never really see. Even now, I am conscious that so much has been lost that the crevices of history never can be filled. West and northwest of the Hackensack River is a kind of "No Man's Land," a great white space on even the best of modern highway maps.

To the uninitiated there is every indication, preposterous though it must be, that the "Great Duel" was fought at the top of the Palisades, rather than on the shore below, in days when there were trees, a more ample shore, and grass that was cut down before the fatal shot was fired. Even so, in the enclosure of a little park where the bust of Alexander Hamilton presides, there is this inscription on a bronze marker:

Hamilton-Burr Duel

Here on the King Estate
July 11, 1804, Alexander Hamilton
was mortally wounded in a duel
with Aaron Burr. His son, Philip
Hamilton, had been killed
in 1801 in like manner
on the same spot.

"Here on the King Estate . . ." has given too many, especially children, the idea, however absurd, that participants in
the Hamilton-Burr duel made their way with difficulty to the
top of a rocky ridge and then, when the affair was ended, at
least one with his aides made his way down, as precariously,
to the Hudson shore. Having been assured of this on many
occasions, I deliberately sought contradiction without finding
it. Where was "the Duelling Ground"? I have asked. "Right
here," I have been told, or with gestures, "Right over there!"
It seems to me that only a few moments' consideration would
make participants in a duel, painstakingly seeking settlement
of differences in secret, seem foolish in climbing to a pinnacle
where they could make a production of it all. Historians for
the most part respond, of course, that the little park with
Hamilton's bust is not meant to indicate that here is where
the duel took place but that any such memorial, even if it were
many times the size of this one, would be lost or never seen
among the docks and wharves and timbers of abandoned ferries down along the shore.

That is probably true. I say that as one who has walked like
Banquo's ghost in and out of silent, dusty, but once palatial
waiting rooms of long-cherished ferries only to return two or
three years afterward to find them so many heaped-up timbers,
like the roots of teeth withdrawn from the oozy gums of mud
and tossed aside. New Jersey has held valiantly to its own
place name Palisades, below Fort Lee, even as New York proclaims its own, just off the Palisades Interstate Parkway, but
these gestures are by no means enough to recall the boundary
lines of old Bayonne, Greenville, Hoboken, West Hoboken, or
North Bergen as they used to be less than a century ago.
Names like Bergen Point, Saltersville, Communipaw, or even
Castle Point, find even the most avid uncertain—and I have
reason to know. I asked no fewer than a dozen persons in the
area of North Guttenberg where Bull's Ferry used to be, and
none was less than confused.

This bust of Alexander Hamilton commands a tiny park on the New Jersey Palisades of the Hudson River. An earlier memorial of the Hamilton-Burr duel was close by the river, where the duel was fought, but vandals made off with it in pieces.

Inasmuch as it may not be readily available to you, let me give you first a description of the place called the Dueling Ground as it was written down by John W. Barber and Henry Howe in the early 1840's, and then, by good fortune, tap one source of their information published as *A Collection of the Facts and Documents Relative to the Death of Major-General Alexander Hamilton,* issued in New York in 1804, the very year of the duel. The deceptive title on the spine of the book is *Coleman's Collection,* to which Barber and Howe confess their debt. That the compiler, the editor of the *Evening Post,* was in a hurry to get everything he could into print is revealed in a few repetitive passages in the text and the appendices. He wrote in his preface:

"This Collection of Papers, and the comments and remarks which will occasionally accompany them, are offered to the public no less in gratification of my own feelings, than in compliance with the request of those whose wishes I have long been accustomed to respect.

"In the death of Hamilton, I have lost my best earthly friend, my ablest adviser, and my most generous and disinterested patron. And all that is now left to me, is to pour forth my gratitude in unavailing sorrow; and to evince my regard for his memory, by defending it against the cruel attacks of those, who, not contented with having deprived him of his life, seem bent on pursuing him beyond the grave, and destroying his fame. A belief is confidently indulged, that when this series of Numbers is completed, enough will have appeared to silence the voice of calumny forever. . . ."

There follows, among the orations, editorials, and resolutions from all over the country, the exchange of correspondence which led to the duel itself. The alleged slanders involved were trivial as compared to accusations made almost everywhere and every day in the politics of today, and, what is more, no instructor of mine ever pointed out that so much to which Aaron Burr took offense was based on hearsay. These reflections came at a time when, wandering along the Palisades, I did not know that I was to meet Dr. William J. Snyder, who in those days lived within walking distance of the Dueling Ground. Nor did I know that I was to see Dr. Snyder's prized dueling pistols, elegantly encased with the legends of what really happened. In fact, I am told that the number of "authentic" pistols of the Great Duel seems to have multiplied with the years. Those of Dr. Snyder were found, he confirmed, in the mansion, now removed, that graced the King Estate.

The record of the *Historical Collections of New Jersey* appears under a drawing of an area of the Palisades precipice in marked and confusing contrast to anything found now in the lofty enclosure. That there once was a monument, but on the shore level, is revealed in the text that follows:

"A short distance above Weehawken, and about three miles above Hoboken, overhung by the Palisades on the bank of the Hudson, is the spot famous as the 'duelling ground.' Here several have paid the forfeit of their lives to a custom at which humanity shudders, and which all laws, divine and human, condemn. Here it was that Gen. Alexander Hamilton fell in a duel with Col. Aaron Burr, Vice-President of the United States, July 11th, 1804; an event at which a nation mourned. A monument was erected to the memory of Hamilton on the spot where he fell, by a society in New York, of which the annexed view, taken many years since by J. C. Ward, Esq., is a representation. . . ."

There are boulders, a wind-torn tree, and the monument, fit for a tomb and all fenced in, with the New York City of its time in the distance. This monument, indicating that the disease of the willful shattering of stone memorials is no mere contagion of today, "was destroyed by the hand of violence, and the pieces carried off as relics. The piece bearing the inscription was found in a low groggery in New York, where it had been pawned off for liquor. . . ."

There follow more than two pages of fine type, credited to *Coleman's Collections,* more properly *Coleman's Collection,* as the name appears on the outside cover but not on the title page of the book (a copy of which Bill Augustine found in Georgia). Here the expected and expanded subtitle declares that here also are *Comments: Together with Various Orations, Sermons and Eulogies That Have Been Published or Written on His Life and Character*—meaning Hamilton's, of course. "By the Editor of the Evening Post" was all the compiler provided as he turned the bundle of manuscript over to Edward Dunscomb "on the twentieth day of August in the Twenty-ninth year of the Independence of the United States of America. . . ." The Great Duel had taken place little more than five weeks earlier. Whether hastily assembled or not, this is the text from which I will give you some of the more graphic portions. Because of his haste, the editor, William Coleman, allowed his name to appear, perhaps by accident, at the bottom of a letter from Hamilton's surgeon, a descriptive piece worth the price of the entire book.

On the heights above the river front, there is an enclosure with a gate, just down the drive that follows the contours of the rising Palisades, with a large rock which served, or so the legend in the vicinity still maintains, as the makeshift pillow for the dying Hamilton. Part of the crowded residential areas of Weehawken adjoin the miniature park and plot, but three hundred and thirty feet below there is a tangled maze of roads and tracks and wharves and offices. As for the rocky pillow, I would say that Alexander's passing from this world was a journey rough enough without it, and furthermore, I doubt if any inducement whatsoever would have inspired anyone to drag it up the steeps.

Before I give you, abridged from the text that was forty years old when Barber and Howe came along, what I believe to be one of the best contemporary accounts of the Hamilton-Burr affair, I must report on statements readily made in the vicinity, thereby adding to the more than occasional bewilderment. "The marker," I once was told, "isn't where Hamilton fell—simply because the road is." Which road? The drive that swings gracefully along the top of the Palisades, close by the memorial enclosure which only those traveling slowly enough see at all, or the road, or roads, at the bottom of the cliffs. I had voted for the latter even before it was stated that a memorial of the duel had been displaced by a ferry terminal which, in its turn, has gone. Even though there is an impressive "carriage-lift" or the tracks that supported the ungainly contraption not far away, this hoist, cut upward through solid rock, was the development of a later era.

I have found only one man willing to recall the "lift" in action—Frederick J. Pixlee, who lives in Belleville. "When I was a small boy," he told me, "we used to visit friends on Weehawken Street in what then was called Union Hill. The upper end of this carriage lift was at the cliff end of this street and was in operation until 1913. There was a large drum in the upper house with a steel cable on it, and there were two lifts, actually. When one ascended the incline, the other one descended. Huge steel gates protected the entrance when the cars were in motion. There was a steam engine in the upper gatehouse operating the drum.

"The car beds themselves were level, and the outer wheels of the cars were at the end of two long vertical beams, because the roadbed, as you have seen, was very steep. The lift was used mostly by heavy horse-drawn drays in those days. I do not recall seeing any automobiles use it. My mother once asked one of the men if we could ride on it and was met with a polite but firm refusal. We were told to use the steep stairway a few yards to the north of the lift.

"I used to call it a Funicular Railway because there was a model of one in a catalogue of a popular construction toy of the day known as 'Meccano,'" Fred Pixlee went on. Even I remembered the "Meccano" device, a car that could travel up an incline with a level platform because the wheels at one end were much smaller than those at the other. "As far as I know," Fred said, "the lift was discontinued some time during World War I. Our friends moved from that neighborhood in 1914, and I did not visit the place again."

This is but an interlude, recalling a cleft with stone supports for tracks that too often goes unexplained in these days. There is a building now at the bottom where the steel gates used to be, and there it was, tongue in cheek, that I asked what the cut through the rocks had been. The man to whom I addressed the question said he did not know. But as absurd and out-of-time schedule as the notion is, nothing less than a lift of this or similar design could have conveyed a dying man and his attendants to the heights of the King Estate.

"My father," John Ehrhardt once told me, "could remember the old King (or King's) Mansion that stood in what we always called King's Woods, which were obviously part of what the historical marker called the King Estate. This was atop the high knob that overlooks the Hudson River and stands between the shore and the Lincoln Tunnel." When John told me that, we went off together looking for the site of the foundation. We found traces of it behind a high wire fence through

This "Carriage Lift" of another day can still be traced in a cleft in the rock of the Palisades at, approximately, Ferry Street in Jersey City. Until 1913 horses and wagons and other vehicles were hauled up and down by drum and cable.

which we could see the swarming tunnel traffic and what remained of something that may have been a stone tower. No
longer were there any woods, and the trees there are still associated in my mind with those having a distinctly unpleasant
smell in a city backyard of long ago. This was all that remained
of the King Mansion, I was assured even later; no one remembered what the tower, if it was a tower, had been, and
even the legend of duelling pistols found inside the house
seemed more unreal by comparison.

"The story goes," John assured me, "that Alexander Hamilton was carried to the King Mansion after he was wounded and
not taken to New York until later that day." This, surely, would
be something of a tall tale, to say the least, and nothing more
than neighborhood gossip, or even less, if the account in the
Coleman collection is accurate, which I have every reason to
believe it is. "It is generally agreed that Hamilton made no
attempt to hit Burr, but it also has been said that he was not
as much against duelling as you think." No one had ever
asked me to think anything about it at all up to that time, but
certainly Hamilton's own words, found in a written statement
in his own writing after his death and presented as part of
Coleman's Collection, are conclusive enough.

"There is something of an expert on the duel who lives not
far from where Hamilton was fatally shot, and I will tell you
where to find him," John changed the subject before I could
go further into the fine type of the narrative. "He has a pair of
dueling pistols received from a member of the King family—
although he has not been able to establish with finality that
one was the weapon that caused Alexander Hamilton's death."
Nor had he, I was to discover and admire in the manner of a
cautious and competent physician, very much to say about
any other details still put down by many as debatable.

It was known, John told me, that the pistols were made by
the same man who fashioned those used in the Great Duel,
that Hamilton had no pistols of his own, and that he borrowed

the set from a friend before the journey to Weehawken. "The present owner of the pistols," he explained, "has traced the descendants of the friend from whom the pistols were borrowed. They have a bill of sale but no tradition at all as to what happened to the pistols themselves. My friend thinks that in the excitement they simply were forgotten at the King Mansion, or King house."

Soon after that I found Dr. William J. Snyder, owner of the pistols, at his home which was then, as I told you, at 74 Columbia Terrace, virtually around the corner from the little park where the Hamilton bust serves as a centerpiece. The good doctor, a thoughtful and soft-spoken man, lost no time in showing me the legendary pistols, as perfect in their craftsmanship as was the red-satin-lined box from which they were lovingly taken. The physician informed me quietly that his father-in-law, Henry D. Mueller, "bought the pistols from some people in Weehawken many years ago." The family, as far as he could find out, was from "lower Weehawken" and might have had some association with the King's Mansion. The story of the pistols having been discovered in the old house seems to have been a part of a New Jersey legend that ebbed and flowed. "There are people," Dr. Snyder told me, "who have a bill of sale for the pistols—made by J. E. Evans, of Philadelphia, according to the name on the set." The box, or cabinet, made obviously for matched weapons, also provided spaces for a pack, ramrod, paper, powder, and a measure for the quantity of powder desired.

Even so, piecing out the story from what John Ehrhardt remembered his father saying, and what the self-effacing doctor was able to tell me, those who have the bill of sale have no pistols, the possessor of the pistols has no more than fragments of the King Mansion story, and so time, with so many gaps to fill in the legend, has filled them in. The summation would seem to be that Dr. Snyder's pistols, if indeed they were those that Alexander Hamilton had borrowed, were left at the King's Mansion for someone, or anyone, to pick up in the excitement that clearly took its time dying down.

Dr. Snyder proved to be a collector of ancient weapons, among them a murderous-looking scimitar used by the Turks in one of their conquests. He knew the story of each piece in his collection, but he felt, I'm sure, that his dueling pistols had as much claim to authenticity as anything else, especially others that have turned up with their own appropriate legends —but, after all, what did it matter this long after? Somehow I could not shrug it all off as easily as that: It seemed to be the buildup for a great letdown. And if the records in the *Collection* quickly thrown together by William Coleman meant anything at all, *it is certain that the pistol which Hamilton had used was in the bottom of the barge on the return journey to New York, made without delay while it was still early in the morning.* You will see that for yourself in what records remain and, more to the point, in what the surgeon, Dr. Hosack, had to say:

"It was nearly seven in the morning when the boat which carried General Hamilton, his friend Mr. Pendleton, and the surgeon mutually agreed on, Dr. Hosack, reached that part of the Jersey shore called the *Weahawk*. There they found Mr. Burr and his friend Mr. Van Ness, who, as I am told, had been employed since their arrival, with coats off, in clearing away the bushes, limbs of trees, etc., so as to make a fair opening. The parties in a few moments were at their allotted situations; when Mr. Pendleton gave the word, Mr. Burr raised his arm slowly, deliberately took his aim, and fired. His ball entered General Hamilton's right side; as soon as the bullet struck him, he raised himself involuntarily on his toes, turned a little to the left (at which moment his pistol went off), and fell upon his face. Mr. Pendleton immediately called out for Dr. Hosack, who, in running to the spot, had to pass Mr. Van Ness and Colonel Burr; but Van Ness had the cool precaution to cover his principal with an umbrella, so that Dr. Hosack should not be able to swear that he saw him on the field."

There follows a report of the surgeon, Dr. Hosack, actually a letter in reply to a note from the editor of the *Evening Post*. I have found it most interesting for a variety of reasons, not the least of which is the surgeon's reference to a pistol in the bottom of the boat and Alexander Hamilton's belief that it had not been discharged and therefore, still cocked, was dangerous. Dr. Hosack wrote:

". . . I will repress my feelings while I endeavor to furnish you with an enumeration of such particulars relative to the melancholy end of our beloved friend Hamilton, as dwell most forcibly on my recollection.

"When called to him, upon his receiving the fatal wound, I found him half-sitting on the ground, supported in the arms of Mr. Pendleton. His countenance of death I shall never forget. He had at that instant just strength to say, 'This is a mortal wound, Doctor'; when he sunk away, and became to all appearances lifeless. I immediately stripped up his clothes, and soon, alas! ascertained that the direction of the ball must have been through some vital part. . . .'"

Except for the change in a word here and there, the Barber and Howe account follows the text precisely. At this point, however, Dr. Hosack seems to have inserted, or added later, a footnote, reading in the same missive, dated August 17, 1804:

"For the satisfaction of some of General Hamilton's friends, I examined his body after death, in presence of Dr. Post and two other gentlemen. I discovered that the ball struck the second or third false rib, and fractured it about in the middle; it then passed through the liver and diaphragm, and, as nearly as we could ascertain without a minute examination, lodged in the first or second lumbar vertebra. The vertebra in which it was lodged was considerably splintered, so that the spiculae were distinctly perceptible to the finger. About a pint of clotted blood was found in the cavity of the belly, which had probably been effused from the divided vessels of the liver. . . ."

This was omitted from the text of the *Historical Collections of New Jersey,* and the compilers, I suppose, sought to spare the feelings of the readers of their day. No such niceties were observed in relation to the Indian barbarities at Swartwout's (now Swartwood) Pond, in which they spelled out the details submitted by one of their collaborators in the field, Nelson Robinson, Esq., of Newton. Although some of the adjectives are omitted in the 1844 revision, Dr. Hosack wrote further, speaking of Hamilton:

"His pulses were not to be felt; his respiration was entirely suspended; and upon laying my hand on his heart, and perceiving no motion there, I considered him as irrecoverably gone. I however observed to Mr. Pendleton that the only chance for his reviving was immediately to get him upon the water. We therefore lifted him up, and carried him out of the wood, to the margin of the bank, where the bargemen aided us in conveying him into the boat, which immediately put off. During all this time I could not discover the least symptom of returning life. I now rubbed his face, lips, and temples, with spirits of hartshorne, applied it to his neck and breast, and to the wrists and palms of his hands, and endeavored to pour some into his mouth. . . ."

There is no evidence of lingering here in New Jersey, on the King Estate, in the King Mansion, or anywhere else. Dr. Hosack insisted on *immediate* return to the New York side and, inasmuch as the Great Duel had taken place early on a summer's morning, the hour was not, as some of the lingering legends indicate, later in the day. The surgeon went on:

"When we had got, as I should judge, about 50 yards from the shore, some imperfect efforts to breathe were for the first time manifest; in a few minutes he sighed, and became sensible to the impression of the hartshorne, or the fresh air of the water. He breathed; his eyes, hardly opened, wandered, without fixing upon any objects; to our great joy he at length spoke: 'My vision is indistinct,' were his first words. His pulse became more perceptible; his respiration more regular; his sight returned. I then examined the wound to know if there was any dangerous discharge of blood; upon slightly pressing his side, it gave him pain; on which I desisted. Soon after recovering his sight, he happened to cast his eye upon the case of pistols, and observing the one that he had had in his hand lying on the outside, he said, 'Take care of that pistol; it is undischarged, and still cocked; it may go off and do harm; Pendleton knows (attempting to turn his head toward him) that I did not intend to fire at him.' 'Yes,' said Mr. Pendleton, understanding his wish, 'I have already made Dr. Hosack acquainted with your determination as to that.' He then closed his eyes and remained calm, without any disposition to speak; nor did he say much afterwards, excepting in reply to my questions as to his feelings. . . ."

In view of the small talk of the comparative few who pause at the little park with the Alexander Hamilton bust, this is as good a place as any for the questions that persist, in spite of answers which from my point of view are obvious enough. Did the case of pistols go to New York and come back again? The legend on the New Jersey side clings to the notion that the "authentic" brace of weapons was forgotten in the ancient house on the King Estate; however, Dr. Hosack has made it more than clear that the case was in the barge and that there was no visit to the King Mansion at all. If the pistols had been borrowed, as these records close to the time and place of the duel point out, would it not have been natural to return them to their owner? Of course, it is possible that the owner did not want them back under the circumstances. Whatever other uncertainties clinging to the Great Duel there may be, of this I am convinced: The pistol in the bottom of the barge that Hamilton saw and warned about was never aimed and was discharged only by reflex action in Weehawken.

The account of the surgeon, Dr. David Hosack, which, I have been delighted to discover, impressed Professor Broadus Mitchell, an authority on the Great Duel, as much as it has impressed me, is straightforward throughout the conclusion of his description of the return to the wharf in New York and the tragic hours that followed.

I may as well tell you that I had planned to allow my great-grandfather, Abraham Clark, the last word inasmuch as, after all, he is the one who really got me into all this. But suddenly I have concluded that this honor should go to Professor Mitchell, who in referring to the *Collection* of the compiler Coleman indicates that the contents originally were issued as a series of pamphlets. "The dueling ground, a narrow ledge of the Palisades some twenty feet above the river, years since was cut away to make room for railroad tracks," he said. "The monument in the small park above commemorates Hamilton's fall, but does not mark the spot. Several possessors of sets of pistols identify them as the weapons used in the Burr-Hamilton duel." (*A New Jersey Reader,* Rutgers University Press, 1961.)

Chapter XIV

REQUIEM FOR THE FERRIES

If ever there had been a shred of lingering doubt as to where the Weehawken "dueling ground" was, it was dispelled for all time when I set out to compose a requiem for ferries up from Communipaw along the Hudson River shore. When I had been there earlier, blackened bones were being dislodged in the dismemberment of the skeletons of once elegant ferry-houses, and others were all but forsaken, gathering a carpet of dust that softened echoes of intruding footfalls. It was then that the editor of the Erie Railroad's monthly was writing: "On the very spot where the West Shore ferryhouse still stands, Alexander Hamilton was mortally wounded by Aaron Burr, of New Jersey. The monument marking the site was moved to the Weehawken cliffs in 1882, making way for the construction of the ferry building. . . ."

If only the historical marker on those cliffs had not read, "Here on the King Estate. . . ." It would have been as easy to have begun the inscription, "Below these cliffs on the waterfront. . . ." As a result, many of the literal-minded have been led needlessly astray. "Waterfront" would still be accurate though the New York Central's once-impressive facilities, closed, cavernous, and gathering grime even in 1959 when I was there, had been swept by a raging fire before I returned in early 1962. The Erie's terminal had also been taken down, with only weed-grown tracks, empty platforms, and tunnel entrances to mark its demise. Charred pilings that jutted from the water like burned fingers recalled the Central, and, oddly enough, a fragment of the covered entrance.

That the monument "on the very spot" where the celebrated

duel was fought was moved to the top of the Palisades provides a basis for any number of new reflections. Is the monument, actually a bust of Hamilton properly mounted in a fenced enclosure, overlooking the cluttered shore, the one that was moved? After all, there is a record of how the first memorial was defaced, its inscription carried to New York as the price of a drink or two. But was there, as some rumors say, another monument in the years between?

The Reverend Herman J. Engelken, of New York, told me one day that there was every need to underscore the proper site of the duel before too many, some of them teachers, accepted and propagated false ideas without knowing it. He told me:

"We lived within sight of the Hamilton monument, and I saw it almost every day when I was a boy. You are right in emphasizing that the duel was *not* fought where the monument stands but down at the bottom of the Palisades. Even so, two national magazines of outstanding reputation within the last ten years have printed pictures of the monument with captions stating that it was here that the duel was fought.

"When you write about the King Estate of Weehawken and the West Shore Ferry area on the bank of the Hudson, you touch on places with which I am familiar and which awaken happy memories. I used to walk through the King Woods on my way to Weehawken School Number 1, from which I was graduated in 1899. My father was one of the first to build a house on the development of Highwood Park, Weehawken, and we lived on Duer Place, named for the Duer family which had some historical fame in that region. My brother and I did our swimming on the west bank of the Hudson, almost directly below the monument. Did you know that Highwood Park was a real estate development that came into existence after the breakup of the ill-fated Eldorado Amusement Park?"

I replied that I did not, but that even this debacle, perhaps coming toward the close of a time when railroads and trac-

My requiem for the ferries is in a minor key. Very soon it will be hard to remember a time when people could travel in leisure and even elegance between the New York and New Jersey shores of the Hudson River.

tion companies went into the amusement park business to drum up trade, well might have been a segment of the disease of passing days, as it manifested itself then, or the gradual fading out of one era after another. Along New Jersey's Hudson river front, an age had been dying while our backs were turned—a kind of death by inches. There are few mourners except the few who choose to go that way, easing down a road with horseshoe bends, wandering out to the end of broken wharves, invading dark sheds, or peeping into boarded windows of once elaborate and ornate ferry terminals, or gazing on empty tracks through bars of gates often idle. Since those wanderings first began I have counted myself fortunate to have been among the curious who have looked down upon piers in time to see some of the last of the ferryboats—tethered and silent, with nowhere to go.

With the coming of this death on the river shore, psychological as well as physical, much that has been history and almost as much folklore slides into the murky water and tends to be forgotten forever. Surely it is more than disturbing that the past drops into the Hudson on one side of a state which is now intent upon erasing memories of yesterday with the Delaware's new reservoirs on the other.

The New York Central's Hudson River ferry service between Manhattan's Forty-second Street and Cortlandt Street terminals and Weehawken ended March 24, 1959. The Erie Railroad's New Jersey-Chambers Street ferry made its last run in the first dark of evening December 12, 1958. When I went there last, the Erie's boats were using the Lackawanna slips at the terminal labeled Erie-Lackawanna-Hoboken, behind the statue of Sam Sloan, surrounded by the usual flock of disrespectful pigeons, cars parked by special permission, trucks, and buses that came down to the edge of the cobbled square. Sam, the inscription said, extending its reminder from another time, was born in 1817, died in 1907, and for thirty-two years was president of the Delaware, Lackawanna, and Western Railroad from 1867 to 1899.

The Lackawanna and Erie ferryboats were still running, and so were those of the Jersey Central, further down, crossing to New York's Liberty Street, although a lone conductor and a shoeshine man were the only signs of life in the terminal described as palatial in 1890. Proceeding up the Hudson, I began my meandering at what had been celebrated as Communipaw, a name still retained by a tugboat I saw secured among the ice cakes below the adjacent wharf. Two of the Central's boats were on duty, and, because it was Saturday, only two or three automobiles were in line between the crossings at any time. There had been ten or twelve trucks when I went snooping three years before, and there was a man selling tickets in a single booth. Now there was no one, and I wandered about at will. Gates were still numbered from one to seventeen, although the first two tracks leading in had been removed for concrete paving on which automobiles of visitors, so defined by a nearby sign, were parked.

Coaches marked "Business Car" were at the end of three tracks, dark and belying their distinction. I asked a man at the only open ticket window what a "Business Car" was, and he said solemnly that they were used by officials of the road "for business as they traveled along." No trains were in action, and there was just enough light by which to read with renewed fascination the words of Gustav Kobbé's *Jersey Central*, probably written in 1899. Gustav said:

"It may be said that thousands of the best citizens of New York are not citizens of that city at all; in the evening they ebb away. They are citizens of New York insofar as the city owes their brains and energy a great share of its prosperity; they are not citizens, in that they live and vote elsewhere. If this great suburban army of intelligent men lived in New York, we would probably hear less of the necessity of municipal reform, for there would be just so much more intelligence among the voting population—which brings us back to our starting point: that of New York's best citizens thousands are, unfortunately for it, citizens of New Jersey, Long Island, and other suburban districts. . . ."

These are the words of a loyal New Jersey commuter speaking out before his time in a day of no income tax, much less a tax for the privilege of working in New York—even though *Jersey Central* was published in New York, in contrast to the imprint of *Jersey Coast and Pines*, Short Hills. I note that Gustav Kobbé's concern was for an "army of intelligent men." Working women commuting to New York were in all probability unknown to Gustav in his day. After some rosy words on behalf of those who were "among the most intelligent and progressive of these non-citizen citizens" who with a knowing nod from the author in the direction of the book's sponsor, came to the city "by the Central Railroad of New Jersey," he went on:

"The New York station of the Central Railroad of New Jersey is at the foot of Liberty Street. The ferry to Jersey City, known as the Communipaw Ferry, was the first legally established ferry between Manhattan Island and the Jersey shore. It was erected at the foot of Communipaw avenue in 1661, William Jansen being licensed to take charge of it. Jansen at once endeavored to establish a monopoly, claiming that under his license every one was obliged to cross in his boat. On the other hand, the people claimed that he had violated his license by refusing to ferry certain parties. Jansen's answer was that he had never refused those who would pay. The Governor and Council neatly solved the problem by deciding against both parties—ordering the Sheriff to assist Jansen in getting his pay, and threatening Jansen with dismissal if he refused to ferry anyone who was willing to pay. The ferry was to be in operation Mondays, Wednesdays, and Fridays, but for an extra compensation, 'four guilders in wampum,' Jansen was obliged to ferry any person at any time. For more than a century thereafter there is no record concerning the ferry, but it probably continued to be patronized. At the close of the Revolution, in 1783, Aaron Longstreet & Co. advised that the ferry would, at 3 p.m., convey passengers to Communipaw for the stage for Newark, whence they could proceed by 'the Excellent New York and Philadelphia Running Machines' to Philadelphia in one day. When, however, the enemy evacuated Paulus Hook, the line of travel swerved that way, and the Communipaw Ferry, falling into disuse, was not revived until the Central Railroad of New Jersey was extended from Elizabethport to Jersey City, the old flat-boat ferry being suddenly rehabilitated in all the improvements of a century of progress. The act authorizing the extension was passed in 1860, and the railroad was opened to travel August 1, 1864.

"The ferry being the most southerly of those crossing to the New Jersey shore, no finer view of New York Harbor is had from the boats of any other of the Jersey railroads.

"At the Jersey City terminus is a depot of the best modern construction. Its high clock-tower and gables are conspicuous features of the river front. Arched corridors lead from the ferry-house to the waiting rooms. The general effect of this room and its accessories is spacious, yet graceful. It is 60 feet from the tiled floor to the apex of the roof, held by ornamental rafters of iron. A sky-light and the windows provide perfect light and ventilation. The walls are of buff glazed imported brick; the tiling of the floor is marble. The building is lighted by electricity. A stair-case and gallery lead to the offices on the second floor.

"On the further right-hand corner of the waiting-room (entering from the ferry), is a luxuriously furnished ladies' parlor, while on the same side, but near the entrance from the ferry, is a smoking-room. Among the accessories is an excellent restaurant.

"The train-shed boasts one of the finest sky-lights in the country. Some idea of the size of the shed may be gained from the statement that there are twelve tracks which will hold fifteen cars each, or 180 cars might start at once and carry away 12,600 people, seated, and another 2,000 might occupy the aisles and platforms; 190 trains arrive and depart from the station every twenty-four hours, and if each one had the full number of cars that might stand under the roof of the car-shed there would be 2,850 cars come and go every day, capable of seating 199,500 passengers every twenty-four hours. . . .

"From this station straightaway an important branch runs into Newark. It traverses Bergen Neck through a cut, with stations at some of the most pleasant residential districts of Jersey City, crosses the Hackensack and Passaic and then enters Newark with stations at East Ferry and Ferry Streets (in the heart of the manufacturing district) and at Broad

Holding on, Lackawanna ferries combined service with the Erie, forgetting old rivalries. Here the likeness of Sam Sloan presides over the customary congregation of pigeons in the palatial Lackawanna-Erie terminal square.

Street, the last being the most central of any railroad station in Newark. From Newark a branch runs to Elizabethport, Elizabeth and Roselle, connecting at the first-named for the Jersey coast and Pine resorts and Freehold, and at the second for places on the main line and its connections. The trains for the track of the New Jersey Jockey Club run part of the distance over the Newark branch and the balance over the Newark and Elizabeth branch. . . ."

It is well to remember at least two things here: first, that this was a record of rail transportation as it was in the late 1880's, far less than a century ago; and second, that few riders were upset by changes from one train to another, and, when the time came, from one trolley car to another. Time was not always of the essence:

"The main line follows the shore of Bergen Neck and crosses Newark Bay to Elizabethport, where connection is made for Perth Amboy and intermediate stops, for all points on the New York and Long Branch Railroad (the famous resorts of the Jersey coast and the race-course at Monmouth Park); on the Freehold and New York Railroad, and on the Jersey Southern Railroad (Lakewood and Atlantic City).

"From Elizabeth the main stem proceeds through a series of beautiful and thriving suburban villages and towns (Roselle, Cranford, Westfield, Fanwood, Netherwood, Dunellen) and the city of Plainfield to Bound Brook. To this point the road is four-tracked to accommodate the Philadelphia, Baltimore, and Washington express trains run by the Central Railroad of New Jersey in connection with the Philadelphia and Reading and the Baltimore and Ohio Railroads, and also the trains of the Lehigh Valley Railroad, which come in near Roselle. Bound Brook is the junction-point for the Philadelphia, Baltimore, and Washington trains. Two stations beyond is Somerville, the terminus of the suburban system and the junction for the South Branch Railroad, which runs to Flemington. From Somerville the main stem continues through the flourishing manufacturing settlement of Raritan and a number of small villages to Phillipsburg, sending at High Bridge a branch to Schooley's Mountain, Budd's Lake, Lake Hopatcong, and a line of rich mines in the Jersey Highlands. Then, having crossed the Delaware, the railroad reaches the rich coal and iron fields of Pennsylvania via Easton, Bethlehem, and Allentown to Scranton."

I have quoted extensively from Gustav Kobbé's little book in an effort to achieve a number of things, none of them to the edification of rail buffs who, for the most part, do not like comparisons even as I made them that day, with *Jersey Central* in hand, a surprise for any interloper. Fortunately, there was none. The stillness that was outside in the area of the train shed which still upheld what had been called "one of the finest sky-lights in the country," was intensified in the terminus with its clock tower, gables, and the high-ceilinged room where, in the gloom, I could discern the "ornamental rafters of iron" so impressive to Gustav. Here was an idleness unfamiliar to passengers who knew a skylight and windows that had provided "perfect light and ventilation," a waiting room with galleries all around which now seemed smaller, and polished seats as broad as the room itself. Now there were no seats.

When I dawdled in and out, I saw that the dining room was closed, and I doubt if Gustav would have recognized it—although a lunch bar (that would have been a new term even to him) was open for the wayfarer in search of a cup of coffee. The stairs to the galleries and upper decks of the ferryboats were chained off and marked "Closed." Only a courageous barber was open for business on the river side. As elaborate as were the fixtures shown in the pen-and-ink sketch of F. A. Farraud, they had been replaced by something more "modern" long ago; the waiting room shown by the artist, crowded by women in bustles and men with valises instead of "Madison Avenue lunchboxes," was filled instead with only a memorable, touchable, quiet, fit companion for gray shadows that reached up into the half dusk. Outside there was the hiss of steam escaping from a coupler or two; inside the dust of dying seemed to be everywhere.

Howard E. Johnson, of Plainfield, already has told me, from a collector's array of trains and trolleys, that he was sure I had visited the old terminal in what he called "non-rush hours." "The rush hour of the Jersey Central's concourse is still tremendous," he assured me. "Then you will find that half of the seventeen tracks are in use and also that stairways to the upper levels of boats are open. With the removal of the Baltimore and Ohio trains the Central has lost some of its glamor, but they still run more than a hundred trains daily. William R. Wright, of Cranford, argued that with the merger of the Erie and the Lackawanna "the Hoboken terminal is now about as busy as the Jersey Central was in the 1940's." However, even Warren Crater agreed that the days of the ferries were numbered and that children and grandchildren should be taken quickly on what would be "their only ferry ride in a lifetime."

I pushed on to the next ferry, the old Pennsylvania. Here, against a background of foundations, only one ferry-slip was left almost entire beside the swaying vertebrae of a long dead companion. Rails in passenger yards were being torn up.

Where once I had wandered into the ghostly dark of the dust-laden Erie terminal, with its newsstands closed and ticket windows rolled down for the last time, demolition was already in progress in the summer of 1959. Less than two years later the building had vanished, weather-worn entrances to the Hudson tubes loomed up in empty yards like grotesque mausoleums, and although tracks were still down, weed-grown, the old ferry-slips were offshore, buffers for barges tied snugly behind them. Old sheds led to nothing at all, contradicting live steam in overhead pipes, as caked ice of a difficult winter mingled with the ragged remains of old buildings. Cracked concrete of once-smooth walkways ended at the water's edge. When I had come there before, some of the old signs were still up, and in one of the vacant slips a bridgeman's wheel rocked up and down in oily water, reluctant to make a crossing on its own.

In those earlier days only a few tracks were torn up where the Erie's commuter train schedule ended at the terminal. One passenger coach was orphaned at the end of the line, a forlorn and forsaken prophet. Two men I saw, intent upon errands across the twisted rails that once were straight and had led to barges in their day, told me, when I went there last, that the Erie boats used the slips of the hospitable Lackawanna but that there were rumors of the building of a new pier. In this lament for the passing of the ferries, something of a true requiem has crept in, a kind of echo of something heard before. Such memorials should be important, it seems to me, to a generation that will never know the adventure of crossing a river on a ferryboat, that never was fully aware of the importance of the ferries themselves, and is already incredulous when I, with words alone, put steam locomotives and lumbering coaches on cinders of empty roadbeds, barges in what used to be business-filled canals.

"What was a ferry?" "Where were the canals?"—or, as they say it in some regions of the state, the "canawls"? "Why did the railroad stop running here?" These, and many, many more are honest, earnest questions deserving sympathetic answers. Those who ask them have missed so much, I felt as I quietly closed the pages of *Jersey Central* and stood with mixed emotions at the foot of the worn stairways in the gathering gloom of a ferry terminal that once held the continuing hum of commerce and the sight of fashion. Even from the first it has not been what some people, in varying circumstances, call "a good death."

The Erie, which had been operating ferries across the Hudson from Pavonia Avenue since May, 1861, had twice posted notices of cessation of service—first on August 14, 1957, and then on September 14, 1958—at last gave up just before Christmas of that year. After that the raging fire, which in many aspects was a funeral pyre, swept the New York Central's unaccustomed emptiness into lasting silence—even though long lines of new automobiles awaited loading beyond the blackened sheds the last time I went there. That in itself was "rubbing it in." By then Erie passengers of the Northern Branch had been shifted to Hoboken. After a last look through boarded windows of a boiler room and a glance at an old-fashioned lunch car, in which a light betrayed lingering life, I walked away. I won't go back.

Literature that was put into the hands of the last of the Weehawken ferry commuters in March, 1959, provided what should have been recognized as a fairly complete autopsy report: Bridges and tunnels had done to death some of the most historic of the ferries and would eventually get them all—after all, the New York Central's ferry had been operating more than one hundred and thirty years.

"It seems amazing," said E. C. Nickerson, vice president for passenger sales and service on the Central at that time, "that less than a generation ago forty-five thousand riders used these ferries every day, but that today there remain only five thousand, of whom only three thousand use our West Shore rail service. In other words, eight out of ten commuters have been siphoned off to the use of auto and bus, after three decades and three hundred and fifty millions of public authority spending for bridges and tunnels. . . ."

With other less official pallbearers the spokesman went on to prophesy the eventual collapse and abandonment of *all* rail facilities, of which, naturally enough, ferryboats were looked upon as an offspring. You took a train to the edge of a river and from there you took a boat to the other side of the river—it was, as they say, as simple as that. However, symptoms of creeping paralysis already were evident. Here, perhaps, is another theme to ponder: The full color of history began fading long ago because folklore—history as it was and was remembered by participants who, in many instances because they could not write, were compelled to pass on what they knew, verbally, to their descendants—was dismissed as incidental and virtually despised as unreliable and unimportant.

For instance, it was from railroad men that the reminder came of the Weehawken Ferry's birth, traceable to "the United States Supreme Court's most quoted decision and nurtured by the most famous gun duel in American history."

It seems that it was Chief Justice John Marshall's "epic *Gibbons* vs. *Ogden* decision" of March 2, 1824, that freed the Hudson River for interstate commerce and, ironically enough, as the authorities put it, laid the legal groundwork for the Transportation Act of 1958, under which the Central's and other ferry services were discontinued. Before this far-reaching decision ferry service between mid-Manhattan and the North Hudson area of the state was limited to for-hire sailing craft. Railroad men are prone to spell the name *pirogues*, but I have seen the alternate *piraguas* as frequently. Whatever the spelling, these ships were fashioned with blunt prows, decks well forward, and cabins after for passengers. These vessels maintained no schedules and made the mile-long crossings only when pay, weather, and the ferryman's inclination added up to what he concluded were favorable conditions.

Feuding between the residents of New York and New Jersey continued as if it were part and parcel of crossing the Hudson. It was steam, however, and the rival steamboat patents of Robert Fulton and John Fitch that brought on a near-naval war between the two states, something passingly referred to in schoolbook histories as the New York-New Jersey border war; and this led to the Gibbons-Ogden decision. The Fulton steamboat interests, headed up by Aaron Ogden and Robert Livingston, obtained at the end of the century an exclusive right from New York State to run steam ferries between lower Manhattan and Hoboken. The monopoly went unchallenged until 1802, when the Fitch combine, under John Stevens, Thomas Gibbons, and Cornelius Vanderbilt, obtained a sim-

Before the days of steamboats, sailing vessels were often pressed into service as Hudson River ferries.

ilar grant from New Jersey. Cornelius later transferred his principal interests to steam railroads and thus became the builder of the New York Central itself. I often have wondered if he foresaw the day when every railroad would seek to add competition with a ferry to New York.

"Each State, claiming the tide line of the other's shore," the records point out, "the ferryboat captains became in point of fact blockade runners. With violence and anarchy threatening, the dispute came before the Supreme Court. . . ." Behind Ogden was arrayed the team of Fulton, Livingston, and the State of New York. Behind Gibbons were Stevens, Vanderbilt, "and the best-known attorney in the land, Daniel Webster." Any monopoly was ruled out, but as railroads were extended, those with rivers to cross added ferries, each rivaling the other in equipment as well as service. Gustav Kobbé proved that with his rosy description of the terminal that must have impressed him personally, quite apart from the obvious source of his book's subsidy.

Although I am glad Gustav never saw the contrasts that I have, I cannot help but think that his may have been among the phantoms I felt about me that day I wandered the water front for the last time. Uncertainty and something more were in the stillness that day, down from the lower Palisades, as if throwing a gray pall over an empty casket. Now that I recall it, the recollection is not excessively kind, even as an analogy; all of this suddenly took me back to the sight of a gilded but voiceless circus calliope, shrouded in the cobwebs of untold years in a forgotten livery stable.

Not until I was returning did I remember that I had not seen old Marmaduke. Most important among the unsung passengers of even the last boat in service at the old Erie terminal, the "Arlington," was Marmaduke—although actually he never was a passenger at all. Marmaduke was a sea gull that probably had not seen or smelled the sea in many a year, if ever in his long life. Whenever a ferry whistle announced a boat's departure, Marmaduke rose lazily from his hidden perch, circled the boat twice, and then flew proudly across the Hudson ahead of it. When I last inquired, on behalf of some of the last ferry-riders who remembered him kindly, no one knew what had happened to the silent, shabby, but dutiful bird that for so long was an unofficial, and unrewarded, pilot of the ferries.

I am glad that the Hudson River ferries, as I write, are not quite dead, and especially that the Lackawanna terminal is still part of a tradition that has from the beginning had its own color and, yes, adventure. As one who rode the ferryboats between Camden and Philadelphia with boyish delight—even that worn and much-repaired paddle-wheeling "Wenonah"—I have watched the ferries close and vanish along the Delaware River, and now there is a void that nothing in this world can refill. There is much more to it than the eagerness or boredom or companionship of commuters, much more than the rusting or removal of tracks that led the way to the river's shore, and certainly much more than the little hotels and cafés and emporiums frequented by sailormen and strangely in tune with an old and cobbled river front.

In none of these ruminations do I willingly turn my back on ferryboats of the Erie, now given haven in slips of the Erie-Lackawanna-Hoboken end of the line, or the Jersey Central, still persevering from its own darkening terminal. I am merely stressing the fact that this is not the usual kind of obituary but rather an unfinished requiem. Perhaps in many ways it is akin to those obituary notices, written in advance by sinister habit, about outstanding personalities, and then filed away to await the moment of death. When the end comes, the notice is withdrawn from its hideaway in newspaper libraries or composing rooms, for the addition of the two or three lines, called a "lead," to which all the rest can be quickly appended. In some instances the "hold for release" obituaries, set in type and stored away, have appeared by accident and those involved have come to a premature end, at least in print. However and whenever the announcement is made, death will come hardest of all in Hoboken, for this will be the end of many a dream on the "Seacoast of Bohemia."

I came upon the name when there was some lingering argument as to whether "Sybil's Cave" remained evident or if "Sybil's Spring" still bubbled up from the earth beside the old River Walk. Then, even as I was being reassured by one who had played on the stairway inside the cave, refreshed by clear, cold water of the spring before the great rocky precipice below the site of Stevens Castle had been sealed for safety's sake, Janice Wheeler, of Breton Harbors, near Toms River, told me of a drawing of the cave itself. It had appeared in *Gleason's Pictorial Drawing-Room Companion* of 1852, which had been used, she said, as an illustration in the late Christopher Morley's *Seacoast of Bohemia*—a little book of some sixty-eight pages of which she owned a copy. I hastened shoreward to examine it.

The drawing showed the gallants of their day with their ladies in a little park provided with scattered tables, all at the bottom of a rocky steep from which trees and flowers managed to draw precarious life. "Sybil's Spring" was shown to be covered over in its own ornate pavilion, beside which another building had been erected, two stories high with something above, which we would call a sun-deck. Under the caption, "Sybil's Cave, Hoboken, New Jersey," was this description:

"Hoboken is beautifully situated in New Jersey, on the Hudson River, directly opposite the south end of New York City, and is, together with Staten Island, the quickest resort of the New Yorkers. You take the ferry at the foot of Barclay Street, Canal Street, or Christopher Street, and in five minutes you are in the country. Thousands visit this 'paradise of Gotham' daily. The shore is wild and rocky; it is beautifully laid out into walks, promenades, and parks, overshadowed by the richest foliage. It has one or two churches, several first-rate hotels, and contains a thousand or more regular inhabitants; it also possesses a very large shipyard. The whole is owned by W. L. Stevens, Esq., to whom belongs the immortality of not only making, but keeping the finest spot adjacent to any city in the world. Sybil's Cave, Hoboken, is one of the principal attractions of the place. No one visits Hoboken without seeing it. It has been hewn out and excavated from a solid rock to the depth of thirty feet. In the middle is a spring of pure and sparkling water, thousands of glasses of which are sold daily in the summer, for a penny per glass. The cave was designed by the owner, W. L. Stevens, Esq. In the engraving Hudson River and Weehawken are seen in the distance. The small building adjoining is a place for refreshments."

I compared this description with another, far better known in the New Jersey volume of the *American Guide Series* of

1939—even as I sent out a call for a copy of Christopher Morley's *Seacoast of Bohemia,* which by some good fortune I was soon to own.

"To seamen, as well as to visiting New Yorkers, River Street is the heart of Hoboken. An almost unbroken row of saloons, with cheap hotels and flats above, stretches along one side of this broad, paved street. On the other side are the entrances to the piers on Hudson River, protected by high wire fences. During the arrival and departure of the great liners, River Street resounds to the rattle of innumerable trucks and taxis, the footsteps of excited, hurrying travelers and their friends. Between times, the street is a Rialto of the seamen of all nations, interspersed with stevedores and longshoremen. The swinging doors of the many saloons admit tieless workers in blue denim shirts, or loitering sailors looking for a berth. In larger back rooms the seafarers meet the local citizenry to dance at night to the music of small jazz bands, mechanical pianos or phonographs, or drink beer at small tables with checkered cloths. . . ."

"Through this same area," the description goes on a little later, after a somewhat unkind interval, "are taverns and dance halls of a different type where a respectable German clientele finds quiet entertainment reminiscent of Continental cafés, and excellent food, served in the best German tradition. There are larger places with old-fashioned fixtures, decorated mirrors, and cut-glass doorways outside swinging doors. Hoboken has been famous for its beer since 1642, though none is brewed here today. . . ." This paragraph, coming after a long skip, perhaps caught my eye in connection with another colorful interval in the life of the Hudson River ferries:

"During 1928 and 1929 Christopher Morley and his associates brought back the sophisticated New York crowds that once pressed into the two old theaters by presenting the melodrama of another generation. *After Dark* and *The Black Crook* kept the Rialto and Lyric alive with eager sightseers. 'Seidel over to Hoboken' became a national phrase. But the competition from Harlem was too strong in 1929. The novelty-seeking crowd drifted away, and the theaters were closed, to reopen as third-run moving picture houses."

My copy of *Seacoast of Bohemia* came from a dealer in rare books in Jersey City, although others were offered on loan, and I saw at once that its jacket, in red and green against a yellow background, was worth the price of the book. For worked into the design were River, Hudson, and Washington Streets, with Newark Street leading up from the Hudson, so that locations of hotels like Meyer's, the Riverview, and the Continental were easily picked out in their relationship to the Lackawanna ferry and the all-important Rialto Theatre. Assigned to seeming lesser importance by the artist with the name "Clam Broth" and an arrow was what now has become the Clam Broth House, which, it was apparent when I was there, was not only among the survivors, like the Continental Hotel, but had expanded to take in a corner. The Hofbrau Haus, obviously a favorite of Christopher Morley and his cronies, wore a new mantle, as did so much more, with even a new name.

"This is the history of four infatuated adventurers," says the jacket blurb of *Seacoast of Bohemia*, whose principal sale was in the lobby of the Rialto and was published in 1929 "for the old Rialto Theatre, 118 Hudson Street, Hoboken, New Jersey, by Doubleday, Doran, Inc." These "adventurers" included the author of *Thunder on the Left*, Cleon Throckmorton, Conrad Milliken, and Harry Wagstaff Gribble, "who rediscovered the old Rialto Theatre in Hoboken, refurnished it for hilarity, and made 'the pagan old playhouse' both famous and financially successful in one of New York's most disastrous theatrical seasons."

All the text of the little book is interesting to me, but here I must be limited to excerpts under the heading of buried history and fading folklore. Chris Morley in his preface said that the original predecessor of the Rialto, "as far as we know, was Weber's Germania Garden, erected about 1863. It was a two-story building," he went on, "numbered 68–74 Hudson Street (the numbers have since been altered), and had a beer-garden adjoining. The ground floor was used for vaudeville performances, the hall upstairs for meetings and dancing. Among the earliest performers remembered . . . [in Morley's day were] the Mullers; part of the attraction of this team was that the lady had very short skirts and rather massive legs in white stockings. . . . Some time in the early '80's, no one knows just when, the Germania Garden became Wareing's Theatre, from which time numerous delightful old playbills have been preserved. Wareing was evidently ambitious, for

One can stand on the once famous River Walk below the Stevens Institute in Hoboken without knowing that rocks conceal Sybil's Spring— what remains of a circular iron staircase and ornate pavilions where hundreds came to take their ease and buy a penny glass of the crystal-clear water in the 1850's. Warehouses now line the river shore, and Sybil's Cave is merely a drawing in *Gleason's Drawing-Room Companion* of 1852.

about 1887 he built another theater in the next block on Hudson Street, which still exists under the name of the Lyric. Siegfried Cronheim presently took over the senior house, restoring its original name of the Germania.

"There is some confusion in the records and it cannot positively be stated whether Hoboken's greatest dramatic evenings took place in Wareing's new house or in the older one. There are partisans of both theories. What is certain is that in April, 1887, Mrs. Langtry appeared on Hudson Street for a week in three plays: *The Lady of Lyons, A Wife's Peril,* and *Pygmalion and Galatea.* These were the great days of the Hoboken stage. Among other attractions of '87 and '88 were Bronson Howard's *The Banker's Daughter,* Hoyt's *A Parlor Match,* Kate Claxton and Charles Stevenson in *The Two Orphans,* Edwin Thorne in *The Black Flag.* Harrigan and Hart played here, and Weber and Fields, in their salad days, billed far down the variety list as knockabout comedians in *The Crazy Dutchman.* Another star was Mme. Janauschek, who was programmed as having 'power and emotional force greater than Ristori, a nervous and fiery intensity equal to Rachel, and a skill for elaboration and finish only equalled by Sarah Bernhardt. . . .'

"A reminiscent citizen signing himself 'Old Timer,' recalling the Cronheim era in the Jersey *Observer,*" Chris Morley continued later on, "specially mentions 'a large Juno-like woman' who sang only in German and who was sometimes accompanied by a Robert Ganzberg, who had a show of his own around on Washington Street between First and Second Streets and who, 'Old Timer' declared, was the father of thirty children. . . ." In old Wareing programs a café "in a tunnel under the theatre" was mentioned, with this added note:

"It is earnestly requested that the patrons of this theatre will refrain from eating peanuts; it mars the performance and annoys the audience."

Participants in the Hoboken theater adventure, already

members of what they called the Three Hours for Lunch Club in New York, paid little attention to matters of lesser interest beyond cuisine and the stage—although I would have wanted to go aboard the "Leviathan," then lying dingy and derelict, "a memento of bad times" at one of the piers. Christopher Morley, in calling *Seacoast of Bohemia* an intimate scrapbook, indicates that such notables as St. John Ervine, J. Brooks Atkinson, R. Dana Skinner, and David McCord ferried over to Hoboken, enjoyed drama at the Old Rialto, and commented on their adventures pleasantly in their columns. "It would have been amusing," he added, however, "to quote from an article in which a Manhattan journalist let on that he himself of course had been going to Hoboken for years; but alas he gave himself away by saying that it was done 'by dropping five cents in the slot.' Anyone who has actually traveled our humid old Hudson Tube knows well that it costs a dime; and it isn't a slot, but a sort of perforated catch-all in which your money makes a delicious tinkling. This same jovial pretender did himself gruesome wrong by describing the Hoboken resorts, which he plainly never had seen, as 'quaint,' with 'candles on the tables.' He was mixing us up with Greenwich Village. There isn't room on a Hoboken tavern table for any candles; and 'quaint,' thank God, is the last thing Hoboken will ever be. . . ."

Most memorable, I think, is that this chapter in the Hoboken story, or even a requiem for the ferries, owed so much to a ferryboat crossing to the Lackawanna Terminal, on the Hudson shore which to producers and patrons alike became the Seacoast of Bohemia, where so much has changed. Perhaps some names would be familiar on River Street or Hudson Street, down from the old typically German pork stores that cling to what used to be; others, I fear, would not, in an array in which it is sometimes difficult to tell, without trying old doors, which taverns are open and which have closed forever. The Café Antwerpen and the Seven Seas Bar rub elbows with the Cherokee, the Paddock, Peggy's Tavern, and Eleanor's

Harbor Lights. On a corner there was a little sign, pinned to a curtain, which announced that the Christian Seamen's and Immigrants' Home was closed and out of business. The Holland-America Line and the American Export Lines were among those still determined to uphold the reputation of the old port.

I showed my copy of *Seacoast of Bohemia* to the proprietor of the Clam Broth House, distinguished enough to have won the recent commentaries of Clementine Paddleford, just as I had shown Gustav Kobbé's *Jersey Central* to the man in the ticket booth outside the Central's terminal when there was one. He was surprised, indicating that he never had seen the Morley book before or that his establishment had been indicated on the jacket, for all that the Clam Broth had been there since 1898. He was uncertain where the Rialto had been, but, outside, I asked a man who said his name was Joseph Siemes how long he had known the neighborhood. "Been here sixty-three years," he replied amiably, adding that he would point out where Christopher Morley's theater had been.

The Rialto's site is now a parking lot, reached irregularly through from Hudson Street to Washington.

Chapter XV

UNDERCLIFF

It was not until I was aboard a New York Central train, on its way to Buffalo along the opposite shore of the Hudson River, that I thought of ways in which to begin the story of the Palisades and Undercliff.

Undercliff was the "Fishermen's Village" of more than eight hundred souls, a scattering of cottages that stretched along the base of a wall of rock jabbing jagged pinnacles into the sky from above Fort Lee to well beyond the New York line. Across the river I realized suddenly that spring truly must come sooner on the New Jersey side and that in spite of all the reasons ichthyologists must give, I put greater credence on the legend of the first shad. Fish know more than men anyway—at least they know enough to swim up a river on the side protected by the purples, grays, and blacks of boulders etched by the season's earliest greens.

The story goes, you see, that when the first shad is caught at or near Alpine Landing, where the last worn pilings recall the ferry that crossed to Yonkers, word is flashed to New York City in what has been called "a rite that for more than two hundred years has marked the coming of spring." There is no record of how the first shad fishermen of Undercliff transmitted the news or if, when it was received, there was an immediate flurry in Wall Street. Nor am I more certain now how the word travels to New York to become, when it is not crowded out, a few paragraphs in boxed blackface type on front pages of daily newspapers. However, persistent wandering for more than a decade over and through the Palisades Interstate Park—suddenly in focus by sustained observation through the window of a moving coach across the water—convinced me that "this barricade of rock, given the form of columns when the molten mass cooled," has guarded secrets of its past far better than Undercliff families considered possible.

This was one way in which to begin, with the comforting reflection that even as I had walked forsaken paths along the stony overhang that seemed to crowd down like frowning foreheads on the cover of dry and crunching leaves, I had not been alone. Nor was I in any sense alone when I was shown the way to a small burial place, fenced in with barbed wire reaching out of walls of stone. Here were headstones bearing names familiar to Undercliff, and spring once again was heralding her approach with more than myrtle's green, fronds of fern gently uncurling, and where the ground was wet, the more flagrant skunk cabbage. However, on the New York side, in spite of the coming and going of urban encroachments that the families of Undercliff had feared, long stretches of the Hudson's shore had seemed, by comparison, as bleak and barren as a hard winter could make it. Up from Ossining there were cakes of ice, floating on the tide; north of Peekskill, the surface remained more and more unbroken.

Another way to begin, I thought almost as quickly, wondering if someone just might tell me when the first shad *was* caught—they never did, although I watched many an April come and go—was with a photograph, one of many in my bag, included in the hope that there might be inspiration for the poetry required for at least the first paragraphs on Undercliff. This one had been taken from an old post card, one of many sent to me by at least a hundred new friends surprisingly aroused by what the historians had written and rewritten of the area. Although it had been titled "Fisher's Village, Foot of Palisades," by its publisher, the old Albertype Company, of Brooklyn, only close observation revealed all of it: the Undercliff houses (not huts or shanties) as they lined the shore, nets hung out to dry, an anvil perched atop a beer keg, and a

Undercliff, often called "The Fishermen's Village," was shown on an old postcard, with nets out to dry, little white houses with picket fences, and (perhaps) the famous tree of the Pear Tree Farm.

bearded fisherman, certainly one of the solid citizens of the village in his day.

In the midst of all that I, too, nearly missed a salient feature, one that had served as a landmark through many a day (as the names of Allison and Huyler ever will for me)—a fruit tree, probably a pear, already in bloom. One of the last houses of Undercliff, outdistancing all but two others even as the fishermen's wives seem to have outlived their men, had been fondly and frequently referred to as "The Pear Tree Farm."

Still another way to begin I thought, as the train moved opposite the Monastery of the Holy Cross in West Park above the New Jersey line, might be with the name of Allison: Allison—not as it had been given to one of the formal lookouts of the Palisades Parkway (so arranged, I think, that they induce those who pause to gaze far off rather than immediately below them, in the manner of a man who never knows when his shoes need a shine), nor in the name of John Allison. It was John who discovered a sheaf of notes by his father William in time to produce a most creditable series of articles on Undercliff by one of its natives. No, I was thinking of the name Henry Allison, as we found it at last in the small and almost hidden cemetery within walking distance from a picnic area. Henry's stone, I recalled, had fallen over and was broken, so that only his age, seventeen, was revealed without a date of death.

It has been suggested that there are more graves in the walled-in plot, riverward from Englewood and close by where boulders of appreciable size have come plummeting down from the Palisades themselves, than are indicated by the limits of the wall. Thick myrtle continues to creep down closer to the river shore, and many notable Undercliff names are conspicuous by their absence. It may be, as some have said, that falling stones covered much that was there in the beginning, but from the first time I heard it, this seemed unlikely. Perhaps many of the last of the pioneers of Undercliff never owned stones at all or, in some instances, buried their dead on the highlands beyond the Palisades.

These, then, are some of the other names and dates you will find up from the drive to the parking place and picnic area and not far from where trickling waterfalls give the first greenings of the year so early a start: Samuel Woodhams, who died in 1865 at fifty-seven; Julia, the wife of Theophilus H. Bloomer and daughter of the Reverend John and Sarah Smith, who died at twenty-one in 1837; William Whitlock, who died in 1837 when he was only eight; Belinda Woolsey, the wife of George Bloomer, who died in 1815; Peter VanWagoner, who died in 1811 when he was six months old; and Jane VanWagoner, who died in 1812. One small stone bears only this legend: "Our Little John. Departed this life, 1872—two years and ten days." From the number of mounds in the enclosure, mostly screened from the world and the hilarity that comes and goes with the seasons downhill, I would say that there are about twenty graves in all.

So, in cataloguing ways in which to begin, I seem to have begun.

Actually, I began long ago on the crest of the Palisades where, as it seems to me now, the coming of the Interstate Park was of sufficient surprise all of sixty years ago to have caught at least some of the owners of the great estates of another era off guard and almost unaware of Undercliff. That is one reason why there remain, just off the dual Palisades Parkway or the paralleling but older 9W, carriage houses that briefly became garages, as well as elaborate gateways of ornamental iron or stone. Some of these, with parts of adjoining walls, are to be found orphaned when change came quickly as in the strip that divides the two strands of parkway. Here lookouts are provided, formally laid out yet descended from the far less formal "pitching places" of days before such distinguished identification as Allison Park—there's that name again! —or Rockefeller and Alpine Lookouts, certainly before sign-painters were enlisted to limit parking, prohibit picnicking except in designated areas, and point the way to foot trails far older than those who use them.

More than twenty years ago John Allison wrote:
"Near the ferry dock of the present-day Alpine Landing stands a house which has nestled at the foot of the wooded talus for nearly two hundred years. At one time a tavern where, it is said, Lord Cornwallis tarried on an evening in the fall of 1776, the house and one other are all that remain of Undercliff. You may well be amazed, as you contrast the aspect today with that of a hundred years past, that Undercliff as a prosperous community has vanished as completely as have some of our western bonanza towns.

"Walk two miles north from the Englewood Dock (Dyckman ferry landing) and you are under the prominence Clinton Point. A house and farm stood there—one of the earliest of the Undercliff homes. Today the spot is marked by a gigantic pear tree which tops a grassy bank a dozen yards above the river. Seventy-five years ago old residents proclaimed that their grandparents knew the pear tree as an equally hoary sentinel standing as mute reminder of some shore-dweller before their time. Not far from this spot, in the spring of 1856, the last catamount seen in the regions of the Palisades was brought to bay.

"The Pear Tree Farm may ante-date the coming of the Huylers who early made their abode on the shore beneath Alpine. One of the Huyler houses still stands on the river-bank, a mile north of which the first road reaching the cliff summit wound its way perilously upward through a steep ravine. It is the road up which, during the Revolution, Cornwallis led his battalions of Hessians, Yagers, and English reserves in his march along the Palisades to Fort Lee.

"Perhaps you have noticed steep ravines hard by some jutting prominence as you gaze upward along the far-flung line of cliffs—'pitching places' were what the Undercliff people called them. There was one near the Green Brook, known as Jeffrey's Pitching Place, and another above the Englewood Dock.

"Lands on top of the Palisades were at one time owned by prominent families of New York City for the sole purpose of providing firewood. During the early 1800's men were sent with ax and ox-team to cut fuel destined to warm the stately mansions of the rich. Felled timber was hauled to the precipice—the pitching place—and tossed over, to be picked up by a waiting schooner. Great must have been the crashing and rending of wood as huge logs of hickory and oak were sent hurtling down these rocky ravines. Other pitching places were Cordtland-Jay's and Mott's. DePeyster's was located at Alpine while slightly south of the present Undercliff Bathing Beach was a pitching place appropriately named High Tom's.

"Visitors in the Park today might find it difficult to realize that the Hudson River, now of somewhat somber aspect from the Palisade shores, once teemed with life and activity upon waters as clear as the far reaches of Long Island Sound. In those times sloops and schooners prevailed. It was a common sight to see as many as one hundred and fifty grouped, their sails flapping, while they waited for the turn of the tide. There were brick boats from Haverstraw, dockstone sloops of Undercliff, and the 'pickle' boats. Also the market sloops touching at Tarrytown and the Alpine Dock on the opposite shore. Here the farmers from the hinterland west of the Palisades brought their produce down the steep slopes to be carried to New York markets.

"Literally colorful was the river-scene then, for it was a fashion among the boatmen to paint their craft in alternate striping of varied hue. Much rivalry concerning this colored banding of boats prevailed among the captains, and it is told that Captain Jake VanWagoner's sloop, *The Sailor's Fancy*, eclipsed all others among these winged rainbows of the Hudson. . . ."

Concerning these paragraphs and those that follow, I must point out that Jim Ransom had referred occasionally to what he called "The Allison Papers." He had not more than his own name for them, and it was only natural that until I saw them I had concluded that they were part of a vast bundle, like dozens of other private papers I had seen in as many collections of county historical societies, awaiting careful editing. Not once did it occur to me that what was involved was a series of three newspaper articles, delightfully illustrated with pen-and-ink sketches by John Allison, an Englewood artist and collector. Even now I am limiting my quotations because I hope that someone will make a permanent brochure of this colorfully presented material from an original and unique source, the notes of John's father William who was born in Undercliff in 1840.

The first settlers of Undercliff, the Allisons recalled, were for the most part of Dutch descent. There were Huylers at Alpine, they said, and toward the south end of the settlement, Bloomers, with Westerveldts, Bleekers, Beckers, VanScivers, and VanWoerts in between. John wrote:

"It has been told of a family coming down the river from Haverstraw who, first settling in Manhattanville on the New York side, found it 'too lonely,' subsequently moving to Undercliff for the 'sake of society.' Again, as if to prove that what is New York City was a desolate abode for any man, it is told that 'Great Grandfather Norman' who kept the Black Horse Tavern at Tubby Hook (Dyckman Street), eventually came to the Palisade shore for the same reason.

"During Undercliff's early days, fishing held first place as an industry. Fyke nets were set for Tom cod and other finny inhabitants of the once clear waters. Hudson River Shad appeared on hotel menus throughout the country and shad catches proved by far the most profitable, often enabling a fisherman to lead a lounging existence on a single season's income. But while the season lasted, the fisherman's life meant plenty of hard work with the long boats and nets to be kept in condition. There was little time for loafing then when sharks and sturgeon often played havoc with the nets while on occasions a sea-dog might become entangled with the meshes.

"At intervals along the shore-line stood the powder houses, flat-roofed structures of red brick, some of them storage magazines for the Hazard and duPont Companies. Abandoned, one of these buildings served the dual function of a religious meeting place and a play-party hall. Dances and other amusements were gotten up and held in the Old Powder House, where the ladies of bonnet and shawl would vie with one another in providing refreshment. Pompey and Sheepshead, Negro boatmen by day—the latter a slave of the Bloomers— provided music, scraping out jigs and hoe-down tunes. Among the favorites were 'Sugar in the Gore' and 'Brennan on the

Moor' while now and again Pompey would break in with a refrain:

> Workin' on a bumboat, two shillins a day,
> Pick up oakum—Pick up oakum.
> Rooted here for life, I'll never get away,
> Johnnie can't you pick upon de banjo.

"Should the evening wax more than usually gay, Captain Crum might sing 'The American Boy' or 'Butternut Hill,' for many and merry were those parties in the Old Powder House. Winter evenings were spent in swapping yarns—and some were mighty—or in listening to shoemaker John Park read from Fox's *Book of Martyrs* and *The Arabian Nights*. The only 'story' paper known to Undercliff in those days was the New York *Ledger*. From its pages John would spell his listeners with a serial, 'Orion the Gold Beater.'

"There were occasional excursions to New York City. Following a fifteen-mile sail down the river, 'the boys' would walk along Broadway to Benson's [sic] 'place' at Lispenard Street, where Benson, erstwhile resident of Undercliff, would regale the home-town friends with champagne. . . .

"In Undercliff there were certain families known for that kind of hospitality in which an almost universal welcome prevailed. Many were the newcomers and often odd characters sharing a catholicity of good will. Among them were iron-jawed Jimmy Mulholland who, it was said, would win wagers by biting ten-penny nails in two; 'Crazy' Allen, who made and sold sticking plaster throughout the community; and John the Babe, a quarryman whose nickname derived from his propensity to burst into tears for no particular reason.

"But there was one who topped all the others. He was an Irishman and the town tippler—one who 'worked around' and who was known universally as Old Whack-me-Jug. Stimulating drinks were not procurable in the south end of the settlement and, bearing a gallon-sized brown jug on a stick flung over one shoulder, Whack-me-Jug would make regular trips to Annette's in Fort Lee. Singing his way home along the shore, he bore good-naturedly the brunt of ridicule from many. He had a kind of standard stunt which consisted of placing his jug on the ground and jumping over it. Following each leap, he would take a swig and cry in a husky voice, 'Whack-me-Jug,' continuing this performance until the jumps petered out into a mere straddling. But the children liked him; he would amuse them with fantastic tales of fairies and little 'Danes' of Ireland.

"Whack-me-Jug was found dead on the beach by a group of these same children. Jug beside him, he was buried in a little cemetery now overgrown with myrtle and foxgrape. It lies half hidden at the foot of the slope just north of High Tom's Pitching Place and a little to the south of the present Undercliff Beach."

There is no doubt in my mind that Old Whack-me-Jug lies in a grave in what, even in the time of William O. Allison, was a larger burial place than the present one but equally obscure for all that. Without a recorded surname there is no way of telling whether Whack-me-Jug was given a tombstone, but if John Allison's statement means what it says, his jug is with him wherever he lies. John made no reference to the stone fence or the barrier of wire that seems to sprout from it and so I feel sure when the graves that remain in evidence were given added protection, the stone that had been there earlier than the dates I saw had disappeared or may have been covered over. John Allison went on:

"A half mile north of the Englewood Dock were grouped the Bloomer houses. Beyond them stood the first schoolhouse in Undercliff, a tiny whitewashed building, part of its foundation consisting of a sea-wall that skirted the shore. Here the bearded Samuel Moses held forth as schoolmaster to the community's towheads, while it is said of Moses that he was meek as his Biblical predecessor. During the 1840's he was paid a salary of $125. per year.

"In the 1850's came a rich man to the cliff-top, building a mansion of Palisade stone. Trees were felled and sloping lawns reached gray trap rock, edging the sky and the river. Oak framing, rich wainscoting, and stained windows were laboriously hauled to the summit from schooners below. It was here, on the present site of Englewood Cliffs, that William B. Dana and his wife made their lonely abode in a stately stone dwelling. It was here where 'The Lady of the Hill' conducted the first Sunday school for children of Undercliff. . . ."

The location of the Dana mansion is shown on the map John Allison provided for the first of his articles; it lies in from Bloomer's Dock and Pickletown, so named after the villagers of Undercliff made the most of a wrecked ship whose hold had been filled with cucumbers. Locating Ruckman Point, Closter, Alpine, Tenafly, Englewood, and Englewood Cliffs, these, no matter what they have become today, appear on John's map only in relation to Cape Flyaway, Excelsior Dock, the old quarry sites, and the pitching places. Thus they attain their own lost importance.

I had come upon the region of Undercliff on "the top floor"; or, as you might say, my entrance by way of a floral "penthouse" had been so challenging, even captivating, that I ignored the "floors" below without meaning to. John F. Schuetz, of Bergenfield, had asked a question many years before that had set my own probings in motion beyond the pinnacles of the Palisades when Undercliff was no more than a name hastily spoken. To the best of my recollection, it was not mentioned at all on the heights where my first Palisades wanderings began and, where for many years, they had ended. However, it was the reading of the Allison sketches, first printed in the Hudson *Despatch*, that inspired a determination to find what remained of Undercliff and, after that, to find those who might remember more than eyes might see in straining across the river from the Lookouts on the New York side.

I have given you this much of the Allison "papers" merely to set the stage.

"Do you know," John Schuetz had asked, "the legends, or at least the background, of the stone towers in the Alpine Woods just west of the Palisades Interstate Park?" "That must have been the Rio Vista tower, not towers," someone said at last after I had repeated the query in all the wrong places. I dimly remembered a tower, but now I drove in boldly to see a great variety of old buildings sprawled across a landscaped terrain through which passed a number of curving roads. Then, abruptly, there was a truly startling house, as well planned as any I had seen in a long while. Almost as quickly we were talking with Mrs. Manuel E. Rionda, and it was almost as if we had come across a moat and into a castle from a world far, far away.

Deep inside the house Mrs. Rionda spoke freely of the estate next door, as if anything could be really next door. *That* had been Rio Vista, she said. The name of *this* estate, the one in which we were talking together, was Glen Goin—and the name was still on the gateposts beside the drive off 9W when I last went by that way. Mrs. Rionda's husband was the nephew of Manuel Rionda, who had come from Spain in 1904. "He still had a sugar plantation in Cuba when he lived there," she explained.

Manuel died in 1942. In addition to holdings in Cuba and the estate high above the Hudson in an era when the view of New Jersey from New York already was something more than the view of New York from New Jersey, Manuel maintained an office in New York City. "But he loved Rio Vista," Mrs. Rionda said, as if to herself. "Of course the name means River View, as you must know, and Manuel loved to make the most of it. . . ." Yes, there *was* a tower on the old estate. There was a chapel, too. After all, Rio Vista in its heyday covered more than two hundred acres when bridges and tunnels were on drawing boards, and when supermarkets and superhighways, or even an unfriendly Cuba, had not been heard of or at least were no more than fantasies, glimpsed and unreal through billowing mists of the future.

For some reason I felt at this precise moment that I was on the brink of something more, as dramatic and even as tempting as the brink of the Palisades themselves. I can remember the question hurrying through my mind, as furtive as John's concerning "the towers." "What was there on the narrow shore below, what and who had been down there, unseen from the long gallery of overhanging rocks and the thick wild growth of trees, in times before rich men had come to build their palaces, gay times of Rio Vista and Glen Goin, now haunting reminders?" I came back to earth in time to hear Mrs. Rionda granting permission to see the tower about which John Schuetz had asked and of which the lady spoke so lovingly. Back along curving roads, still picturesque as they led through formal gardens, by this time overgrown, we came upon other houses of stone but much smaller. Mrs. Rionda said that these in the beginning had been houses for the help—maids, gardeners, and the rest of an impressive staff.

The tower proved to be one hundred feet tall, very much like something built for a Graustark motion picture, but much more formidable. At the top was a weather-beaten clock which had stopped long before, no one knew how long. Gold leaf had curled up from the face and hands. There was a wide arch under the tower with a doorway leading to rooms on each side. The stairs were gone, and an elevator, in ruin, stood forlornly in its shaft, beyond reclamation.

The place had not been used in many years, that was evident. Windows aloft had been broken, and those on the ground level had been boarded up against the intrusion of vandals. Standing below the arch and gazing off in the direction of the Hudson, I saw another building at the left, completely closed and with its heavy door protected by a massive lock and chain. A workman told me that this had been the library and that another building of the same general design and massive stone had been the chapel. No one ventured there any more.

We moved on that day, seeking more towers without saying so, and thus came to a large cellar hole, so impressive in the size of its emptiness that I wonder why the house was taken down and some of its appurtenances left behind as tombstones. Mrs. Rionda had said that the great manor house, Rio Vista, had gone, and that it had been removed at last by the Park Commission. Then, without warning, we came upon a small stone building such as a gatehouse must have been in

Towers of the Rio Vista estate and others like them are reminders of days when industrial magnates and other notables built palaces along the Palisades, sometimes with rustic summer houses on cliffs overlooking the Hudson. Quarrying for dockstone and paving blocks destroyed pleasure and peace of mind for fishermen and millionaires alike in the nineteenth century.

the same era. Peering through windows long dirty, I knew that I had been there before, for there were drawing boards and blueprints and other equipment of engineers. I could not help but think how utterly ironic it was that a gatehouse, perhaps more than one, which had served the needs of yesterday was being used by men concerned principally with an alien tomorrow—broadening the dual highway, extending the lookouts, and landscaping acres adjoining the very areas where planting and landscaping had come and gone before. Here, however, was a contradictory quirk of the engineering mind, tacitly admitting defeat by leaving the impressive gates and walls of yesterday where they had been and so making them mementos to excite imaginations of today.

Undercliff, out of sight and thus out of mind in even palmier days, had nothing in common with what had come to the upper levels behind the Palisades—it is quite possible that those who lived along the river shore and those beyond the peaks gave thanks for the barrier in between. It was not until 1869 that the elegant Palisades Mountain House was erected on the bluff above Englewood Dock. Part of a new age, it was a palatial structure that accommodated five hundred persons who made the most of what was said to have been a cuisine renowned throughout the entire country. The Mountain House was owned by Senator Lydecker, of Englewood, and William B. Dana, mentioned in the Allison papers and no newcomer to the ridge, but by now editor of *The Financial Chronicle*. Patrons came by ribbon-trimmed steamboat from New York City to a landing at the foot of the cliffs, making their way to the top in carriages whose sweating horses labored up a narrow, steep, and winding road.

"Some," Jim Ransom admitted on one occasion, "came by train to Englewood, and from there by horse and buggy. But as was the case with so many resort hotels, the life of the Palisades Mountain House was short and ended in a disastrous fire not long after its operation had begun. So many have been content to know little more about the Palisades than the name, no matter which side of the Hudson they've been on. Actually, they extend from Bergen Point in New Jersey to Piermont in New York, roughly a distance of some thirty miles. Their altitude varies from a maximum of five hundred and fifty-five feet above sea level at the southern terminus; the mean elevation over most of the ridge is two hundred and sixty-nine feet. They vary in width from two miles to less than a mile and average one and a half miles across. . . ."

Jime goes in for details like that, and it's a good thing that someone does. Turn to *The Legislative Manual of the State of New Jersey,* and this is what you will find:

In the New Jersey section "the (Palisades Interstate Park) Commission maintains and operates seven refreshment stands, two motorboat basins at Englewood and Alpine"—by now they may be *marinas*—"two sunbathing and picnic areas at Alpine and Bloomers, six large picnic groves and many small ones, six parking spaces and about 20 miles of trails. The Henry Hudson Drive, built with funds specially appropriated by the State of New Jersey, is the main artery of traffic in the New Jersey park along the river. Other important highways are the Englewood and Alpine approaches to the drive. With the assistance of the Palisades Nature Association, Greenbrook Sanctuary, in which are located Greenbrook Dam and a 7½-acre pond, continues to be developed by nature groups. . . ."

There is not, as you can see, the slightest reference to Undercliff. Nor, for that matter, is there a nod toward the days after the Civil War when many of the wealthy started building mansions with a kind of competitive fever, as if they intended to transform the land, from which timber had been shorn to heat the New York of long before, into a little Newport-on-the-Hudson. With the continuing development of the park, showplace after showplace began bowing out, some vanishing in holes lined with jagged masonry, some leaving behind great columns and other fragments of ruins for the curious to discover and wonder about. Although I was there soon enough to see the evidence of what for a time must have been another Millionaires' Row, most of that has gone. Here and there the shrubs and perennials of old gardens continue to bloom in strange places, mute memorials to those who planted them and equally silent when park planners assume the credit. Only when an incautious intruder stumbles on ends of Doric columns or a crumbled section of mortared bricks, lost in the long grass, do names come back to revive the old stories once again—legends of the Dales, the Danas, the Goins, and, of course, the Riondas, with at least as many more. Some have said that many of these were better acquainted with the shad and other fish of the Hudson than they were with the man of Undercliff who caught them.

Only a few in all Bergen had spoken openly of Undercliff. Certainly no one but Jim Ransom had referred to it even in passing as "the old Fishermen's Village." For me at this point there were still many gaps in the backdrop—and as many questions. One question that stood out from many in my mind was: Which had outlasted the other, the humble houses along the river shore or the ornate and pretentious castles which had come years after on the heights? The answer is this: Doom came to both at about the same time. The reason is still there, covered over with so much more: the quarries. John Allison wrote:

"Quarrying for dockstone and paving blocks developed into the final and most lucrative occupation in Undercliff. The first black powder blast to send the Palisade trap-rock crashing to the river took place on the Mott property midway between Huyler's Landing at Alpine, and Pickletown at the south end of the settlement. As profits mounted, boarding places accommodating the quarrymen flourished while Mrs. Kearney's tavern under Alpine presented a scene nightly of sloopmen and quarry workers. . . .

"At Buckingham's quarry were made the first paving blocks known as the Russ and Reed which were laid in Fulton Street, New York. Other quarries along the line of the Palisades were Dan Croley's, under Clinton Point, and Jordan's and Van-Sciver's at Alpine, where stood also a general store and oatmeal mill. Captain Becker for years used to say that half of New York City was widened into both rivers on cribs filled with Palisade stone. There were government contracts too; the Maynard quarry, during the 1840's, disgorging hundreds of tons of 'blue trap' which was shipped to New Orleans for the breakwater then in construction. The average price paid for Palisade stone was a dollar a ton.

"Trig and sturdy must have been the sloops and other craft which slid down the ways of the Undercliff boatbuilders. Staunch indeed to stand the wear of the treacherous cargo on which New York City was gradually spreading itself. Peter and Garry Huyler conducted a shipyard under Alpine, as did George Bloomer in the Pickletown section. . . .

"From the boatyards came Josh VanWagoner's *Spy*, a two-master, Billy Allison's *Active*, Pony Jordan's *Guide* and Pete VanWagoner's *Dockbuilder*, all sloops. Among the finest of the schooners built in Undercliff was Captain Becker's *Ajax;* she was considered 'a beauty with a high bowsprit and figurehead' while it is told that 'she later went a-slaving.' . . .

"Following the Civil War, dynamite and improved equipment found its way to the quarries. By 1870 the actual cliff front was threatened, while previously only the talus or fallen rock had been quarried. . . .

"Justifiably, an undercurrent of 'save the Palisades' sentiment began to reach the surface. Many of the Undercliff people sensed early this feeling on the part of the public with the result that interest in maintaining their houses and properties began to wane; it was the beginning of a decadence. Englewood, inchoate suburb on the western slope of the hinterland, offered opportunities to some, while during the decade following many families deserted the community to make their homes in that part of New Jersey known as Northern Valley.

"A gradual exodus took place. During the final years of the century there remained but two families in Undercliff—and they of the first settlers—the VanWagoners and Crums. . . . About them were tumbling porches, rotting wharves, and hollyhock and tansy running wild. Gone were the boatmen and quarry workers—gone the good ladies of bonnet and shawl. . . ."

Not all were gone, I think. In one of myriad letters that have come to me, which I intend to share with you, there were eight to ten cottages there in 1911, with the women, widows of fishermen, ready with their own welcome of tea and cakes. Otherwise I have found nothing anywhere to compare with the record of John Allison, snatched for posterity from the notes of his father, and I do not fault it now. He concluded: "On Christmas Eve in 1900 the pounding crushers of the quarry under Fort Lee were silenced; the dust settled, the mercenary quarrying of Palisade rock ceased forever. The Palisade Interstate Park had begun to function, and a portion of the west bank of the Hudson River was to become one of the great recreational beauty spots of a metropolitan area."

My own feeling is that Millionaires' Row began to shudder, literally, with the persistent blasts of the quarries just over the ledge, and then, when the "save the Palisades" cry went up from two states proposing a park, the closing of the great houses began, even as hope began to die down by the river, in Undercliff itself.

After tossing old names, names of old places and names of pioneer families, in almost every direction, much like an old-fashioned farmer sowing seed, the response was overwhelming. It was as if each name had touched off a fuse. In each mail came letters, post cards, picture post cards processed in Germany, and even a share of long-distance telephone calls. None of these writers or callers had compared notes before offering to supply a portion of the picture that was fading; no one hesitated to send along the segment, no matter how small or large, concluding that it would be needed to catch the rich color and detail of the landscape. Unable to express my own appreciation, or yours, except in these lines, I have looked upon it as the most extraordinary and spontaneous chorus of joy that Undercliff was being remembered again, and honored, and understood. New friends in Rutherford, in Ridgewood, New Milford, and North Bergen joined others (without knowing it) in Closter, Little Falls, the Highlands, Cranford, and even as far off as Los Angeles, with both folklore and questions. Over and over again word came from descendants of Undercliff families who said they had been repeatedly assured that "there was no more to see."

Albert Crum wrote that his ancestors had lived along the Hudson's shore since the late 1600's and that the little walled cemetery of Undercliff, discovered at length with the help of Mrs. Robert Bassford and her son Lance, of Ridgefield Park, had been established there by his own great-great-grandfather. The Weisses in Hillsdale told me about Al Jordan, one of the last shad fishermen descended from the first in The Fishermen's Village and remembered that there were more tombstones in the little graveyard that were not there when I went back, blame vandals, or rock-falls, or what you will. Captain Leon W. Older, of Haworth, said:

"About the Huyler Landing—we lived there when I was a boy, and I climbed to the top of the 'hill,' which was rough going, to school in Alpine. There were four houses here at this time, about 1908: the Brown Cottage; Uncle Tom, Kate, and Charles Older's; John Older's—he lived in the house still standing—and that of my father, Obadiah Older. A cottage further south was that of the VanScivers. . . . My father ran the first ferry between Yonkers and Alpine. My grandfather owned a great deal of the Palisades (from the then dirt road known as

Sylvan Boulevard and now Route 9 to the west shore), whence various sloops and other boats carried produce and much more to New York.

"Did you know that just north of Alpine, at what was known as Riverside Landing, a world's championship fight was held privately for a side bet? The patrons were brought up from New York City on two excursion steamers. Also, have you heard of a family there brought up principally on oatmeal, tea, and fish, or of an industry that made coffee from pea beans, split and colored to look like coffee?"

No one, I admitted quickly, ever had mentioned the fight or the spurious coffee. Paul Syren, of Closter, was one of many who, as if with one accord, remembered where, long ago, they had come upon the Undercliff graveyard "or what was left of it." Almost as many, more timorous, urged that I wait for spring's return "when the lower road would not be officially closed." If I had waited, not risking a sheathing of ice, I would have missed the Huyler Dock House, one of the two remaining houses of Undercliff, frequently referred to but not often identified. The other, I knew, was the Cornwallis house, half hidden behind the parking, boating, and other facilities at Alpine Landing, and little more than a tavern until the General, in moving his troops across the Hudson, spent most of a night there.

Caryl W. Harwood, who said she had been one of the Westervelts, long natives of the area, added "we always understood that our mother was born at Huyler's Landing," but "we didn't know until you mentioned it that there was anything left to see or that we could go there. I know the Huyler Homestead, as they call it in Cresskill, and I have been there. But no one said anything about the Huyler Dock or the Huyler Dock House."

This brought Ernest G. Hansing, who with Mrs. Hansing lives in the Huyler Homestead in Cresskill, to the surface,

Close by where the catch of the first shad heralds the coming of Spring, we found the old Huyler Dock House, almost hidden except from the lower road along the Palisades shore. Boy Scouts turned it into a Sunday museum for a time, but park officials say that its interior is now unsafe.

probably as I was viewing the Huyler Dock House with its windows boarded up tight. He told me:

"The Huyler House on the shore of the Hudson is about one mile south of the old Alpine Ferry. You cannot see it from the top of the road which runs half way between the top of the Palisades and the river unless you leave your car at the entrance of Huyler's Landing Road, which is very steep and blocked off, no cars allowed. This road originally ran from the river over the Palisades to what now is known as Madison Avenue, Cresskill, which at one time was part of the Huyler property. A few years ago Robert Huyler, now deceased, Mr. Dobson, then president of the Bergen County Historical Society, and I were granted permission to visit the house by the river. We found a sixteen-room house, built of brick, with a slate roof—in excellent condition on the outside but in deplorable condition on the inside. There are eight small rooms on the third floor or attic, no doubt where the help slept who worked in the shipyard—four rooms each on the first and second floors, double entrances, with stairs leading up directly behind the front doors.

"This old house is about seventy-five feet from the river. Like it, Huyler's Landing is also going to rack and ruin. The house could easily be restored and a caretaker placed in one side, rent free, to look after it."

I did not see the inside of the Huyler Dock House. As cooperative as park police were, they advised against it. I concluded that they felt that if it was opened for me, and someone saw us, there would be other similar requests. In spite of the fact that the house was an informal museum opened for a small fee by Boy Scouts on week ends as recently as 1939, the interior, I was assured, literally has fallen apart. Once when I returned, a troop of Boy Scouts hiking along the path that follows the river shore paused to rest in the shade of trees that all but envelop the Dock House, and I took occasion to tell them some of its story, stressing the Boy Scout museum chapter. Ernest Hansing went on:

"The property we live in was confiscated by New Jersey after the Revolution from a Tory who fled to Canada, and it was purchased by John Huyler. The small part on the right, probably built before 1770, was the original. The larger section was added in 1836 by Peter, son of John. The roof extends six feet over the front and back, and the position of the house is facing south. At high noon the shadow of the roof drops below the lower windows, so no sun can shine in during the summer months, keeping the rooms cool. Apart and to the right is the slave house. No doubt, when the larger part of the house was added, the cooking was moved to the slave house and our fireplace was cut down from six to four feet to allow for a side entrance. . . ."

I lost no time in visiting the Hansings in the Huyler Home-

Mrs. Ernest G. Hansing, of Cresskill, showed me many treasures in the Huyler Homestead, which she and her husband regard as a museum. The earliest part of the house was built before 1770.

stead, as much a museum as a home and the more delightful for it. There, in spite of time's punctuation by one hundred and fifty-five clocks, I learned that other Huyler houses had been everywhere in the neighborhood now designated as Cresskill but in Tenafly as recently as 1876. After all, the Huylers were among the giants of Undercliff, especially when The Fishermen's Village turned to quarrying and the building of ships which the transport of paving blocks demanded. However, not until a letter came from Laura Huyler, living in Los Angeles, was I made aware of such much of the family's history. Laura wrote:

"I am the last of the children of John H. Huyler and Annie A. Post—they were married in 1873 in Paterson, New Jersey. John H. Huyler was born in 1852 and died in June, 1891.

"Byron Huyler died July 20, 1937, at the Old Homestead. He was president of the Tenafly Trust Company. George Huyler died in Connecticut. J. Grover Huyler died in St. Petersburg, Florida. I, Laura Huyler, have been living in southern California since 1947. There were two George Huylers in this generation. As the oldest child was George, named for Grandpa Huyler—George died at the age of eight as did the next children, Phillip and Holister, and they all were buried within a week of each other—Grandpa Huyler insisted on another George when the next boy was born. This is the reason for two Georges in one generation.

"All these records will be found in the cemetery at the South

Mr. Hansing said that the Huyler Homestead was confiscated after the Revolution from a Tory who fled to Canada and that it was purchased later by John Huyler. I must go back sometime to hear more stories about the Huylers and see the tiny graveyard where pioneers of the Fishermen's Village, Undercliff, lie buried.

Church, Bergenfield, with the exception of Byron Huyler's. He is buried in Brookside Cemetery, Englewood, new part. The picture that they told you was that of Peter Huyler was John, my father, in his early years. Sometimes there is confusion."

There is nothing here, at any rate, to indicate that any of the Huylers were buried in the Undercliff cemetery, which, I feel very sure, once extended beyond where the stone fence indicates now. Nor should anything I have written here indicate that I am a genealogist. Climbing family trees can lead to more than the breaking of a leg.

As we come to the end of our journey, high in the pinnacles of the Palisades, or down along the shore where the tides of the Hudson patrol the timbers of old ferries and landings of Undercliff with greater intimacy than a patrolman of the park, I will introduce Ethel Dunbaden, of Cranford. Enclosing a photograph of The Fishermen's Village taken in 1911, she wrote:

"I visited the fishing village, by then a town of about eight or ten houses. We used to enter by the gate, which is open, as you will see, in the picture. Every cottage was occupied by a fisherman's wife—all between the ages of seventy and seventy-five. We as teen-agers loved 'the Palisades,' and there was an old ruin or pillars, as if a gate had been there. We found many plants, and some of them we transplanted to our own gardens. It was a veritable Garden of Eden in which to get old worn-out bulbs, plants, rose bushes—everything in a state of decay, up to 1915—my last visit to what had been Undercliff. We never went beyond these cottages and were usually invited in for tea or milk or cookies by these old ladies, whose husbands for the most part were dead. They all spoke of the fear that their homes would be razed.

"The old school of which you spoke was used many years as the home of an artist who did oils of the Palisades—a Mr. Perrine. One of his pictures was hung in the White House in Washington, and the government gave him permission to use the building as a home. His houseboy was Japanese. He later married a distinguished pianist.

"I have a book of poems by Dr. Thomas Dunn English, who lived on the extreme west side of Coytesville, the closest village to that part of the Cliffs. You may remember that he wrote 'Ben Bolt' and many poems of historical happenings in that part of New Jersey—one called 'The Raid on the Ramapo' mentions Pete Huyler's daughter, Betty, being one of the helpers with a gun. . . ."

Another poem, Ethel Dunbaden said in her letter, written in dark green ink on light green paper, strung together old names of the region. The poem, titled "Kinderkamack," was fifty-two verses long, she warned, listing Willem Van Brockhuizen, Elias Van Klinker, and Gerbraed Van der Groots with such tongue-twisters as Cornelis Van Stavoren, Pieter Van Poots, Hermanus Van Schoop, and Wouter Van Schecker. However, inasmuch as Dr. English pointed out that the Dutch names along the Palisades could be pronounced properly "only by people of Belgic extraction," I must make a respectful bow, promise to come this way again, and take my leave.

A NOTE ON THE AUTHOR

by John Cunningham

HE WAS a concert violinist, an author, an Episcopal priest. He taught in a one-room school, labored as a young Camden newspaperman, won state-wide fame as a folklorist. He led tours in the Pine Barrens and lectured everywhere. He was the first to write extensively about the state, and he wrote with such warmth and enthusiasm that at least two generations of people who believe in New Jersey fell under his spell and owe an enduring debt to him. Despite his accomplishments, he never became pompously serious. He was Henry Charlton Beck.

Two careers beckoned to him after graduation from Haddonfield High School: the ministry and music. He enrolled at Virginia Theological Seminary after high school but never attended because of lack of money. He played in concert orchestras for fifteen years, but he never made it to the big time of music. Extremely bright, but without formal qualifications, he taught in a one-room school immediately after leaving high school.

When Henry Beck was twenty, he joined the Camden *Courier-Post* as a cub reporter. He saw his typewriter as an instrument of expression; shortly before his death he defined his career: "I just sit down and tap it out like any rewriteman." The "tapping" turned out six detective novels, all published but none distinguished. Assigned to write about South Jersey in the early 1930s, the young newspaperman found himself enthralled by tales spun to him in Penny Pot, Apple Pie Hill, and Ong's Hat, in Batsto, Calico, and Crowleytown. He had found his life. He listened, he tapped out his stories, and he became known to a limited *Courier-Post* readership. Then, in 1936, E. P. Dutton gathered together his early newspaper stories

337

and published them as *Forgotten Towns of Southern New Jersey*.

It was a smash hit. Other books followed on New Jersey, six in all. His knowledge of the state made him the logical choice to be editor of Rutgers University Press for a brief tenure (1945–1947). His emphasis on folklore led to the founding of the New Jersey Folklore Society, with Henry C. Beck the only possible choice for president.

His desire to be a minister never waned. He studied for the Episcopal priesthood while at Rutgers Press and received ordination in 1949. He preached and he ministered, and did so very well, yet he continued writing a weekly full-page article for the Newark *Star-Ledger*.

A listing of his accomplishments, however distinguished, does Henry Beck only slight credit. It tells little of this gentle, witty man except that he worked far beyond the capacity of most of us. It tells nothing of his charm as a guide through the Pine Barrens, nothing of his kindnesses to the few of us who were just beginning as writers when he was at his peak.

He was often called a historian but he insisted that he was "only a folklorist." His goal was to seek out those who have lived history, have them tell it in their own terms. He was, in fact, an oral historian long before the National Endowment for the Humanities poured out funds to make oral history academically respectable. Because of his books, Father Beck may be regarded by some as a historian. But his leg often was pulled by those whom he interviewed, and he, in turn, could put entertainment above scholarship. Above all, be sure of this: he never wittingly gave less than his best.

Henry C. Beck died in 1965. Those of us who knew his varied, parallel careers and who encountered his name from High Point to Cape May were surprised to learn that he was only sixty-two years old when he died. Few persons accomplish so much in so short a time.

INDEX